D1255614

Mothers
of the
Nation

Women's Political Writing in England,
1780–1830

Anne K. Mellor

Indiana University Press
Bloomington & Indianapolis

This book is a publication of

Indiana University Press
601 North Morton Street
Bloomington, IN 47404-3797 USA

http://www.indiana.edu/~iupress

Telephone orders   800-842-6796
Fax orders   812-855-7931
Orders by e-mail   iuporder@indiana.edu

© 2000 by Anne Mellor

PR
468
.P57
M45
2000

The paper used in this publication meets the minimum
requirements of American National Standard for Information
Sciences—Permanence of Paper for Printed Library Materials,
ANSI Z39.48-1984.

Manufactured in the United States of America

Library of Congress Cataloging-in-Publication Data

Mellor, Anne Kostelanetz.
    Mothers of the nation: women's political writing in England, 1780–1830 /
Anne K. Mellor.
        p.   cm. — (Women of letters)
    Includes bibliographical references (p.   ) and index.
    ISBN 0-253-33713-5 (alk. paper) — ISBN 0-253-21369-X (pbk.: alk. paper)
        1. English literature—19th century—History and criticism. 2. Politics and literature—
Great Britain—History—19th century. 3. Politics and literature—Great Britain—History—
18th century. 4. English literature—Women authors—History and criticism. 5. English
literature—18th century—History and criticism. 6. Women and literature—England—
History—19th century. 7. Women and literature—England—History—18th century. 8.
Great Britain—Politics and Government—1760–1820. 9. Great Britain—Politics and
government—1820–1830. 10. Women authors, English—Political and social views. I.
Title.   II. Women of letters (Bloomington, Ind.)

PR468.P57 .M45 2000
820.9'358—dc21
                                                            99-047328

1   2   3   4   5   05   04   03   02   01   00

For Ron

"separate rights are lost in mutual love"

Contents

Illustrations

Acknowledgments

I gratefully acknowledge the generous permission received from the following journal and press to publish here in revised form material that originally appeared under their imprints: The Johns Hopkins University Press, for "A Criticism of Their Own: Romantic Women Literary Critics," in *Questioning Romanticism,* ed. John Beer, Johns Hopkins University Press, 1995, 29–48; and The Trustees of Boston University, for "The Female Poet and the Poetess: Two Traditions of British Women's Poetry, 1780–1830," *Studies in Romanticism* 36 (Summer 1997): 261–76, and for "Joanna Baillie and the Counter-Public Sphere," *Studies in Romanticism* 33 (Winter 1994): 559–68.

I wish also to thank the many colleagues and students who have helped in profound ways to shape this book: the readers for Indiana University Press, the UCLA Romantic Study Group, the members of my National Endowment for the Humanities Summer Seminars for College Teachers, my graduate students at UCLA, and in particular those whose trenchant comments on earlier versions of these chapters sharpened my thinking— Isobel Armstrong, Stephen Behrendt, Ann Bermingham, Joseph Bristow, Julie Carlson, Ellen DuBois, Paula Feldman, Sandra Gilbert, Susan Gubar, Anne Janowitz, Greg Kucich, Peter Manning, Felicity Nussbaum, Carole Pateman, Leilani Riehle, Johanna Schwartz, Paul Sheats, Clifford Siskin, Susan Wolfson, and above all, Kevin Gilmartin, whose ongoing dialogue with me on Hannah More has greatly influenced this work.

The Clark Library and the Center for Seventeenth and Eighteenth Century Studies at UCLA have generously provided research assistance for this book.

I dedicate this book, on our thirtieth wedding anniversary (7 June 1999), to the person who has endured much, given more, and never let me down, my deeply loved husband, Ron Mellor.

Mothers of the Nation

Introduction

Women and the Public Sphere in England, 1780–1830

Social historians and literary critics who have analyzed British culture in the late eighteenth and early nineteenth century have tended to assume the existence of a "doctrine of the separate spheres" based primarily on gender, which powerfully shaped the lives of both men and women. Men inhabited the public realm of government and commerce; women were confined to a private, domestic realm of the family, the emotions, and spirituality. Jürgen Habermas's influential *The Structural Transformation of the Public Sphere* (1962, trans. 1989) both critiqued and at the same time powerfully reinforced this conceptual paradigm.

On the one hand, Habermas insisted that the public sphere must be theoretically distinguished from the machinations of the political state. He defined the "public sphere" as the arena of what he called bourgeois "civil society," a public space where the common good is debated and promoted, and where a public opinion based not on status or traditions but on the free and rational exchange of ideas can be developed. Habermas further argued that this public sphere emerged for the first time in Britain and France in the eighteenth century as an emancipatory reasoned discourse enabled by the growth of print culture (newspapers, periodicals, books), postal services, coffee houses, and salons. As Nancy Fraser precisely summarizes the Habermasian concept of the public sphere,

> it designates a theater in modern societies in which political participation is enacted through the medium of talk. It is the space in which citizens deliberate about their common affairs, and hence an institutionalized arena of discursive interaction. This arena is conceptually distinct from the state; it is a site for the production and circulation of discourses that can in principle be critical of the state. (Fraser 70)

Habermas further insisted that the public sphere must be conceptually distinguished not only from the state but also from the economy—it is an arena of debating and deliberating rather than of buying and selling, of discursive rather than of market relations. But as Keith Baker has rightly emphasized, this literary or discursive public sphere had its own economic foundations:

> Its existence depended upon the commercialization of culture in a capitalist society. Private persons could be constituted as a reading public, Habermas maintains, only through the postal services, periodicals, and other communications sytems that had grown in regularity with a market society; their individual access to the printed word could be sustained only insofar as it fed the commercial expansion of the printing and publishing trades; their personal taste for culture could be satisfied only in the coffee houses, salons, reading societies, theaters, museums, and concert halls opened to them in the urban centers of a bourgeois society; their collective judgment could be informed only by the new class of writers and critics whose livelihood now depended upon the production of culture as a commodity. (Baker 184–85)

On the other hand, as such feminist scholars as Joan Landes, Nancy Fraser, and Leonore Davidoff, among many others, have pointed out, Habermas limited participation in this eighteenth-century bourgeois civil society or public sphere—in this discursive community whose rational debate generated public opinion—to men of property. According to Habermas, women and unpropertied workers (or servants) could gain entrance to the public sphere only as *readers* (Habermas 56). As Leonore Davidoff rightly concluded, "Habermas' 'privatised individual' in these constructions is consistently, if unconsciously, masculine" (Davidoff 1995: 239).

In this book I argue first that Habermas's conceptual limitation of the public sphere in England between 1780 and 1830 to men of property is historically incorrect. During the Romantic era women participated fully in the public sphere as Habermas defined it. They openly and frequently published their free and reasoned opinions on an enormous range of topics, from the French Revolution and the abolitionist campaigns against the slave trade through doctrinal religious issues and methods of education to the economic management both of the individual household and of the state. Their views were openly circulated not only through the economic institutions of print culture (newspapers and journals, books, circulating libraries) but also through the public forums of debating societies and the theater. Not only did women participate fully in the discursive public sphere, but their opinions had definable impact on the social movements, economic relationships, and state-regulated policies of the day. Because women writers participated in the *same* discursive public sphere and in the *same* formation of public opinion as did their male peers, I have resisted using the concepts of a "counter" public sphere, proposed by Rita Felski, or of "competing" or "alternative" public spheres, endorsed by Bruce Robbins, Geoff Eley, and others. While useful in giving a more nuanced view of the multiple ways in which women, workers, and other marginalized groups participate in social movements, such theoretical formulations of competing "counter-publics" have resulted in the erasure of the historical fact of women's full participation in the very public sphere theorized by Habermas himself.

In support of my argument that women, both as writers and as educators, philanthropists, and social reformers, participated fully in the discursive public sphere and in the formation of public opinion, I cite as evidence the sheer bulk of their literary production. We know of more than 900 female poets (Jackson xv), at least 500 female novelists (the Corvey Library alone contains more than 300), and numerous other female playwrights, travel writers, historians, philosophers, and political writers who published at least one volume in this period. Their writings received exceptionally wide attention and distribution through the literary reviews, the many new ladies magazines (as documented by Margaret Beetham), and the fast-growing circulating libraries.

The success of the circulating or lending libraries, which spread rapidly throughout England during the late eighteenth century, ensured that women dominated both the production and the consumption of literature. Hitherto prohibitively expensive books were now available to a new and ever-growing readership, a readership composed in large part of increasingly literate and leisured upper- and middle-class women who preferred to read literature, and especially novels, written by women. The contents of the ten leading circulating libraries in London in 1800, tabulated by the London Statistical Society (cited in Richard Altick's *The English Common Reader: A Social History of the Mass Reading Public, 1800–1900*), suggests that the bulk of the writers for and the subscribers to these libraries were female. Three-quarters of the two thousand books in circulation were either "Fashionable Novels, well known" (439 volumes) or "Novels of the lowest character, being chiefly imitations of Fashionable Novels" (1008 volumes). Two additional categories also appealed primarily to women readers: "Romances" (76 volumes) and "Novels by Miss Edgeworth, and Moral and Religious Novels" (49 volumes). A cursory scanning of the literary journals of the period suggests that by 1830 over five hundred living women writers could claim authorship of at least one published and reviewed novel, and that by far the most prolific novelist of the period, as Mitzi Myers has observed, was the anonymous "A Lady." After surveying both the number of editions of individual novels and their reception in the leading literary reviews, Ann H. Jones concluded in *Ideas and Innovations: Best Sellers of Jane Austen's Age* that the most popular novelists of the period from 1800 to 1820 were women: Maria Edgeworth, Elizabeth Hamilton, Amelia Opie, Mary Brunton, Jane and Anna Maria Porter, and Sydney Owenson (Lady Morgan). Only two men are on the list, Walter Scott and Thomas Surr. By 1830, seven more women rivaled these nine in popularity: Ann Radcliffe, Mary Shelley, Susan Ferrier, Marguerite Gardiner (Countess of Blessington), Elizabeth Le Noir, Jane West, and, posthumously, Jane Austen.

Women writers' words and ideas were disseminated orally as well as in print. The popularity of the privately organized or commercially sponsored debating society has been documented by Lawrence Klein as a site, along with the coffee house and the newspaper, of the development both of what Habermas called public opinion and of what Klein, following Norbert Elias, calls "politeness" or "good form" (Klein 1993: 110). Recent research on London's debating societies by Donna Andrew documents that women participated equally with men in these commercially supported and extremely popular public events. They debated and voted affirmatively on such questions as: "Do not the extraordinary abilities of the Ladies in the present age demand Academical honours from the Universities—a right to vote at elections, and to be returned Members of Parliament?" (17 March 1788, *London Debating Societies, 1776–1799*, #1331: 223). So well known were these female debaters that Hannah Cowley could openly invoke them at a meeting of a gentleman's debating society in her one-act interlude *The School of Eloquence*, performed at the Theatre Royal, Drury Lane, on 30 March 1780. One of Cowley's "Sons of Oratory" brings a "commission" from the ladies, to thank these gentlemen for enabling them

> to leave the ancient fields of Female Eloquence—to soar above the curtain Lecture, the tea table chat, the kitchen brawl, and boldly leap into the Publick Forum, to debate, to discuss, the most abstruse subjects with a degree of success allmost [*sic*] equal to your own.

As this speaker then comments,

I am for my own part Sir, particularly rejoic'd at this, as I hope the Ladies in future will take upon themselves the troublesome office of instructing the world, which has so long lain heavy on the Men. (Hannah Cowley, *The School of Eloquence,* Huntington Library ms. LA 515, 6 recto and verso)

1. *The Female Moderator,* from George Alexander Stevens's
A Lecture on Heads, 1802.

George Alexander Stevens included the Female Moderator of a Debating Society among the caricatures in his wildly popular public performances of his *A Lecture on Heads* in the early 1780s. As re-enacted and published by Charles Lee Lewes in 1785, Stevens first displayed wigged and costumed, painted wood-and-pasteboard busts and then delivered speeches with gestures appropriate to each head. The 47 "heads" included such familiar public figures as the "Young Blood," the "British Tar," the "Connoisseur," "the Materialist," and the "Female Quaker." That the political claims of female orators or debaters were widely disseminated by 1785 is documented by Stevens's "head of the Female Moderator" (figure 1) whose recorded speech I quote in full:

This is the head [*takes the head*] of a FEMALE MODERATOR, or president of the Ladies' Debating Society; she can prove to a demonstration that man is an usurper of dignities and preferments, and that her sex has just right to participation of both with him: she would have physicians in petticoats, and lawyers with high heads and French curls; then she would have *young* women of spirit to command our fleets and armies, and *old* ones to govern the state:—she pathetically laments that women are considered as mere domestic animals, fit only for making puddings, pickling cucumbers, or registering cures for the measles and chincough. If this lady's wishes for reformation should ever be accomplished, we may expect to hear that an admiral's in the hysterics, that a general has miscarried, and that a prime minister was brought to bed the moment she opened the budget. (Stevens 35–36)

Moreover, many women writers and orators transformed their theoretical views and political opinions into social practice. As we shall see, Hannah More was a leading figure in the Sunday School movement, establishing several schools in the Mendip region to educate the children of the rural poor and thus to increase literacy among the lower classes. Amelia Opie helped to organize and run the Anti-Slavery Society in Norwich. They were joined in these enterprises by many other women, of course. As Clare Midgley has argued in her persuasive account of the role of women in the Abolitionist campaigns, *Women against Slavery: The British Campaigns, 1780–1870* (1992), women played a formative role in the successful drive to end both the slave trade and the institution of slavery in the British West Indian colonies. The powerful role of women in the burgeoning philanthropic voluntary associations has been documented by F. K. Prochaska (*Women and Philanthropy in Nineteenth-Century England,* 1980), while their dominant role in the charity-school movement, both as founders and as teachers, has been analyzed by such social historians as Thomas Laqueur, David Owen, and M. G. Jones.

This is not to claim that women's participation in the literary public sphere was not contested; as we well know, the opposite was the case. Numerous conduct books and other forms of public discourse—from sermons to literary texts to public debates—urged women to remain silent, to stay at home, to devote themselves exclusively to the activities of raising children and pleasing their husbands. But these masculinist discursive productions existed in open dialogue with women's published arguments which vigorously contested, qualified, or even on occasion endorsed them.

∾

Working within a different intellectual tradition, feminist historians and literary critics of both British and American culture have long assumed that women inhabited a distinctly differentiated domestic realm in the eighteenth and nineteenth centuries. For the disciplines of both women's history and women's literary criticism, the conceptual doctrine of separate sexual spheres has proved formative. Numerous scholars have followed the lead of Mary Poovey, Sandra Gilbert and Susan Gubar, Elaine Showalter, Nancy Cott, Nancy Armstrong, and Leonore Davidoff and Catherine Hall in exploring the ramifications of a domestic ideology which confined women to the private sphere in England and America in the late eighteenth and nineteenth centuries, and the ways in which it shaped a "literature of their own" by women.

But if women participated fully in the discursive public sphere and in the formation of public opinion in Britain by the late eighteenth century, then the assumption that there existed a clear distinction in historical practice between a realm of public, exclusively male activities and a realm of private, exclusively female activities in this period is also erroneous. At the very least, the conception of a hegemonic "domestic ideology" propounded by Davidoff, Hall, and others must be fundamentally revised to include women's active role in the discursive public sphere. I would further suggest that the theoretical paradigm of "the doctrine of the separate spheres" is now getting in the way of a richer, more complex, and accurate understanding of the varied nature of the daily lived experiences of both men and women in England between 1780 and 1830, together with the literary culture they produced. It may be time to discard this binary, overly simplistic concept of separate sexual spheres altogether in favor of a more nuanced and flexible conceptual paradigm that foregrounds the complex intersection of class, religious, racial, and gender differences in this historical period.

Several historians and literary scholars have recently begun to challenge the notion that fixed boundaries were in place between the public and the private spheres in England at this time, although their arguments have relied on a much broader and looser definition of the public sphere. They have extended Habermas's notion of the strictly discursive public sphere to a concept of the public sphere that includes the apparatuses of state government and the functionings of the marketplace. John Brewer has discussed the ways in which the public sphere (in which he includes government agencies) had during the eighteenth century in England "provided both the grounds and the means by which [the private sphere] could be colonized and invaded" (Brewer 1995: 18). A radically expanding print culture had subjected the hitherto private letter to public scrutiny, the newly developed domestic architecture of the Georgian townhouse had created a "front room" designed to be seen into as well as out of, and the growth of the novel had rendered interiorized subjectivity a matter of public discussion. As Brewer rather pessimistically concludes:

> All that was needed were the political circumstances that permitted the multivalent views of the private expressed in the public sphere to be reduced to the single gaze of the revolutionary state. The Pandora's box of private life had

already been opened. All that the Committee of Public Safety had to do was look into it. (1995: 19)

As noted earlier, rather than seeing the public sphere as monolithic, several scholars have suggested that we should think rather in terms of "competing," "alternative," or "counter" public spheres (see Bruce Robbins, Jeff Weintraub, Geoff Eley, Rita Felski). Weintraub, for instance, clarifies four distinct ways in which the public sphere interacts with the private sphere: (1) as a state administration regulating the private economy; (2) as state sovereignty taking account of the public opinion of private citizens; (3) as the symbolic display or theatrical representation of social power independent of state power; and (4) as a public economy opposed to the private economy of domestic production and reproduction (Weintraub, cited by Robbins xiii).

Other scholars have argued that it is simply impossible to separate the private from the public sphere in a consistently meaningful way. Introducing their useful collection of essays on this issue, *The Intersections of the Public and Private Spheres in Early Modern England* in 1996, Paula Backscheider and Timothy Dykstal conclude, borrowing their terminology from the work of the anthropologist Victor Turner, that the existence of a "liminal space" between the public and the private sphere is now widely established. More precisely, the contributors to this volume and to two other important collections of essays on this topic, *Habermas and the Public Sphere,* edited by Craig Calhoun (1992), and *Shifting the Boundaries: Transformation of the Languages of the Public and Private in the Eighteenth Century,* edited by Dario Castiglione and Leslie Sharpe (1995), detail many of the ways in which the distinctions between a public sphere (whether discursive or state regulated) and a private domestic sphere break down on linguistic, economic, and social levels.

The issue of gender only complicates the attempt to separate neatly the private realm (supposedly inhabited by women) from the public realm (supposedly inhabited by men). As Amanda Vickery has forcefully argued in an important review-essay that trenchantly critiques the public/private division, the definition of labor solely in terms of market-oriented production fatally obscures the "organisational and administrative" work that women did in household management at all class levels, work that she has described in detail in her *The Gentleman's Daughter: Women's Lives in Georgian England.* Linda Colley has provided extensive evidence of the ways in which the conservative backlash against the French Revolution in England in the 1790s enabled greater female participation in a more highly publicized political life of electioneering, loyalist parades, and patriotic subscriptions to the war effort, on the one hand, and abolitionist petitions and evangelical crusades against vice and intemperance on the other. As Colley concludes,

"At one and the same time, separate sexual spheres were being increasingly prescribed in theory, yet increasingly broken through in practice" (250, and chap. 6 passim).

Moreover, during the eighteenth century, women emerged as the primary consumers of an increasingly consumer-oriented market culture. As John Brewer and his co-editors Ray Porter, Susan Staves, and Ann Bermingham have amply demonstrated in the three large volumes of essays published under the general title *Consumption and Culture in the 17th and 18th Centuries* (1992–1995), by the end of the eighteenth century Britain's economy depended on an ever-expanding consumption by all classes of what would have hitherto been regarded as wasteful "luxury goods": textiles, home furnishings, teas, spices, and opium imported from the East, sugar and rum imported from the West Indies, leather and furs imported from the Americas, together with textiles, pottery, furniture, and objets d'art produced in England, Europe, India, and China. Since women were then as now the primary "shoppers" or "consuming subjects" (in Elizabeth Kowaleski-Wallace's phrase), their direct control over the workings of the market economy grew exponentially during this period, and as a direct consequence, so did their social power. Increasingly, women came to determine the social status—and thus the access to political influence—of other women and their husbands. One marker of this control, as Jennifer Hall-Witt has recently shown, was access to the highly coveted boxes at the Covent Garden Opera, which were bought and traded almost exclusively among upper-class women.

Between 1780 and 1830 in England, women participated in this more broadly defined public sphere of discourse, political activity, work, and the market in unprecedented numbers: as political canvassers, electioneers, and the organizers of jubilees; as workers in all areas of the economy (domestic, industrial, and commercial), as Maxine Berg has shown; as philanthropists and administrators of charitable organizations and voluntary societies; as educators and writers; and as consumers. The women writers of the British Romantic era on whom this book focuses saw themselves and their female readers as active members of this more broadly defined public sphere. Not only did they participate fully in the discursive or literary public sphere conceptualized by Habermas, self-consciously defining themselves as the shapers of public opinion. Insofar as they represented the interests of women, children, and the family, they also saw themselves as peculiarly *responsible* for defining the future direction of public policy and social reform. Their numerous and widely disseminated writings—poems, plays, novels, critical essays, political tracts—asserted both the right and the duty of women to speak *for* the nation.

In asserting their literary and political authority, these women writers consciously drew on the tradition of the seventeenth-century female preacher, those Dissenting and Quaker female prophets who identified themselves as the voice of Christian virtue, answerable to no merely mortal male. Invoking biblical precedents for female judges (Deborah), female rulers (Queen Esther), female military leaders and saviors of their people (Judith), these female preachers claimed divine authority for their words, both spoken and written. Romantic women writers translated this religious authority into a more secular literary authority, claiming that they spoke on behalf of morality and "right feeling" (or *true* sensibility).

Finally, we can turn to popular culture for further evidence of women's participation in both the discursive and the more broadly defined public sphere. The "Blue Stockings" and such electioneering women as the Duchess of Devonshire and Mary Robinson were widely attacked in satirical prints, as Dorothy George, Linda Colley, and Diana Donald have demonstrated. The enormous popularity of Richard Polwhele's lampooning satirical poem on the leading women writers and artists of the day, "The Unsex'd Females" (1798), testifies both to the familiarity of their work and to the anxiety roused among men by their views. The development of such "rational amusements" as board games designed for the moral or educational improvement of both sexes which feature women prominently in their pictorial vignettes further testifies to women's participation in the public sphere. In a typical example, *The Delicious Game of the Fruit-Basket, or Moral and Intellectual Dessert* published by William Darton in 1822, the players proceed from prison to the "Muse of Learning" (figure 2). In the vignettes along their path, females are portrayed as attending public chemistry lectures and art exhibitions, purchasing goods in the bazaar, nursing in hospitals, visiting the poorhouse, educating children in a national school, patronizing a school for the blind, dispensing wisdom (and university degrees) in the guise of "Glory inciting an Exonian and a Cantab student to Emulation, Learning and the Arts," attending a Bible Society meeting, and leading a march through the streets under the banner of the "Female Benevolent Society." As the anonymous author of the accompanying Rules of the Game explains this last vignette:

> Numerous are the benevolent institutions in this metropolis, and among them many entirely supported by the fair sex. It is a beautiful part of their character, and cannot be too highly prized. When we read of women renowned for deeds of courage and magnanimity, we question if they were as well versed in domestic duties, and that tender consideration for the sorrows of others which distinguish our own countrywomen.
> The noble Roman ladies did not visit prisons, or reprove the guilty, soothe the penitent, and instruct the ignorant: they did not meet to clothe and feed the aged and destitute, or rescue their fellow creatures from the horrors of a gaol,

2. *The Delicious Game of the Fruit-Basket, or Moral and Intellectual Dessert,* published by William Darton, 1822. Reproduced with permission of the V & A Picture Library, Victoria and Albert Museum, London.

and lead them into the path of rectitude. Yet these are deeds which bear comparison with all their boasted ones. (*Delicious Game* 47)

Significantly, in this board game, a player has "won" when he or she has married, produced a contented and well-fed family, learned the Bible, helped the poor, and thereby gained wisdom.

To sum up, in this book I argue that women writers had an enormous—and hitherto largely uncredited—impact on the formation of public opinion in England between 1780 and 1830. Rather than seeing the public sphere "invading" and "colonizing" the private sphere, as John Brewer does, I see the values of the private sphere associated primarily with women—moral virtue and an ethic of care—infiltrating and finally dominating the discursive public sphere during the Romantic era. As a result of women's published writing in this period, generations of children were taught to see the role of the nation differently. Women writers were primarily responsible for insisting that the conduct of the British government must be *moral*—that political leaders should demonstrate the same Christian virtues that mothers and daughters—and fathers and sons—were expected to practice at home. It was this transformation in public opinion, in the political culture of Britain, that made the financial excesses and sexual promiscuity of George IV increasingly less acceptable to his subjects and ensured that no future monarch of England during the nineteenth or twentieth century would be permitted to indulge in such fiscal and moral irregularities.

1

Hannah More, Revolutionary Reformer

3. John Opie, *HANNAH MORE*, eng. J. C. Buttre for
The London Repository, 1861.

Hannah More was the most influential woman living in England in the
Romantic era. Through her writings, political actions, and personal relationships, she promoted a successful program for social change from *within*

the existing social and political order. In this chapter, I make five claims concerning the historical impact of More's career. (1) Her writings contributed to the prevention of a French-style, violent revolution in England. (2) They did so by helping to reform, rather than subvert, the existing social order. (3) This reform was four-pronged: it was directed simultaneously at the behavior of the aristocracy, at the behavior of the clergy, at the behavior of the working classes, and at the education and behavior of women across all classes. (4) In an era of greatly expanding imperialism and consumption, she *moralized* both capitalism and consumption. (5) So profound were these social changes that one can plausibly say that Hannah More's writings consolidated and disseminated a revolution, not in the overt structure of public government, but, equally important, in the very culture or mores of the English nation. These are bold claims which I must now try to support.

Before I do, I should enter one caveat. In this book, I use the term "revolution," as in my deliberately provocative chapter title, to refer to cultural and social revolutions, as well as to political revolutions. If a verbal campaign has the effect of markedly transforming the everyday social practices and lived experience of the majority of the inhabitants of a community or nation, then that campaign has brought about an overturning, or revolution, in the culture or mores of that nation, even when no change in the constitutional structure of the state government has occurred. I here draw on the specific valence that the word "revolution" carried in the late eighteenth century. As Raymond Williams has noted in his *Keywords*, in the 1790s "revolution" meant "making a new social order," either through the violent overthrowing of the old order increasingly associated in political discourse with the French Revolution or through "peaceful and constitutional means," as the result of profound and effective social reform (229).

The enormous influence of Hannah More on her contemporaries was widely acknowledged in her lifetime; as Georgiana, Lady Chatterton, commented with some asperity in 1861, "half an hour's conversation with any Somersetshire octogenarian, whose memory of events can go back clearly into the last twenty years of the last century, will convince anyone (not grossly prejudiced) that Hannah More rendered national services of unappreciable extent" (Chatterton I: 146). Sixty years after More died, Canon Overton, writing on the history of the English church in the nineteenth century, insisted that "It is hardly too much to say that she was the most influential person—certainly the most influential lady—who lived at that time" (Overton; qtd. in Meakin x–xi). Her fame spread far beyond England. The early American feminist Elizabeth Cady Stanton, a woman in a position to know, best summed up More's contribution to her age in 1848:

> It has happened more than once that in a great crisis of national affairs, woman has been appealed to for her aid. Hannah More one of the great minds of her

day, at a time when French revolutionary and atheistical opinions were spreading—was earnestly besought by many eminent men to write something to
counteract these destructive influences—Her style was so popular and she had
shown so intimate a knowledge of human nature that they hoped much from
her influence. Her village politics by Will Chip, written in a few hours showed
that she merited the opinion entertained of her power upon all classes of mind.
It had as was expected great effect. The tact and intelligence of this woman
completely turned the tide of opinion and many say prevented a revolution,
whether she did old Englands poor any essential service by thus warding off
what must surely come is a question—however she did it and the wise ones of
her day gloried in her success. Strange that surrounded by such a galaxy of
great minds, that so great a work should have been given with one accord to a
woman to do. (Stanton 112–13)

Nineteenth- and twentieth-century biographers have continued to affirm
More's overwhelming impact on the British nation during her lifetime.
Clara Balfour observed in 1854 that despite her "comparatively humble
station" and the fact that her age was "not favorable to women's mental
elevation," Hannah More nonetheless became a "person of such influence,
that no contemporary female name ranked higher in the list of educational
and literary benefactors" and further, "came to be the favorite companion
of the learned and the noble, and the monitor both of peasants and princes"
(Balfour 4–5). F. K. Prochaska, in his definitive study of women and philanthropy in nineteenth-century England, again concluded in 1980 that Hannah More was not only "the most influential female philanthropist of her
day" but also "probably the most influential woman of her day" (6). Almost certainly, as A. D. Harvey comments, she was "the most successful
propagandist of the 1790s" (1978: 106).

Why then has Hannah More been so relentlessly condemned by, even on
occasion *erased* from, the most widely read historical accounts of England
in the early nineteenth century? This is so much the case that the recent,
and very fine, study of Hannah More's life and works by Patricia Demers in
1996 begins with an apology for taking her work seriously (Demers, preface). My answer, albeit speculative, is simple. The leading historians of eigh-
teenth- and nineteenth-century England have emerged from a theoretical
tradition grounded on Marxist or left-wing socialist ideologies: they *hate*
Hannah More because in their eyes she did far too much to stop a liberat-
ing French-style political revolution from occurring in England. In the mid-
1790s, More's widely disseminated *Cheap Repository Tracts* were often credited with preventing rebellion and thereby saving the monarchy in England.
Numerous commentators—Henry Thompson and Thomas Taylor in 1838,
Marion Harland in 1900, Sam Pickering again in 1976 (Thompson 158;
Taylor 154; Harland 176–77; Pickering 35)—have noted that in 1795, rioting colliers both at Bath and at Hull were calmed by a singing of More's
cautionary ballad "The Riot, or, Half a Loaf is Better than No Bread." As

Ford K. Brown observes, More's friends considered her to be "the chief agency in checking the flood of philosophy, infidelity and disrespect for inherited privilege that poured fearfully across the Channel from 1790 on" (123).

The negative press on Hannah More has been deafening, from British social historians and literary critics alike. E. P. Thompson summed up the charges against More in *The Making of the English Working Class* in 1963, in which he accuses More and her allies of nurturing a fear of social change among the landed gentry so powerful that "in these counter-revolutionary decades . . . the humanitarian tradition became warped beyond recognition" (61). He further denounces her most philanthropic project, the construction of Sunday Schools for workers, as an exercise in "discipline and repression" in which the bourgeoisie brainwashed the working classes into submission (441). Here Thompson joins the assault on More begun fifty years earlier by John and Barbara Hammond, who in 1917 in their *The Town Labourer* condemned the entire Evangelical movement as well as the Sunday Schools it fostered as an attempt to reconcile workers to their misery on earth and to persuade them to let the rich "do their thinking for them" (Hammond x). As the Hammonds powerfully concluded their critique of More and her allies:

> The working classes were therefore regarded as people to be kept out of mischief, rather than as people with faculties and characters to be encouraged and developed. They were to have just so much instruction as would make them more useful work people; to be trained, in Hannah More's phrase, "in habits of industry and piety." Thus not only the towns they lived in, the hours they worked, the wages they received, but also the schools in which some of their children were taught their letters, stamped them as a subject population, existing merely for the service and profit of other classes. (51)

So persuasive has been the Marxist claim that Hannah More participated in an oppressive project of "social control," as Robert Hole and Morag Shiach have recently defined it (Hole 135–41, Shiach 86), in what Foucault would call a discourse of discipline and punishment, that to date no British social historian has defended her career. Some, like Philip Corrigan and Derek Sayer in their *The Great Arch: English State Formation as Cultural Revolution* (1985), simply omit her from their account. But most follow E. P. Thompson in seeing her as opposed both to reform and to free thought, as do R. K. Webb, V. Kiernan, and M. J. Crossley Evans. In *The British Working Class Reader*, Webb dismisses her *Cheap Repository Tracts* as "anti-reform" (42, 56). Kiernan, in an influential essay on "Evangelicalism and the French Revolution" that appeared in *Past and Present* in 1955, focuses entirely on the "negative" aspects of the Evangelical movement as a social agent which contributed to "preserving an essentially static social order"

(44); while Evans more broadly condemns her as "anti-Enlightenment" (460).

Even her humanitarian efforts as a philanthropist have been downplayed by David Owen in his highly regarded study *English Philanthropy 1660–1960* (1964). Owen condemns Hannah More's and Sarah Trimmer's Sunday Schools as "patronising" the poor and putting a "sinister stamp on nineteenth century charity," although, he claims, luckily they were on the "losing side" (92, 99–100). The rancorous undercurrent to much of the historical commentary on More's career erupts into full view with William Richardson's description of her in 1975 as a "necrophiliac . . . opportunist" who "flattered and fawned" her way into society, whose *Cheap Repository Tracts* were "designed to instill anti-intellectualism, intolerable pride of class, and complacent awareness of their own virtue" among the "middling sort," and whose ideal woman Mrs. Simpson is a "singularly repellant female Job," "the prototype of all the long-suffering soap opera heroines who ever . . . castrated a male a week upon the altars of their implacable virtues" (230, 232, 235).

On the whole, Hannah More has fared no better at the hands of literary critics, even feminist ones. Elizabeth Kowaleski-Wallace defined her as the quintessential "daddy's girl," a willing participant in a patriarchal order who used the Evangelical movement to position herself as "the social 'superior' to her lower-class sisters" (1991: 56–93). Lucinda Cole reads her as advocating the *silencing* of women (120–24), while Cannon Schmitt invokes her as the leading propagandist for an almost Gothic "internal surveillance" of the "unruly" female self (28–32). Alan Richardson defines her educational program as "anti-feminist" and designed to support a traditional patriarchal society rather than to alter woman's social position (1994: 180–81). Gary Kelly sees her writings as an apologia for "rural paternalism" (1987: 150), while Claire Grogan similarly responds, in the face of recent efforts to gain a more sympathetic hearing for More's career, that she was relentlessly anti-Jacobin and pro-patriarchal (100). And Mary Waldron, introducing a recent paperback reprint of More's novel *Coelebs in Search of a Wife*, can barely contain her irritation with More's propaganda for "the stability of the existing order," for "quietism and stasis," concluding that the novel is now no more than a "sometimes slightly horrifying, historical curiosity" (Waldron vii, viii, xxx). Elisabeth Jay again condemns More's literary gifts, insisting that More "accorded little of the aesthetic respect to her tool [the novel] that we might expect from the committed artist" (4).

This judgment on More's literary achievement echoes many of her contemporaries' view of her writings. The poet Peter Pindar [John Wilcot] in 1799 condemned Hannah More as a "rhyme-and-prose Gentlewoman, born at Bristol" whose genius is of a "metallic nature," so much so that he "solemnly protesteth that he cannot wade twice through Miss Hannah's Works, deeming them, as Dr. Johnson would have expressed himself, pages of puerile vanity and intellectual imbecility" (Pindar 5). William Shaw, writing as the Rev. Sir Archibald MacSarcasm, denounced More's "information and genius" as entirely "factitious," insisting that "there is neither invention, genius, plot or description in her dramas," that her poetry consists of "eight volumes of inanity, much chaff and little wheat," and concluding that she suffers from "meanness of mind and a maliciousness of heart" (MacSarcasm 6, 25, 7, 89). The influential *Edinburgh Review* in 1809 dismissed *Coelebs* as an "uninspired production" (145). This negative view of More's literary efforts culminated with Augustine Birrell's claim that she was

> one of the most detestable writers that ever held a pen. She flounders like a huge conger eel in an ocean of dingy morality. . . . Her religion lacks reality. Not a single expression of genuine piety, of heartfelt emotion, ever escapes her lips. (qtd. in Silvester 119–20)

Reviewing More's *Complete Works* in 1894, Birrell concluded that these nineteen volumes constituted an "encyclopedia of all literary vices" which, being unreadable and unsellable, he had *buried* in his backyard (1894: 71).

Recently, however, More's achievements have been evaluated more positively by feminist scholars. Beginning with Mitzi Myer's robust recuperation in 1982 of Hannah More as an effective advocate for the rational education of women on a par with Mary Wollstonecraft, feminists have begun to understand the ways in which More's writings historically advanced the cause of women's social empowerment. Kathryn Sutherland in 1991 persuasively argued that More positioned women at the center of a political campaign for domestic and national reform, while Dorice Elliot brilliantly analyzed *Coelebs in Search of a Wife* as a representation of a new professionalization of women as philanthropists. Most recently, Patricia Demers, in her *The World of Hannah More,* and Charles Howard Ford in his *Hannah More: A Critical Biography,* also published in 1996, have provided finely nuanced and sympathetic—if sometimes overly defensive—reassessments of More's career. My view of Hannah More's historical achievement is very much in accord with these critics.

I

Rather than promoting the political revolution urged by the French Jacobins or the proletarian revolution of the workers later envisioned by Marx, Hannah More devoted her life to reforming the culture of the English nation from within. She called for a "revolution in manners" or cultural mores, a radical change in the *moral* behavior of the nation. Writing in an era which she considered one of "superannuated impiety" (*Estimate of the Religion of the Fashionable World* II: 316), of notable moral decline marked by "the excesses of luxury, the costly diversions, and the intemperate dissipation in which numbers of professing Christians indulge themselves" (II: 309), More set out to lead "a moral revolution in the national manners and principles" that would be "analogous to that great political one which we hear so much and so justly extolled" (II: 296). In so doing, as Gerald Newman recognized, she powerfully criticized, rather than supported, the existing social order (1975: 401).

More fought her moral revolution on four fronts. Confronted with the decadent practices of the late-eighteenth-century aristocracy—with codes of behavior that licensed libertinism, adultery, gambling, dueling, and fiscal irresponsibility (Jaeger 54–6)—she first attacked the highborn members of "Society." Although generally overlooked, the *Cheap Repository Tracts* of the mid-1790s contain as trenchant a critique of the morally irresponsible aristocracy as of the revolutionary workers. In *Village Politics*, for instance, Jack Anvil the blacksmith, while warning workers against the evils of violent rebellion, nonetheless recognizes the evils perpetrated by the "great folks": "I don't pretend to say they are a bit better than they should be . . . let them look to that; they'll answer for that in another place. To be sure, I wish they'd set us a better example about going to church, and those things: . . . They do spend too much, to be sure, in feastings and fandangoes." And, he concludes, "my lady is too rantipolish, and flies about all summer to hot water and cold water" (II: 230).

In two major tracts addressed directly to the upper classes, *Thoughts on the Importance of the Manners of the Great to General Society* (1788) and *An Estimate of the Religion of the Fashionable World* (1790), Hannah More directly condemned the hypocrisy of the "merely nominal" Christians among the aristocracy. Since the rich and powerful are perforce the role models for the lower classes, they have an increased social responsibility to set a good example, More argued. She pointed out all the ways in which the leaders of her time were failing in that civic responsibility: they did not attend church, or did so half-heartedly, combining Sunday services with visiting, concerts, and hairdressing; they gambled, even the women, at card parties in their own homes, using their winnings to tip the servants of the hostess; they engaged in a sustained practice of social lying, forcing servants to tell visitors they were "not at home"; they tolerated adultery, especially for husbands; and they systematically failed to develop an appreciation of what was for More the center of personal and social fulfillment—"family enjoyment, select conversation, and domestic delights" (*Manners of the Great* II: 285). Their behavior thus corrupted rather than educated their servants, forcing these servants to lie, encourage gambling, cheat, and steal.

More calculatedly attributed the amoral practices of the rich to their excessive dependence on French fashions and behaviors. By identifying aristocratic English society with France, at the very moment of the French Revolution, she subtly defined the British aristocrats as potential Jacobins, corrupted from within by their adherence to French philosophy—the anti-Christian skepticism of Voltaire—and French culture. With rhetorical skill she invoked the specter of a French conquest of the English character in *Religion of the Fashionable World,* personifying Jacobin France as "scepticism":

> prudent scepticism has wisely studied the temper of the times, and skilfully felt the pulse of this relaxed, and indolent, and selfish age. It prudently accommodated itself to the reigning character, when it adopted sarcasm instead of reasoning, and preferred a sneer to an argument. It discreetly judged, that, if it would now gain proselytes, it must shew itself under the bewitching form of a profane bon-mot; must be interwoven in the texture of some amusing history, written with the levity of a romance, and the point and glitter of an epigram; it must embellish the ample margin with some offensive anecdote or impure allusion, and decorate impiety with every loose and meretricious ornament which a corrupt imagination can invent. (II: 293)

By identifying upper-class social practices not merely as amoral or non-Christian but also as French, More undercut the aristocracy's claim to both political and social authority at the time of the Revolution. If they are to rule the British nation, they must become more British—which More defined as devoutly Christian, rigorously Sabbatarian, pious, chaste, honest, and benevolent in thought and deed.

More's clarion call for the reform of the manners of the rich was heard by many of the aristocracy and landed gentry. As David Spring documented in several articles published in the 1960s, an increase in aristocratic morality in the 1820s could be directly traced to the writings of More and the other members of the Clapham Sect of Evangelicals. This amounted, Spring argued, to "a change in the social type of aristocracy" (1963: 270)—the formation of a new ideal of the British aristocrat characterized by an outward decorum, fewer rowdy amusements, more concern with the pragmatic aspects of business, land use, and the science of agriculture, together with an attendant decrease in a concern for the patronage of the fine arts. As Linda Colley has concluded, the attack on the "cultural treason" of the elite mounted by More and others produced a new ideology of the British ruling class: one marked by "public probity," "regular church-going and conventional sexual morality," and "ostentatious uxoriousness" (188–89).

That More played a key role in this transformation of the British aristocracy is registered in the numerous verbal and visual caricatures of her that proliferated in the early nineteenth century, from William Cobbett's contemptuous description of More as "an old bishop in petticoats" to Byron's invective against her in *Don Juan* as

Morality's prim personification
In which not envy's self a flaw discovers.
To other's share let female errors fall,
For she had not even one—the worst of all.
(Canto I, st. 16, lines 5–8)

In 1808 a satirical print represented the libidinous Duke of York with his mistress, defying Canning by asserting "my Country calls—. . . never mind the Bishop & Hannah, they threaten the spiritual court for F—or—n" (George 8: 11023). Even the defiant old-style aristocrats were forced to acknowledge her impact. At one of the notorious Baby Balls which she denounced in *Strictures on the Modern System of Female Education*—midnight balls at which children between the ages of four and eight danced the latest French minuets in fancy dress—Hannah More appeared as a Bogey, played by a man, cross-dressed, with rod in hand. This Bogey invited the children to attack him: "Rouse the echoes of the hall / With your sportive Baby Ball, / Foot it nimbly on the floor / Nor heed the carping Hannah More" (M. G. Jones 1952: 112).

More's attack on the lax morals and irresponsibility of the upper classes was also aimed at the Church of England. As Alan Gilbert has documented, by the end of the eighteenth century the Church of England was in severe decline, its clergy demoralized and impoverished, heavily dependent on the landed gentry for their support, and marked by religious apathy. Many clergymen did not even live in the parishes they served. In 1812, there were 4,813 non-resident clergy and only 3,694 resident curates; over 1,000 parishes had no assigned clergyman (Gilbert 4–7). By 1820, in the face of the rapid growth of the dissenting sects, both of the Old Dissent (Quakers, Presbyterians, Unitarians) and especially of the New Dissent (Methodists, Wesleyans, Baptists, Congregationalists), the Church of England was "on the point of becoming a minority religious Establishment" (27).

More's impassioned pleas to the Anglican clergy to play a central role in bringing about the moral reform of the nation inspired numerous members of the clergy to join the Evangelical branch of the Church of England—by 1830, over one-quarter of its clergy were openly identified with the Clapham Sect Evangelicals. Their efforts, both as resident clergy and as missionaries, effectively revitalized the Church of England during the nineteenth century, absorbing much of the religious energy that had previously flowed to the New Dissent.

II

Equally aggressively, Hannah More attempted to reform the working classes of England. In her propagandistic *Cheap Repository Tracts* explicitly aimed at workers, of which over two million were sold or otherwise distributed in 1795 alone (Spinney 296), More hammered home her message: if workers would become sober, industrious, thrifty, healthy, and religious, then they could rise into the lower rungs of the middle class. By providing numerous examples of workers who financially bettered their lot in life through sober industry, together with counter-examples of drunken, lazy, immoral workers like Black Giles the poacher and his wife Tawney Rachel the thieving fortune-teller who end up in jail or transported or dead, cruelly neglecting and abusing their children along the way, More attempted to persuade the working classes that they too had a stake in an economically prosperous and politically stable England. She thus contributed directly to arousing that "militant loyalism" among the workers which H. T. Dickinson has defined as the primary cause for the failure of a revolutionary political movement in England at this time (Dickinson 1989, 1990). In effect, she told the workers, you can have the material rewards your employers have; you can *become* the middle class. And at the same time you can save your Christian souls.

Let me take just three examples from the *Tracts*. Intended as a direct assault on the irreligious chapbooks and "penny-dreadful" songs of popular culture that glorified "spunk and luck" rather than respectability and hard work (see Pedersen), written in a plain, direct, vivid, and often overtly allegorical style, illustrated with full- or half-page woodcuts, and sold for a penny or less, the *Tracts* were extremely effective propaganda. They offered a primer in capitalist economics for the uneducated, as well as a crash course in home economics or domestic management for working-class women. In "The Two Shoemakers," for instance, Jack Brown, a "wild, giddy" and idle middle-class boy who has been spoiled by his mother, and James Stock, a poor, modest, industrious, pious working-class boy, are both apprenticed to the local shoemaker. James quickly learns the trade, while Jack becomes a drunkard and gambles away his earnings. When their master—also a gambling drunkard—goes bankrupt, the creditors—impressed with James's sobriety, industry, and technical craftsmanship—lend money to James to buy the shop. In the second installment, "Apprentice turned Master," James is depicted as the ideal tradesman: honest, reliable, and devout. He pays his debts promptly, marries a "dutiful" woman, is kind but firm to his apprentices, and even decides to educate at his own expense the pious poorhouse boy, Thomas Williams. Meanwhile, Jack Brown, in the third installment, has set up his own shop on his father's capital, where he sells cheap, gaudy, badly made shoes; his shop fails, he is disinherited because he was too drunk to attend his mother's deathbed, and his remaining funds are stolen by traveling actors. He ends up in jail, contracts "jail-fever," and is abandoned by his fair-weather friends. Only James Stock attends his deathbed, offering him the final consolations of Christianity. More here offered an elementary course in what we might now call "Christian capitalism," of how to maximize one's material and spiritual welfare by being trustworthy, industrious, and devout.

More was as concerned with educating working women as men in the basic elements of economy. In "Betty Brown, the St. Giles Orange Girl," the kindly Justice and his wife teach the streetwise orphan Betty Brown, who is surviving by selling oranges, that she is being cheated by Mrs. Sponge, who demands 6 pence a day in return for setting Betty up in business by lending her a fruitbarrow and 5 shillings to buy oranges; she also takes the rest of Betty's daily income for food and lodging. After a year Betty has paid £7.10 interest for the loan of a mere five shillings. By lending Betty the money to buy her own orangecart and oranges, money which Betty pays back from her earnings within six months, and at the same time helping her to find cheaper lodgings and better food than that provided by the thieving pawnbroker Mrs. Sponge, the Justice and his wife train Betty effectively in the methods of capitalism. She is such an apt pupil that within a few years she has risen from abject poverty to become the "owner of that handsome sausage-shop near Seven Dials" and the wife of an honest hackney coachman.

In "The Cottage Cook," More turned her attention to domestic economy. Her middle-class philanthropist Mrs. Jones here teaches the poorer women in her parish how to manage better on their limited incomes by buying healthier food, baking their own more nourishing wheat bread, brewing their own beer so their husbands will spend less time and money at the pubs, and sewing and knitting their own clothes. She warns against taking credit from shopkeepers, pointing out how "long credit" mounts up into unpayable debts. The results, as Mrs. Jones observes in her own neighborhood, are cleaner, healthier working-class families where the father spends his leisure time with his family and the wife beams with happiness.

To bring about the reformation of the working classes in a more systematic way, More turned to the institution of the charity Sunday School, recently initiated with success in Gloucester by Richard Raikes, as her primary instrument of social change. Between 1789 and 1799 she and her sister Martha established nine Sunday Schools amongst the rural poverty and social depravity of the Mendips region. Described at length in Martha More's journal (published as *Mendip Annals* in 1859), these nine schools educated over a thousand children and adults a year. Designed to bring literacy (reading, but not writing, since More considered penmanship unnecessary for domestic servants), numeracy, Christianity, sobriety, industry, and good health to the rural poor, combining vocational training with religious instruction, these Sunday Schools have been widely criticized as exercises in the "politicization" or loyalist indoctrination of children (Shiach 86). But as Thomas Laqueur has demonstrated in detail in his study of Sunday Schools and working-class culture, these schools in fact functioned to improve and to empower the working classes. "What appears to have been an imposition from above," he concludes, "was, in fact, a way in which those who spent their lives in disorder, uncertainty, dirt and disease brought some order into this environment. Cleanliness in body, punctuality, neatness in dress and in one's home, and orderliness in one's life style were very much part of the fabric of 'respectable' working-class society and by no means inhibited those engaged in their pursuit from attacking the repressive aspects of the contemporary political and economic system; *rather the reverse*" (170; Laqueur's italics). As he points out, "a highly developed culture of self-help, self-improvement and respectability, which nurtured many of the political and trade-union leaders of the working-class, emerged from the late 18th- and the 19th century Sunday Schools" (155).

By teaching the workers to read, Hannah More's Mendips Sunday Schools for the first time made available to the rural poor of this region the social world of Evangelical middle-class culture, a culture which they on the whole eagerly embraced. Both the *Cheap Repository Tracts* and the Sunday Schools strongly asserted a Christian bourgeois ideology as normative for the entire nation. Together with the widespread growth of voluntary philanthropic societies in the early nineteenth century, they helped to stabilize a class system increasingly controlled, not by the aristocracy and the "Old Corruption," but by a growing and newly empowered professional and commercial middle class which by 1800 included, according to Jonathan Barry, perhaps as much as half of the population. As R. J. Morris observes in his study of Leeds, in this period British society was being remade in the image of the middle class and the voluntary society, "inviting everyone, aristocrats and working class to join, providing of course they obeyed the rules and paid their subscriptions" (331). This shift of economic and political power to an "active middling order" dominated by a professional and commercial elite increasingly committed to Evangelical Christianity was further enforced, as Martin Daunton notes in his recent economic history of Britain in this period, by a new professional police, new poor laws which differentiated between the "deserving" and the "undeserving" poor, and new prisons (501).

It hardly needs saying that More's program for the reform of Britain's social culture was not egalitarian (a position that many scholars today rightly find problematic). She strongly believed in economic stratification, in the prerogatives but also the responsibilities of the better-off to educate, set the moral standards for, and demonstrate charity to the less well off. Her immediate goal was not to tear down a class system as such, but rather to eliminate the immoral sexual and financial excesses found at all rungs of the class ladder, particularly at the top and at the bottom. Thus she argued first for a new definition of Britain as an "imagined community" of ideologically like-minded persons. Both the reformed aristocracy and the "respectable" working class, by endorsing and enacting the same Christian moral code, shared the same British national identity. At the same time, her writings tended to identify this Evangelical moral code with the specific economic practices of Christian capitalism and thus with the material and religious culture of the growing Evangelical professional and commercial middle class (as represented in the Clapham Sect). More implicitly defined what we might now call "middle-class values" as normative for the nation as a whole; in so doing, she subtly undercut the social prestige and political authority of the aristocracy.[1]

At the same time, in her *Cheap Repository Tracts,* she subtly affirmed certain fundamental political rights for all the citizens of England, rights which stood against a royal or aristocratic usurpation of excessive power. In *Village Politics* (1793), after the loyalist Jack the blacksmith has persuaded the pro-Jacobin, Painite Tom the mason of the errors of his revolutionary opinions, Tom "sums up the evidence" against French republicanism thus:

> To cut every man's throat who does not think as I do, or hang him up at a lamp-post!—Pretend liberty of conscience, and then banish the parsons only for being conscientious!—Cry out liberty of the press, and hang up the first man who writes his mind!—Lose our poor laws!—Lose one's wife perhaps upon every little tiff!—March without clothes, and fight without victuals!—No trade!—No bible!—No Sabbath, nor day of rest!—No safety, no comfort, no peace in this world—and no world to come! (II: 235–36)

As Mark Philp has observed, Tom here asserts a set of basic political values: the rule of law, liberty of the press, religious and political toleration, support for the indigent, free trade, military defense of the homeland. These values in effect constitute a set of criteria by which both Jack and Tom can assess and judge both the existing British and French governments and their policies (63). Rather than blankly endorsing the political status quo from a conservative position, More instead articulates her own conception of a just British government, a constitutional monarchy that recognizes its legal limits and that fulfills its economic and religious obligations to preserve the "safety, comfort and peace" of all its subjects.

III

Fundamental to Hannah More's project of cultural revolution was a transformation of the role played by women of all classes in the formation of national culture. Unlike Wollstonecraft, who argued that the two sexes were in all significant aspects the same, Hannah More insisted on the innate difference between the sexes. To women she assigned a greater delicacy of perception and feeling and above all, a greater moral purity and capacity for virtue. Men on the other hand have better judgment, based on their wider experience of the public world; at the same time their manners are coarse, with "rough angles and asperities" (introduction to *Essays on Various Subjects,* 1777, VI: 266). If More's "revolution in manners" was to occur, then, it must be carried out by women.

But first women must be educated to understand their proper function in society. More's *Strictures on the Modern System of Female Education* (1799) laid out her program for the education of "excellent women" (III: 200): a systematic development of the innate female capacity for virtue and piety through a judicious reading of the Bible, devotional tracts, and serious literature, extended by rational conversation and manifested in the active exercise of compassion and generosity. The goal of More's educational project for women was no less than a cultural redefinition of *female virtue.* As summed up in that "pattern daughter . . . [who] will make a pattern wife," Lucilla Stanley (*Coelebs in Search of a Wife,* 1808/1995: 246), female virtue was equated by More with rational intelligence, modesty and chastity, a sincere commitment to spiritual values and the Christian religion, an affectionate devotion to one's family, active service on behalf of one's community, and an insistence on keeping promises. In More's words,

> I call education, not that which smothers a woman with accomplishments, but that which tends to consolidate a firm and regular system of character; that which tends to form a friend, a companion, and a wife. I call education, not that which is made up of the shreds and patches of useless arts, but that which inculcates principles, polishes taste, regulates temper, cultivates reason, subdues the passions, directs the feelings, habituates to reflection, trains to self-denial, and, more especially, that which refers all actions, feelings, sentiments, tastes and passions to the love and fear of God. (*Coelebs* 13)

More's concept of female virtue thus stood in stark contrast to her culture's prevailing definition of the ideal woman as one who possessed physical beauty and numerous accomplishments and who could effectively entice a man of substance into marriage.

More's concept of female virtue also stood in opposition to the prevailing masculine concept of virtue as civic humanism. As J. G. A. Pocock explains, in the eighteenth century the Roman republican concept of virtue as "devotion to the public good," and "the practice . . . of relations of equality between citizens" could no longer be reconciled with the "ideals" of commerce which required an exchange between non-equals, credit, and dependence. Hence masculine "virtue" was redefined as the possession of property and "the practice and refinement of polished manners," manners which would engage the trust and credit of like-minded men of property (Pocock 41–48). This specifically male "commercial humanism" (Barrell 102–103) seemed to More to be soulless and mechanistic, substituting the form of good manners for the substance. Female virtue was not a matter of credit and exchange but rather of spiritual conviction, sincere compassion for the welfare of others, humility, and self-sacrifice.

Embedded in More's program for the education of women was a new career for upper- and middle-class women, as Dorice Elliot has shown: namely, a sustained and increasingly institutionalized effort to relieve the sufferings of the less fortunate. As Mrs. Stanley defines this career: "*Charity is the calling of a lady; the care of the poor is her profession*" (*Coelebs* 138; More's italics). More here conceptualized for the first time the career of what we would now call the "social worker," the organized and corporate, as opposed to the spontaneous and individualistic, practice of philanthropy. As embodied in Lucinda Stanley, this profession involves spending one day each week collecting "necessaries" for the poor—food, clothing, medicine —and two evenings each week visiting them in their own cottages where she can best determine "their wants and their characters" (*Coelebs* 63).

More advocated an even more institutionalized philanthropy, a "regular systematical good" resulting in a "broad stream of bounty . . . flowing through and refreshing whole districts" (*Strictures* III: 270). She urged her women readers to participate actively in the organization of voluntary benevolent societies and in the foundation of hospitals, orphanages, Sunday Schools, and all-week charity or "ragged" schools for the education and relief of the poor. And her call was heard: literally thousands of voluntary societies sprang up in the opening decades of the nineteenth century to serve the needs of every imaginable group of sufferers, from the Bristol Orphan Asylum to the Sailors Home, from the Poor Printers Fund to the Pensioners at Wrington, to name only four among the seventy-one charities to which More herself contributed generously in her will (Henry Thompson 325).

More's Evangelical demand that women demonstrate their commitment to God through a life of active service for the first time gave her upper- and middle-class sisters a mission in life, the personal and financial support of institutionalized charities: from orphanages, workhouses, and hospitals to asylums and prisons. These philanthropic activities contributed directly to the emancipation and increasing social empowerment of women. As F. K. Prochaska concludes his study of women and philanthropy in nineteenth-century England, in an observation so important that I wish to quote him at length:

The charitable experience of women was a lever which they used to open the doors closed to them in other spheres, for in its variety it was experience applicable to just about every profession in England. Through their extensive contact with charitable organisations women increased their interest in government, administration, and the law. Through contact with charity schools they increased their interest in education. Through the system of district visiting they increased their interest in the problems of poverty and the social services. Through their work as hospital, workhouse, and prison visitors they increased their interest in, among other things, medicine and diet. Moreover, as a religion of action philanthropy slowly challenged the complaisancy of women, gave them practical experience and responsibility, and perhaps most importantly, it heightened their self-confidence and self-respect. At the back of their minds, however, was an awareness that if they were to become more useful they would need more knowledge. Philanthropy pointed out the limitations imposed upon women at the same time as it broadened their horizons. It should not come as a surprise that in 1866 women trained in charitable societies were prominent among those who petitioned the House of Commons praying for the enfranchisement of their sex. (227)

Women were particularly suited to the active exercise of charity because, according to More, they possessed greater sensibility than do men. More defined sensibility as an *active* rather than passive sympathy for the sufferings of others, one that immediately attempts to relieve the misery it perceives. As she invoked it in one of her early poems,

> Sweet Sensibility! thou keen delight!
> Thou hasty moral! sudden sense of right!
> Thou untaught goodness! Virtue's precious seed!
> Thou sweet precursor of the gen'rous deed!
> (*Sensibility: A Poetical Epistle to the Hon. Mrs. Boscawen*, 1782,
> lines 244–47)

Secondly, women were more versed in what More called "practical piety," the immediate assessment and relief of the day-to-day requirements of the poor, the sick, the dying. Finally, women who had learned how to manage a household properly could more readily extend those skills to the Sunday School, workhouse, or hospital.

Implicit both in More's *Strictures on Female Education* and in her novel *Coelebs* is the argument that household management or domestic economy provides the best model for the management of the state or national economy. As Coelebs asserts, "my notion of 'household good,' which does not include one idea of drudgery or servility, but which involves a large and comprehensive scheme of excellence . . . is . . . the most appropriate branch of female knowledge. . . . The domestic arrangements of [Milton's Eve] resemble . . . those of Providence, whose under-agent she is. Her wisdom is seen in its effects" (*Coelebs* 9). And as Mr. Stanley later explains, "Retrenchments, to be efficient, must be applied to great objects. The true [domestic] economist will draw in by contracting the outline, by narrowing the bottom, by cutting off with an unsparing hand costly superfluities, which affect not comfort but cherish vanity" (184). Moreover, he continues, such domestic economists "execute their well-ordered plan as an indispensable duty, but not as a superlative merit. . . . It is their business, not their boast" (185). More had earlier spelled out this concept of home economics in greater detail in her *Strictures on the Modern System of Female Education:*

> ladies whose natural vanity has been aggravated by a false education, may look down on economy as a vulgar attainment, unworthy of the attention of an highly cultivated intellect; but that is the false estimate of a shallow mind. Economy, such as a woman of fortune is called on to practice, is not merely the petty detail of small daily expenses, the shabby curtailments and stinted parsimony of a little mind operating on little concerns; but it is the exercise of a sound judgment exerted in the comprehensive outline of order, of arrangement, of distribution; *of regulation by which alone well-governed societies, great and small, subsist.* . . . A sound economy is a sound understanding brought into action; it is calculation realized; it is the doctrine of proportion reduced to practice; it is foreseeing consequences, and guarding against them; it is expecting contingencies, and being prepared for them. (III: 189–90; my italics)

By assigning to women—and their mentor Eve—the capacity to develop and execute a fiscally responsible plan of household management which satisfies the physical, emotional, and religious needs of all the members of the household (servants as well as family members), More effectually defined women as the best managers of the national estate, as the true patriots. As Kathryn Sutherland has argued, More proposed "a practical politics of domestic reformation, which is national in the ambitious scope of its campaign and personal in its focus on the woman in her family as the source of this larger regeneration" (36). Or as More addressed her female compatriots:

> In this moment of alarm and peril [1799], I would call on them . . . to come forward, and contribute their full and fair proportion towards the saving of their country . . . without blemishing the delicacy of their sex: I would call them to the best and most appropriate exertion of their power, to raise the depressed tone of public morals, and to awaken the drowsy spirit of religious principle. (*Strictures* III: 13)

Again invoking Milton's Eve as her model of female propriety and "Those thousand *decencies* which daily flow / From all her words and actions," More urged her sisters to "exert themselves with a patriotism at once firm and feminine, for the general good" (*Strictures* III: 14).

It is in the role of mother that More's ideal of the well-educated, fiscally responsible, and morally pure woman finds her fulfillment. But it is crucial to recognize that More's mother is the mother, not just of her own family, but of the nation as a whole. As More affirmed in *Strictures on the Modern System of Female Education,*

> the great object to which *you,* who are or may be mothers, are more especially called, is the education of your children. If we are responsible for the use of influence in the case of those over whom we have no immediate control, in the case of our children we are responsible for the exercise of acknowledged *power:* a power wide in its extent, indefinite in its effects, and inestimable in its importance. On YOU depend in no small degree the principles of the whole rising generation. To your direction the daughters are almost exclusively committed; and until a certain age, to you also is consigned the mighty privilege of forming the hearts and minds of your infant sons. To YOU is made over the awfully important trust of infusing the first principles of piety into the tender minds of those who may one day be called to instruct, not families merely, but districts; to influence, not individuals, but senates. Your private exertions may at this moment be contributing to the future happiness, your domestic neglect, to the future ruin, of your country. And may you never forget, in this your early instruction of your offspring, that religion is the only sure ground of morals; that private principle is the only solid ground of public virtue. (*Strictures* III: 44)

As Mitzi Myers has noted, no one worked harder than More to define a new ideological mission for women: to "educate the young and illiterate, succor the unfortunate, amend the debased popular culture of the lower orders, reorient worldly men of every class, and set the national household in order," thereby elevating women's "nurturing and reformative assignment" into a "national mission" (1986: 266). Women can become, in More's view, the mothers of the nation. Horace Walpole correctly, if viciously, acknowledged More's claim when he scathingly referred to her as "an Alma Mater with dugs enough to suckle the 365 bantlings of the Countess of Hainault" (344).

Emphasizing women's *public* role as mothers of the nation, More necessarily downplayed their more private sexual roles as females. More has been roundly criticized, by Nancy Cott and many others, for insisting on a new ideal of female "passionlessness." As Cott put it, Hannah More's "work perfected the transformation of woman's image from sexual to moral being," giving women power only at the price of sexual repression (1978: 226). But this is too one-sided a reading of More's campaign. More did not urge women to *deny* their sexual desires, but only to *channel* them into marriage with a morally as well as sexually desirable partner. Michael Mason gives a more nuanced reading of More's attitude to sexual desire. Mason first notes that the strongest push for anti-sensualism in the early nineteenth century came, not from Anglican Evangelicalism, or even Nonconformist Evangelicalism, but rather "from secularist and progressive quarters: from individuals trying to apply the thought of Jeremy Bentham, for instance, from those who might write for the *Westminster Review* and the

Fortnightly, equally certainly from women's rights activists, and even from those who might be found addressing Chartist rallies" (3). He then rightly observes that "To Hannah More belongs the distinction of having written at greater length explicitly about sex than any other leading Evangelical" (77).

More's novel *Coelebs in Search of a Wife* is a lengthy account of the systematic search of a young Evangelical bachelor for an appropriate life-companion: it is clear that this Eve-like woman must and does arouse his erotic desires as well as his moral approbation. When told that he cannot marry Lucilla Stanley for three months, Coelebs manifests what is clearly an experience of sexual frustration (*Coelebs* 244); Lucilla's vivid blush when Coelebs proposes to her signals the same consciousness of physical desire (220), as Ruth Yeazell's fine study of the significance of the blush in nineteenth-century fiction has taught us (65–80). And Lady Melbury, who has won back the affections of her husband by following Evangelical prescriptions, proudly announces that "we became lovers and companions" (254).

By defining the private household and "private principle" as the source of "public virtue" (*Strictures* III: 44), More implicitly endorsed Edmund Burke's concept of the domestic estate as the model for the state of the nation. As Burke had argued in his *Reflections on the Revolution in France:*

> one of the first and most leading principles on which the commonwealth and the laws are consecrated is, lest the temporary possessors and life-renters in it, unmindful of what they have received from their ancestors or of what is due to their posterity, should act as if they were the entire masters; that they should not think it amongst their rights to cut off the entail or commit waste on the inheritance, by destroying at their pleasure the whole original fabric of their society; hazarding to leave to those who come after them a ruin instead of an habitation—and teaching these successors as little to respect their contrivances as they had themselves respected the institutions of their forefathers. (83)

But rather than assigning to our canonized "forefathers" the ultimate responsibility for the moral improvement and sustenance of the family estate (Burke's "little platoon," 41), More explicitly assigned that responsibility to women, to *mothers*. Men may wage battles abroad, but women protect the home front: as she asked rhetorically, "Is it not desirable to be the lawful possessors of a lesser domestic territory, rather than the turbulent usurpers of a wider foreign empire?" (*Strictures* III: 200). This is why her heroine Lucilla Stanley devotes a great deal of time to *gardening*—to nurturing and controlling the native land of England, as Eve cultivated the fields of Eden.

In making the private upper- and middle-class household the model for the national household, Hannah More effectively erased any meaningful distinction between the private and the broadly defined public sphere. She further insisted that it is women, not men, who are most responsible for carrying out moral reforms and thus for advancing the progress of civilization as such: "The general state of civilized society depends more than those are aware who are not accustomed to scrutinize into the springs of human action, on the prevailing sentiments and habits of women, and on the nature and degree of the estimation in which they are held" (*Strictures* III: 12). She here anticipated Lucy Aikin's observation in her *Epistles on Women* (1810) that "men cannot degrade women without degrading themselves." Insisting on the primary role of women in establishing "true taste, right principle, and genuine feeling" in the culture of a nation, More finally claimed for women the dominant role in what Norbert Elias has since called the "civilizing process."

IV

The late eighteenth century in England was a culture of consumption, one marked by the wide availability of a significantly greater range of goods —the results of Britain's rapidly expanding imperial and commercial ventures both in the West (the Americas and the Pacific Islands) and the East (the East India Company's growing trade with India, China, and the Spice Islands in the Indonesia archipelago) (see McKendrick, Brewer [1993, 1995], Plumb, Campbell). Confronted with both an aristocratic emphasis on the ostentatious display of wealth through the purchase of ever-changing fashionable furnishings, clothes, and carriages, and the rising middle-class desire to emulate the elite by similarly acquiring such new fancy goods, Hannah More attempted to define a *moral* method of capitalist investment and consumption.

Together with the male members of the Evangelical Clapham Sect, she developed the concept of what we might now call moral or Christian capitalism. The acquisition of money, of capital, was not in her eyes an inherent evil; rather the reverse: it all depended on how you earned your money and what you spent it on. As David Spring has shown, the Clapham Sect was actively committed to the pursuit of business, using the methods of capitalist investment (1961). As More argued, "the mischief arises not from our living in the world, but from the world living in us; occupying our hearts, and monopolizing our affections. Action is the life of virtue, and the world is the theater of action" (*Manners of the Great* II: 275). Following Adam Smith, the Clapham Sect saw no contradiction between laissez-faire capitalism and the development of moral sentiment. This is because, as Thomas Haskell has argued in two brilliant essays, successful capitalism and humanitarianism in an era of imperial expansion theoretically depend on the same two things. (1) One must keep one's promise to strangers one has never met, that is, enter into a bond (a legally enforceable "contract") with strangers. This immediately produces, Haskell argues, a sense of connect-edness with or indebtedness to strangers. (2) One must attend to the re-mote consequences of one's acts. One thereby comes to feel a sense of obligation for the welfare of people one has never met; one comes to care about the death of a starving stranger. The Age of Contract thus becomes the Age of Principle, where "The defining characteristic of the 'man of principle,' the moral paragon of a promise-keeping, market-centered form of life, was his willingness to act on principle no matter how inconvenient it might be" (Haskell 2:152). Moreover, Haskell continues, "the very possi-bility of feeling obliged to go to the aid of a suffering stranger—whether his suffering was that occasioned by chattel slavery or by what the observer interpreted as slavery to sin—was enormously heightened by the emergence of a form of life that made attention to the remote consequences of one's acts (or omissions) an emblem of civilization itself" (2:155). Theoretically, then, keeping promises and a benevolent concern for others became the touchstone of Christian capitalism (I say theoretically because, as we well know, the churchgoing Christian capitalist was in practice often insensitive to the sufferings of others, as the exploitation of men, women, and children in the mines, mills, glass houses, and factories of Victorian England amply documents).

Hannah More represents such business men and women of principle in several of the tales included in the *Cheap Repository Tracts*. In "The Two Wealthy Farmers," the unscrupulous Mr. Bragwell systematically lies to his clients, deals in stolen goods, gets his neighbors drunk before auctioning off his land or horses so as to reduce their good judgment, takes advantage of the ignorance of others, breaks the Sabbath, and encourages his daugh-ters' love of ostentatious display. He is rewarded with the elopement of one daughter with a traveling actor, the marriage of another to a wealthy but greedy squire who "squeezes" his in-laws to finance ever riskier land deals until this son-in-law runs into enormous debt and kills himself; his wife, in dire poverty, then dies in childbirth. Meanwhile, Mr. Worthy, a man of principle, is content with his station in life, works hard, treats all his cus-tomers honestly, maintains a home with "not so many ornaments," but "more comforts" (I: 43), raises his daughters in the lessons of "humility, economy, meekness, contentment, self-denial, industry" (I: 42), engages in daily prayers at home and church attendance on Sunday, and is rewarded when his daughters all happily marry young men of probity and wealth. More paints a composite portrait of such principled men of business in "The History of Mr. Fantom," where Mr. Trueman joins his fellow trades-men at their favorite club:

> This club consisted of a few sober citizens, who met of an evening for a little harmless recreation after business: their object was, not to reform parliament, but their own shops; not to correct the abuses of government, but of parish officers; not to cure the excesses of administration, but of their own porters and apprentices. . . . In such turbulent times it was a comfort to each to feel he was a tradesman, and not a statesman; that he was not called to responsibility for a trust for which he found he had no talents, while he was at full liberty to employ the talents he really possessed, in fairly amassing a fortune, of which the laws would be the best guardian, and government the best security. Thus a legitimate self-love, regulated by prudence, and restrained by principle, produced peaceable subjects and good citizens. (I: 4)

Lower on the social scale, the honest "Hackney Coachman" who never overcharges his customers sees his business grow so fast that he cannot keep up with the demand and is hence able to marry Betty Brown, the hardworking, thrifty orange girl of St. Giles, and to set up a successful sausage-shop. Tom White, the poor but industrious postboy, is tempted away from honest service by the offer of a position as chaise-boy, a job which brings him into bad company, forces him to whip his horses brutally, and leads him into a riding accident that might have been fatal. Chastened, Tom returns to his former employment, succeeds well enough to be able to buy a farm on credit, marries a "neat, modest, plain" girl and eventually becomes rich. For as More comments, in a summation of her view of Christian capitalism, "the same principles which make a man sober and honest, have also a natural tendency to make him healthy and rich" (II: 93).

The Christian capitalist not only earns money honestly and fairly, but he or she also, More insisted, distributes that money to others through systematic charity. James Stock, the successful shoemaker, decides to educate at his own expense the God-fearing poorhouse boy Thomas Williams. Mr. Trueman, seeing his hardworking gardener's cottage on fire, immediately organizes a water-bucket brigade and even risks his life to save the gardener's son from the burning house. He then gives the gardener's family food, clothing, and the funds necessary to rebuild their cottage. Pleading among her Protestant peers on behalf of the emigrant French Catholic clergy during the 1790s, Hannah More argued that charity is not only a religious imperative to alleviate the sufferings of strangers; it is also good economics:

> the inability to give much ought not, on any occasion, to be converted into an excuse for giving nothing. Even moderate circumstances need not plead an exemption. The industrious tradesman will not, even in a political view, be eventually a loser by his small contribution. The money now raised is neither carried out of our country, nor dissipated in luxuries, but returns again to the community; returns to our shops and to our markets, to procure the bare necessaries of life. (*Address in Behalf of the French Emigrant Clergy* II: 379)

More not only argued for the moral distribution and redistribution of money to the deserving in a Christian capitalist society. She also advocated a concept of moral or Christian consumption. She urged her readers to purchase goods, not just because they were useful or not, beautiful or not, healthy or not, but because it was morally right or wrong to do so. She was an early advocate of the boycott on the use of West Indian sugar. An ardent foe of the slave trade and slavery in the British colonies, she endorsed the arguments of William Fox, who felt that the consumption of West Indian sugar, "steeped in the blood of our fellow creatures," was tantamount to an act of cannibalism that would forever pollute the pure British constitution (Sussman 51–53). As early as 1788, Hannah More urged her friends not to use West Indian sugar in their tea or baked goods (Roberts II: 103; M.G. Jones 1952: 83–84). She thus, as Clare Midgley has noted, joined Lady Middleton and those many female abstention campaigners who extended the abolitionist movement to household practices, further underlining More's argument that social and cultural reform begins at home, under the leadership of women (1992: 16–18; 1996: 142–43).

More extended her concept of Christian consumption beyond the immediate political campaign against slavery and the slave trade. She defined evil consumption as "luxury" and "dissipation" (*Essay on Dissipation* VI: 267–70), the waste of money on fashion, food, and display for its own sake. In her sacred drama *Belshazzar,* she explicitly equated the overt consumption of luxuries with imperial tyranny; as Belshazzar arrogantly proclaims,

> What is wealth
> But the rich means to gratify desire?
> . . . . What is empire?
> The privilege to punish and enjoy;
> To feel our power in making others fear it;
> To taste of pleasure's cup till we grow giddy,
> And think ourselves immortal! (VI:163)

Throughout her *Cheap Repository Tracts,* More waged a campaign against extravagant waste—the excessive, ten-course meals served by Mrs. Bragwell—and in favor of what she defined as morally good consumption: wholesome brown bread, nourishing cheap stews, rice pudding, and home-brewed beer for the working class (*Tom White* II: 108–16); tasty plain food in moderation for the middle and upper classes. Both Mrs. Worthy, who prepares for her guests "a plain and neat but good dinner" with "excellent tarts" (I: 43), and Celia, the woman who wins over the dissipated gentleman Florio in More's poem "Florio," represent More's view of good middle-class household consumption:

> Celia a table still supplied,
> Which modish luxury might deride:
> A modest feast the hope conveys,

> The master eats on other days;
> While gorgeous banquets oft bespeak
> A hungry household all the week.
> And decent elegance was there,
> And plenty with her liberal air. (V: 296)

More calculatedly politicized her campaign for good national consumption by equating ostentatious luxury with French culture and cuisine. Flavia, Florio's aristocratic mistress and "th'acknowledged empress of bonton," presides over a dinner table where

> None at her polish'd table sit,
> But who aspire to modish wit;
> The *persiflage,* th'unfeeling jeer,
> The civil, grave, ironic sneer (V: 301)

and where

> . . . still the natural taste was cheated,
> Twas delug'd in some sauce one hated.
> "Twas sauce! twas sweatmeat! t'was confection!
> All poignancy! and all perfection!"
> Rich *entremets,* whose name none knows,
> *Ragouts, tourtes, tendrons, fricandeaux,*
> Might picque the sensuality
> O' th' hogs of Epicurus' sty; . . .
> Great goddess of the French *cuisine!* (V: 302–303)

V

By moralizing both capitalism and consumption, the daily work of earning and spending, and opposing British Christianity to French Catholic culture and cuisine, More directly engaged in that eighteenth-century project of national self-formation so well described by Gerald Newman and Linda Colley. She equated the ideal British nation with a Protestant Evangelical morality that defined itself in opposition both to French and to Catholic corruptions. Attacking the impiety of M. Dupont's speech to the National Convention at Paris in 1792, in which Dupont advocated that atheism be taught in the new public schools of France, More articulated her nationalist vision of England:

Who, I say, that had a head to reason, or a heart to feel, did not glow with the hope, that from the ruins of tyranny, and the rubbish of popery [in France], a beautiful and finely-framed edifice would in time have been constructed, and that ours would not have been the only country in which the patriot's fair idea of well-understood liberty, the politician's view of a perfect constitution, together with the establishment of a pure and reasonable, a sublime and rectified Christianity, might be realized? (*Remarks on the Speech of M. Dupont* II: 386)

Essential to More's project of national reformation was the assumption that the "public revolution of manners" (preface to *Works* I: ix) she demanded must be led by women, and in particular by one woman, the supposed future Queen of England, Princess Charlotte. Her *Hints towards forming the Character of a Young Princess* (1805), like Thomas Elyot's *Book of the Governor* and Machiavelli's *The Prince,* is a treatise on the nature of good government. Ostensibly a program for the education of the young Charlotte, More's treatise first argues that all citizens of the nation, male or female, royalty or commoners, rich or poor, should be educated according to the same principles of self-discipline, rationality, and Christian morality. After outlining the appropriate subjects that a future monarch should study (history, geography, political theory, Latin and modern European languages, an appreciation of the fine arts), More concludes that the "art of reigning" consists above all in the exercise of "wise . . . judgment" (IV: 24), a judgment which More explicitly defines as being within the capacity of a woman: "Let her ever bear in mind, she *is not to study that she may become learned, but that she may become wise*" (IV: 23; More's italics). To attain such wisdom, More recommends conversation with men and women of mature judgment and critical perception, such rational amusements as serious reading, and the development of memory.

Part of the wisdom which the future female monarch must learn is the limits of her own royal "prerogatives"—even as she must stand firm in endorsement of her own religious beliefs and intellectual understanding, she must acknowledge that her power is constrained by the laws of the British constitution which guarantee the freedom of her people. Tracking the history of fallen empires, More insists that the British constitution is uniquely "favourable to virtue," "congenial with religion, and conducive to happiness" because it seeks to provide for the "well-being of the whole community . . . by effectually securing the rights, the safety, the comforts of every individual" (IV: 67–68). More is here defining a concept of the reformed British nation as based on an ethic of care, a Christian concern to meet the needs of all members of the community.

After detailing at length the myriad practical tasks in the daily business of governance and deportment which the Princess should master, through a close study of historical precedents and a sustained program of reading in both the classics and modern science, More insists that above all the Princess must actively embrace the commandments and teachings of the Bible. She must affirm Christianity as her spiritual guide, and must vigorously support the rituals of the established Church of England. By far the most important duty of the Princess is to set the moral tone of the nation through her own example and through the judicious selection of the bishops who are to lead the Church. In this role, as the moral leader of England, More suggests, "the just administration of this peculiar power may be reasonably expected as much, we had almost said even more, from a female, than from a monarch of the other sex" (IV: 361). More concluded her theoretical treatise on how to create the ideal ruler of England with this exhortation to Charlotte and her tutors:

> she should practically understand, that religion, though it has its distinct and separate duties, yet it is not by any means a distinct and separate thing, so as to make up a duty of itself, disconnected with other duties; but that it is a grand, and universally governing principle, which is to be the fountain of her morality, and the living spring of all her actions: that religion is not merely a thing to be retained in the mind, as a dormant mass of inoperative opinions, but which is to be brought, by every individual, in to the detail of every day's deed; which, in a prince, is to influence his private behaviour, as well as his public conduct; which is to regulate his choice of ministers, and his adoption of measures; which is to govern his mind, in making war and making peace; which is to accompany him, not only to the closet, but to the council; which is to fill his mind, whether in the world or in retirement, with an abiding sense of the vast responsibility which he is under, and the awful account to which he will one day be called, before that Being, who lodges the welfare of so many millions in his hands. (IV: 398)

In this remarkable passage, More subtly conflated the female with the male ruler of England: both have a "vast responsibility," second only to God himself, for the "welfare of so many millions."

By making women the potential embodiment of what Mitzi Myers calls "aggressive virtue" (1982: 209), by addressing her tract on good Christian government to a woman, Hannah More specifically called on women to save the nation. And her demand for a "revolution in manners" was answered. The career of Hannah More, who was virtually canonized as an "Anglican Saint" after her death in 1833 (Cropper vii), made the reign—not of Charlotte—but of Victoria and everything we now mean by Victorianism—inevitable. After the Evangelical campaigns of the early nineteenth century, Britain would not have tolerated the rule of another George IV: a fiscally irresponsible libertine devoted to luxury, stylistic display, and dissipation. The new British nation required that its royal monarch be economically prudent, decorous in appearance and taste, and above all moral (see Brown, Quinlan, Jaeger, Hall). And after the career of Hannah More, the symbolic representation of this new national identity had to be female: only a woman, in the historical case, Queen Victoria, could literally embody and thus transparently represent British national virtue, that Christian virtue that More had everywhere in her writings gendered as female. Only a woman could become the Mother of the Nation, Britannia herself.

2

Theater as the School of Virtue

The leading women playwrights of the Romantic era—Joanna Baillie, Hannah More, Hannah Cowley, and Elizabeth Inchbald—consciously used the theater to re-stage and thereby revise both the social construction of gender and the nature of good government. They were writing at a time when, as Gillian Russell has recently shown, the theater was an intensely political place and its influence on the cultural and political life of the nation widely recognized. Russell focuses on the ways in which the Georgian theater written and produced by men represented British chauvinist self-affirmations during the French Revolution and subsequent Napoleonic campaigns, celebrating the British army and navy and the freedoms guaranteed by England's constitutional monarchy. Women playwrights engaged in an equally political campaign, using their dramatic writings to challenge a dominant patriarchy by providing counter-examples of "a new woman," a rational, compassionate, merciful, tolerant, and peace-loving woman better equipped to rule the nation than the men currently in power. At the same time they challenged the notion that the English monarchy did in fact protect the liberties of her people, especially those of women. Finally, they argued that the theater was uniquely well situated to promote social reform, since it could function as a public school for females, one that could be used to correct the inappropriate or inadequate education many girls received at home.

Joanna Baillie

In her introductory discourse to *A Series of Plays on the Passions* (1798), Joanna Baillie offered the most detailed theoretical statement of this conception of the theater as a school for female virtue and political empowerment. As Catherine Burroughs has shown, Baillie's theater theory subtly erased the division between the public and the private, formulating the ways in which domestic "closet drama" could be staged in public arenas. Baillie begins her introductory discourse by defining human nature's primary motivation or "great master propensity" as "sympathetick curiosity" (4), a definition that contests the assertions of Hobbes, Locke, Burke, and Bentham, as well as modern "rational choice" social scientists, that human beings are primarily motivated by self-interest. Instead Baillie invokes Adam Smith's concept, in his *Theory of Moral Sentiments* (1759), that sympathy is one of "the original passions of human nature" (Smith 2); it is the capacity to *feel* the emotions of another person. Baillie then argues that the subject or self can be constructed only in sympathetic relation to other selves, and that knowledge is produced, not from "objective" or detached observation but rather from empathic identification, an identification that is then articulated through the stories we tell of what and whom we meet, what she calls "tattling." Baillie's epistemology strikingly anticipates contemporary standpoint theory, the belief that valid knowledge can be achieved, not by positing a universal subject removed from local circumstances (as assumed by Habermas and by many contemporary scientists), but only by acknowledging that all knowledge-producers are historically and culturally located, and by attempting to correct for the inherent biases or limited standpoints of a given set of experimenters or observers. For Baillie, it is the drama that uniquely enables the observer to take up different subject positions, to identify with opposing standpoints, and thus to correct the biases of a single point of view.

Baillie's introductory discourse is specifically to *A Series of Plays in which it is attempted to delineate The Stronger Passions of the Mind;* she further claims that the development of the individual is governed most powerfully by feelings and desires, passions which must be held in check by reason if they are not to become self-destructive. Asserting that human character is organic and developmental, growing not from Locke's "white paper" or blank slate but from an inherent "propensity" or seed, she both anticipates William Wordsworth's influential assertion that "fair seed-time had my soul" and also argues that this growing seed takes its final shape from its interactions with its environment. Each of her tragedies studies the growth of a single passion that, unchecked by the rational advice of others, destroys the hero; her comedies hold that obsessive passion up to the derision of others, laughing its possessor back into a more moderated feeling.

Significantly, in Baillie's plays, it is the *male* characters who are prey to unregulated passion, while the *female* characters are the voices of rational moderation (unless they are driven by hostile external forces beyond the range of reason altogether, as in *Orra*, her Gothic tragedy of female persecution, fear, and madness). She thus denies a patriarchal gender definition of the female sex as irrational, impulsive, and uncontrollable. At the same time, like Mary Wollstonecraft, she insists that there is no significant psychological or mental sex-difference between males and females. As she claims in her introductory discourse, "I believe that there is no man that ever lived, who has behaved in a certain manner, on a certain occasion, who has not had amongst women some corresponding spirit, who on the like occasion, and every way similarly circumstanced, would have behaved in the like manner" (36).

The function of drama, Baillie asserts, is to arouse the sympathetic curiosity of the viewer so that the audience will both identify with her characters and learn from their errors. "The theater is a school" (58), she claims, and like the other female literary critics of her day, she wished to use literature to educate her audience to a more responsible morality. In order to do this, she recognized, drama must be probable or "natural"—it must show "the plain order of things in this every-day world" (21), including the way that the passions develop and change *over time*, in their "infant, growing, and repressed state" (59). Despite her claims for the universality of the growth of the human passions, we must recognize that there is a potentially limiting class bias in Baillie's concept of human nature. For Baillie, what is "natural" is what is "middling and lower" class, English, and domestic— she rejects both the "artifice" of the aristocracy and the potentially disruptive "ballad-reading" of the "lowest classes of the labouring people, who are the broad foundation of society, which," she claimed, "can never be generally moved without endangering every thing that is constructed upon it" (57–58).

To achieve a "natural" or probable revelation of the human passions, Baillie devised several specific dramatic techniques: the frequent use of the soliloquy; a focus on but one passion and one plot (with no distracting subplots or unrelated incidents); the staging of processions, balls, banquets, and other social rituals or ceremonies in place of subplots in order to arouse audience attention but avoid distraction; and the confinement of the action to a small, intimate, often domestic space (a house, a town square). Eschewing what she considered to be bad comedy—the rhetorical excesses of satirical comedy, the amorality of witty comedy, the hypocrisies of sentimental comedy, and the contrivances (or "ambushed bush-fighting") of "busy" comedy or farce—Baillie wrote what she called "Characteristick Comedy," a comedy devoted to the representation of the "motley world of men and women in which we live" (49), using ordinary language and focusing on the damage done by emotional excesses.

We must recognize the large cultural authority to which Baillie laid claim. Echoing the sixteenth-century Scottish nationalist, Andrew Fletcher of Saltoun, she suggests that "if I have the writing of its [Drama], let who will make the laws of a nation" (57). Baillie thus positions herself as the unacknowledged legislator of the British nation, superior to the historian, philosopher, and poet. In her view, the dramatist alone can combine an abstract moral lesson with a concrete appeal to our "sympathetic curiosity," an appeal that will—in this first articulation of what we might now call reader-response theory—produce political action, cultural ideology, and meaning itself. Although Baillie employs a conventional modesty topos, craving the "forbearance of my reader" (69), she firmly asserts both the originality and the pedagogical value of her dramatic project: she is the first to attempt to reveal the growth of individual passions, from love and hatred to remorse and sexual jealousy, by writing *paired* plays, a tragedy and a comedy on each passion. By moving the realm of private, psychological feelings from the domestic "closet" to the public stage, Baillie implicitly asserts that a hitherto culturally marginalized "women's realm," the realm of feelings, sympathy, and curiosity, is in fact the basis of all human culture, and especially of political culture. Good domestic management thus becomes her model for good politics; a rational control of passion that produces harmonious and loving family relationships becomes the model for peaceful national and international relations.

Turning now to what I consider to be Baillie's finest play, *Count Basil* (1798), I would like to discuss it briefly as an example of the argument made above. *Count Basil* is Baillie's examination in the genre of tragedy of the passion of love, her response to Shakespeare's interrogation of the conflicting claims of honor and love in *Antony and Cleopatra* and to John Dryden's rehearsal of those same issues in his *All for Love*. Equally important, this play is about the control of the public realm, a debate between two opposing methods of government.

Count Basil begins by staging the meeting of two opposing processions, two genders, two value systems. From one side, accompanied by martial music, comes the military procession of Count Basil and his soldiers, who are hailed for their discipline and military success; from the opposite side, accompanied by "soft music," comes the Princess Victoria and her women, who are hailed for their beauty and their public display of filial devotion and religious duty. Two bodies are here presented for the specular desire of both the audience and of Count Basil: the wounded body of the old soldier Geoffrey and the "splendid" body of Victoria. Overtly, this display stages the tension between military honor and erotic love, between masculine heroism and feminine graciousness. But Baillie is not simply rewriting *Antony and Cleopatra*. Instead, she insists in this opening scene on what is *absent:* Geoffrey's arm ("this arm . . . / Which now thou seest is no arm of mine" [76]) and Victoria's mother ("She is fair, / But not so fair as her good mother was" [79]).

This absence at the center of the public realm is further identified, as the play proceeds, with the amoral, Machiavellian policies of Victoria's father, the Duke of Mantua, who schemes to keep Basil in his court long enough for his secret ally, the King of France, to defeat Basil's Austro-Hungarian Emperor. Pretending hospitality, the Duke employs his daughter as a pawn in his policy. Unknowingly, Victoria graciously urges Basil to stay with her and Basil, infatuated with her beauty, acquiesces.

Basil stays in Mantua one day, two days, three days, despite the urgent demands of his cousin, fellow officer, and chief advisor, Count Rosinberg, that he continue on his march at once. Rosinberg's motives are called into question, however, both by his misogyny (the only woman he knows whose love will never change is his "own good mother" [88]), and by his erotic infatuation with his younger cousin. His "foolish admiration" claims that "when Basil fights he wields a thousand swords" (80–81), and he embraces Basil with the ardor of a jealous lover ("my friend! / I love thee now more than I ever lov'd thee" [161]), when Basil agrees to leave Victoria (Act IV, sc. 3).

As we come to recognize, in *Count Basil* the hero's struggle is not between erotic passion and military duty but rather between three kinds of passion: heterosexual love, homosocial love, and self-love. Basil's heterosexual infatuation with Victoria might well be reciprocated, we are led to believe, as Victoria begins to recognize the difference between Basil's mature devotion and the hypocritical attentions of her previous lovers, and to respond judiciously to Basil's passion for her. But Basil already has another love, as he confesses: "From early youth, war has my mistress been, / And tho' a rugged one, I'll constant prove, / And not forsake her now" (86). As the play unfolds, we see this prior love unveiled as a powerful homosocial bonding of Basil with his men, and especially with Rosinberg, who is passionately devoted to Basil and hostile to any woman who might interrupt that bond. Two bodies are here displayed for Basil's specular desire: the "divine" body of the beautiful Victoria and the scarred body of the old soldier Geoffrey. Weeping with his men over the body of Geoffrey, Basil manifests his deeper emotional bond, with his men. When Basil betrays that bond, when his men mutiny, Basil's self begins to split apart. The "wounded soldier" whose mask Basil wears at the ball is not only the rejected lover of Victoria, as he claims, but also the rejecting lover of his own wounded men.

But the wounded love which drives Basil to suicide is finally neither heterosexual nor homosocial. It is, as Basil admits, "his great love of military fame" (81): the wound to his own "glorious name." His failure to fight at Pavia did no harm to his own men or to his emperor's cause, since the French King was soundly defeated by another general. Nor did it, as Old Geoffrey tells him, do any lasting damage to Basil's own military career, since his previous victories remain untouched and his "soldier's fame is far too surely raised / To be o'erthrown with one unhappy chance" (179). Only Basil's self-love is fatally wounded, and it is that unregulated self-love that causes his self-destruction. Thus Baillie uncovers the dominating passion of the masculine public realm: an egotistic self-love that seeks only its personal aggrandizement, whether through Machiavellian policy or military success. Both the Duke's policy, the profit-and-loss calculations of a "petty tradesman" (107), and Basil's desire for military glory finally overwhelm their possessors: the Duke is betrayed by his own followers, especially Gauriceio, while Basil is betrayed by his own love of fame. Basil's self-love can thus be seen as the ghostly, absent arm of Old Geoffrey: what men seek and most admire is that heroic arm which is but an empty sleeve.

Opposed to this conception of masculine honor in Baillie's play is an alternative sphere of action and value, what we might think of as the female public sphere, the space assigned to the absent mother. This space is filled by the Countess Albini, who "stands in" for Victoria's mother, as Victoria acknowledges: "Still call me child, and chide me as thou wilt. / O! would that I were such as thou couldst love! / Couldst dearly love! as thou didst love my mother" (111). The Countess Albini is Baillie's homage to Mary Wollstonecraft, the ideal woman Wollstonecraft envisioned in *A Vindication of the Rights of Woman* published six years before Baillie wrote this play. She is the embodiment of rational judgment, the one who sees Victoria's faults, the one who unmasks at the ball, the one who can advise all the characters honestly and judiciously, the one who urges Rosinberg to persuade Basil to leave before permanent harm is done (131). She engages in the same revisioning of gender roles as did Wollstonecraft, advocating not the "poor ideal [i.e., "most unreal"] tyranny" of feminine beauty but rather the domestic "duties of an useful state" (109) and a love grounded in "sincerity and truth" (130). In effect, she argues for what both Hannah More and Mary Wollstonecraft defined as a family politics: the model of the well-managed home and a family harmoniously united by the domestic affections as the paradigm for successful political government. As even the misogynist Rosinberg acknowledges, of all women, only the "brave Albini" can "so wisely rule, / Their subjects never from the yoke escape" (163).

But the Countess Albini "disdains" (163) to rule a nation founded solely on self-interest; her reign is over an alternative public sphere, which in this play is associated with the interior or "closeted" spaces of the bedroom, where she advises Victoria, and the ballroom, where she rightly warns Rosinberg. Her rule of reason and the "fettered" control of the emotions does not yet extend to the militarized spaces of the ramparts where Basil meets his mutinous soldiers or to the savage, uncivilized forest where Basil declares his passionate love for Victoria. Significantly, it is in these "wild" or open spaces (of the town street, of the forest) that uncontrolled emotions reign. Basil brings his rebellious men to tears by threatening to shoot himself, while his own heart, as he leads Victoria aside during the hunt, is "bursting" (169) as he "walks up and down with hurried step, tossing about his arms in transport" (stage direction, 171). And it is outdoors, during a dark night, first in a graveyard and then in a hidden cave, that Basil, having learned that General Piscaro has alone defeated the King of France at Pavia, flings aside the sensible arguments of Old Geoffrey and rushes off in a frenzy of wounded self-love to kill himself.

The ending of the play is ambiguous. Basil dies, as his men weep beside him and Rosinberg passionately declares his love for him. Excessive masculine emotion is thus explicitly identified with death, as all who admired Basil "love him fall'n" (192)—love him who has fallen, but also, these concluding words subtly imply, love him *because* he has fallen, because those who endorse a masculinist code of honor can love only themselves or that which is finally not there, the empty sleeve of Geoffrey's arm.

Victoria vows to spend her days grieving in a "dark, shaded cloister" (190), both assuming responsibility and doing penance for having aroused but failed to control Basil's unregulated passion: "I've wrecked a brave man's honour" (175); "I have murder'd thee!" (189). But since we know Victoria to be innocent of any conscious effort to deceive Basil—and even suspect that she might well have returned his love sincerely in time, we cannot endorse her self-blame. While Victoria defines her coming life in a convent as "sad and lonely" and "cheerless" (190), might we not also see it as a possible affirmation of a female public sphere, a space where women reign? At the very least, her cloistered life endorses Albini's view that the female pursuit of the "worthless praise" and "silly adoration" of a male lover does "degrade a noble mind" (167). Finally, I would argue, Baillie suggests that it is men who destroy themselves through an excess of emotion and women who have the ability to free themselves from the follies and prejudices of their youth, to take up all standpoints, and to see a larger truth. As in *De Montfort, The Alienated Manor,* and many other plays by Joanna Baillie, it is finally the wise *woman* who combines rational prudence with sympathetic understanding and thus acts best for the nation.

Hannah More

Hannah More's hostility to the "pernicious ribaldry" (I: 109) and dangerously corrupting influence of the theater, as proclaimed in the preface to her plays first included in her collected *Works* in 1801, has been often cited. Yet she began her writing career as a playwright, continued to revise her plays for performance throughout her life, and included them in every edition of her collected *Works.* What might seem a contradiction is not so if we recognize that More enthusiastically endorsed a drama that would actively reform the morals of the nation, but denounced the actual plays performed on the stages of England during her lifetime, plays such as Susannah Centlivre's *The Bold Stroke for a Wife* and Kotzebue's *The Stranger* that offered "contagious and destructive" scenes of "temptation and seduction" (V: xxvii). As she explained in her "Preface to the Tragedies" in 1801, she had over her twenty-five-year writing career been forced to change her mind. When she first wrote for the stage, in 1773, she believed fervently that "the stage . . . might be converted into a school of virtue" (V: vi). Even in her mature view, drama remained a far more potent agent of moral reformation, one might even say propaganda, than prose or poetry:

> of all public amusements, [a well-written tragedy] is the most interesting, the most intellectual, and the most accommodated to the tastes and capacities of a rational being; nay, . . . it is almost the only one which has *mind* for its object; which has the combined advantage of addressing itself to the imagination, the judgment and the heart; . . . it is the only public diversion which calls out the higher energies of the understanding in the composition, and awakens the most lively and natural feelings of the heart in the representation. (V: vii)

More here anticipated the position of the Cambridge clergyman, James Plumptre, who argued both in his *Discourses on the Stage* and in his preface to *The English Stage Purified* (1812)—a book to which the dramatist Elizabeth Inchbald subscribed—that the theater could be beneficial for devout Christians. As Plumptre put it,

> I maintain that the evils alleged against the Drama arise only from the *abuses* of it, and if you can do those away, Christians may lawfully attend dramatic representations; that it is the duty of Christians to assist in this work,—that we must not be more severe in our censures of this particular species of literature or

amusement, than of others; nor must we expect absolute perfection, or near it, in an imperfect world,—and that we must not expect from the Drama and the Theatre, what we do not see attainable in Sermons and in the Church. An ideal perfection of the Stage may certainly be conceived to exist: let us form this idea to ourselves, and make it our aim, not in wrath and contention, but in a spirit of brotherly love and charity. (I: viii)

Plumptre tried to achieve this aim by amending the most popular plays of the day so as to omit any immoral or corrupting materials they might contain, as did Thomas Bowdler with Shakespeare's plays.

But More came to believe that the moral efficacy of the theater could be realized only after the audience—rather than the plays themselves—had been "purified" (V: viii), that her contemporary English playgoers took no delight in sacred plays or virtuous protagonists, preferring the "holy mummery" of comic medieval mystery plays and the "promiscuous pleasure" of comedies of manners (V: ix, x), and that sincere Christians who attended the popular plays of the day would be forced to spend an unjustifiable amount of time and energy counteracting the pernicious temptations set before them. She therefore urged her peers to stay at home and *read* plays that conveyed moral improvement, to prefer the quiet pleasures afforded by closet drama to the unregulated passions roused by the spectacles of the public theater (V: xxv–xxxi).

Recognizing that the stage possessed a "decided superiority in point of mental pleasure," an ability to "charm the imagination and captivate the senses" provided by no other genre (V: xvi), Hannah More first turned to playwriting to carry out her educational project of useful and moral "instruction as well as pleasure" (V: vii). *The Search after Happiness,* written in 1773 to be performed by an all-female cast at the girls' school in Bristol she ran with her sisters, went through several significant revisions, as Patricia Demers has shown (Demers 26–35). The prologue for the eleventh edition in 1796 emphasizes that More is writing a new kind of drama, one not intended to represent the existing (and corrupt) manners of the age but rather to promote "simple truth and common sense," "plain virtue," and "useful thought" (VI: 228). The final version of the play consciously promotes the new concept of female education that More described at length in her *Strictures on the Modern System of Female Education* in 1799. So sympathetic were the teachers at girls' schools to More's revolutionary program of female educational reform that *The Search after Happiness* became the most widely performed play in England between 1780 and 1830 (admittedly in performances limited to schoolrooms), as well as the most often chosen prize book for girls, second only to the Bible, judging by the number of copies that survive, prize gift-plates intact, in both British and American libraries.

In *The Search after Happiness,* four girls escape the corruptions of the city and the "disease of state" to seek happiness in "pure" Nature (VI: 229–30). More quickly establishes that these four girls are middle class, neither "vulgar" (working class) nor vitiated aristocrats. They visit the wise woman (and Milton's former muse) Urania, a woman who has lost her former rank and fortune and now "shuns the public eye," but who embodies both "maternal love" and genuine wisdom. Urania asks each girl to define her "ruling passion," and also to confess what has most troubled her as she sought to gratify that passion: for Euphelia it is the "pleasures," "pomp," and "dress" of high society, which have only aroused "envy" in her; for Pastorella it is the desire for romance, inspired by the novels of sensibility (such as Charlotte Lennox's *The Female Quixote*), which has led her to live in a fantasy world and loathe "the offices of real life"; for Laurinda it is the pleasures of indolence which have left her with "no principle of action" and no "character" of her own; and most problematic, for Cleora it is fame as a writer and scholar, which has aroused "wonder" but not "affection" (VI: 236–43).

Urania, with the help of Florella, a shepherdess who has sustained the artless simplicity and natural piety of her innocent youth, then counsels each girl. She urges Euphelia to combine her love of beauty and fashion with intelligent mental effort and conscious virtue. She tells Pastorella that she must act, not daydream, and similarly urges the lazy Laurinda to undertake a vigorous program of self-education and religious charity. And she urges Cleora to seek, not learning for the purposes of public admiration, but rather the *domestic* virtues of good sense, practical knowledge, taste, and usefulness, "for woman shines but in her proper sphere" (VI: 251).

Patricia Demers has read this play as a contradiction between a humanist concept of knowledge as a process of organic growth, "a combination of trial and error with amenability to instruction," and a "retrograde," "anti-educational manifesto" that urges women to settle for Florella's pious simplicity rather than to seek learning (32–34). But this very early play may be more coherent, more subtly feminist, and hence more revolutionary than Demers allows. More does not suggest that women either cannot or should not attain a high degree of learning—indeed, Cleora presents herself as a female who has acquired a competent knowledge of British literature, physics, geometry, metaphysics, and the philosophy of John Locke. Rather, More argues that one should not desire learning merely for the purposes of *display,* merely to flaunt one's pedantry and win a spurious public fame. Instead one should combine the pursuit of knowledge with modesty, with the desire to serve others, and thus with a life of active charity. It is not Cleora's learning that More condemns, but the way she uses it. Not fame, but a life of dedicated benevolence, domestic good works, and conscious self-approbation are what both Urania and More advocate for women. As Urania concludes:

> So woman, born to dignify retreat,
> Unknown to flourish, and unseen be great,
> To give domestic life its sweetest charm,
> With softness polish, and with virtue warm,
> Fearful of fame, unwilling to be known,
> Should seek but Heaven's applauses, and her own;
> Hers be the task to seek the lonely cell
> Where modest want and silent anguish dwell;
> Raise the weak head, sustain the feeble knees,
> Cheer the cold heart, and chase the dire disease.
> The splendid deeds, which only seek a name,
> Are paid their just reward in present fame;
> But know, the awful, all-disclosing day,
> The long arrear of secret worth shall pay;
> Applauding saints shall hear with fond regard,
> And He, who witness'd here, shall there reward. (VI: 253)

"Woman shines but in her proper sphere"—by the end of *The Search after Happiness,* More has equated that "proper sphere" with heaven itself. What better model, one might ask, could the British nation as a whole seek to imitate in its quest for a new national identity and purpose than heaven itself? From this perspective, women alone are able to lead the Britain of the future to the promised land, a paradise regained of moral purity, plenty, and peace.

The evangelical principles that inspire Urania's counsel to young women are also applied to men in More's dramas written for the legitimate public theater. As Christine Krueger has perceptively shown, More's three trag-edies—*The Inflexible Captive* (1774), *Percy* (1778), and *The Fatal False-hood* (1779)—all condemn those heroic or patriarchal codes which violate a Christian concept of domestic responsibility and active care (Krueger 97–104). *The Inflexible Captive,* for instance, rather than endorsing the captive Roman general Regulus's insistence that he must be sacrificed to preserve Roman honor—he has been sent as a prisoner of war from Carthage to negotiate a peace treaty he considers humiliating to Rome, with certain death awaiting his return if he fails—instead subtly affirms the opposing views of the two leading women figures in the play. Attilia, Regulus's daughter, tries desperately to save her father's life, first by persuading Regu-lus to remain in Rome (despite his sworn oath to return to Carthage) and then when her plea fails, by persuading first her lover Licinius and then the Roman people as a whole to save her father. Attilia constantly invokes the domestic affections and a daughter's duty to cherish and save her father as the highest human value; kneeling before the Roman consul Manlius, she begs him to ransom or forcibly free her father:

> If ever pity's sweet emotions touch'd thee,
> If ever gentle love assail'd thy breast—
> If ever virtuous friendship fir'd thy soul—
> By the dear names of husband and of parent—
> By all the soft yet powerful ties of nature—
> If e'er thy lisping infants charm'd thine ear,
> And waken'd all the father in thy soul,—
> If e'er thou hop'st to have thy latter days
> Blest by their love, and sweeten'd by their duty—
> Oh! hear a kneeling, weeping, wretched daughter,
> Who begs a father's life—nor her's alone,
> But Rome's—his country's—father. (VI: 82)

But Regulus refuses to be saved from certain death, placing his "honour" above any recognition of paternal loyalty or responsibility to his own daughter.

The Carthaginian slave girl Barce then defines Regulus's self-destructive refusal as "romantic madness" (VI: 94). Barce speaks, as Krueger has noted, from a racially and sexually marginalized position that enables her to see beyond the masculinist heroic code that Regulus, Rome, and even Attilia finally endorse (99–100). Her words open up the possibility of a more humane and universal Christian benevolence, one that demands not sacrifice but rather forgiveness. As Barce concludes,

> This love of glory's the disease of Rome;
> It makes her mad, it is a wild delirium,
> An universal and contagious frenzy;
> It preys on all, it spares nor sex nor age:
> The Consul envies Regulus his chains—
> He, not less mad, contemns his life and freedom—
> The daughter glories in the father's ruin—
> . . . For this vain phantom, for this empty glory.
> This may be virtue; but I thank the gods,
> The soul of Barce's not a Roman soul. (IV: 95)

Barce's words, spoken with passion and authority, suggest an alternative to Roman honor, the same practical generosity and virtue shown by her Carthaginian lover, General Hamilcar, who offers to let Regulus escape. Regulus haughtily refuses this offer, but the racist terms in which he does so—"thy poor, dark soul / Hath never felt the piercing ray of virtue" (VI: 89)—subtly shifts the audience's sympathies to Hamilcar. This is all the more the case because Hamilcar has already equated his effort to free Regulus with Regulus's son's generous return of the slave Barce, and with his own assertion that "The soil of *Afric* too produces heroes. / What, though our pride perhaps be less than theirs, / Our virtue may be equal" (IV: 76). Here More powerfully attributes to the African race a deeper understanding of such Christian principles as pity and generosity than can be found within a Roman republican ideology grounded on masculinist concepts of fame and honor.

Throughout her tragedies, More, like Baillie, consciously uses drama to stage both the greater wisdom and virtue of women and the superiority of a Christian ethic of forgiveness and self-discipline over a Roman republican or medieval chivalric code of honor and fame. As she proclaims in the prologue to *The Fatal Falsehood,* "*self-conquest* is the *lesson* books should preach" (VI: 172; More's italics). And it is her female characters—Attilia, Barce, Elwina Raby in *Percy,* Emmelina and Julia in *The Fatal Falsehood*—who embody that virtue of generous self-control.

Hannah Cowley

As did Joanna Baillie and Hannah More, Hannah Cowley fervently believed that the theater had the potential to shape public opinion, to reform the manners of the nation, and to teach virtue. But in her view, the theater of England in the late eighteenth century had singularly failed to fulfill that cultural responsibility. In the prologue to her comedy *The Town before You,* performed in 1795 at the Theatre Royal, Covent Garden, she deplores the modern taste for slapstick comedy and vulgar pantomimes:

> LAUGH! LAUGH! LAUGH! is the demand: not a word must be uttered that looks like instruction, or a sentence which ought to be remembered.
> . . . I invoke the rising generation, to *correct* a taste which to be gratified, demands neither genius or intellect;—which asks only a happy knack at inventing TRICK. I adjure them to restore to the Drama SENSE, OBSERVATION, WIT, LESSON! and to teach our Writers to respect their own talents.
> What mother can now lead her daughters to the great National School, THE THEATRE, in the confidence of their receiving either polish or improvement? . . .
> O! GENIUS of a polish'd age, descend!—plant thy banners in our Theatres, and bid ELEGANCE and FEELING take place of the *droll* and the *laugh,* which formerly were found only in the Booths of *Bartlemy* Fair, and were divided between *Flocton* and *Yates!* . . . The UNDERSTANDING, DISCERNMENT and EDUCATION, which distinguish our modern actors, are useless to them; strong muscles are in greater repute, and grimace a more powerful attraction. (x–xi)

Although herself guilty of including moments of slapstick in her comedies, as she blushingly acknowledges in this preface, Hannah Cowley nonetheless attempted through wit and humor to reform in subtle ways the gender roles and social mores of her day. While never contesting the established political institutions of marriage and the British monarchy as such,

Cowley consistently represents the success of those institutions as grounded on the actions of *women*. It is the intelligence, moral virtue, and resourcefulness of her female protagonists that prevent her male characters from engaging in acts of patriarchal tyranny, cruelty, and foolishness. We can best read Cowley, I would argue, as a conservative or Tory feminist, one who endorses heterosexual marriage, the British constitution, inherited wealth, and the class system, but who nonetheless envisions women as the agents who can best govern those institutions.

In this sense, her plays are profoundly political. Admittedly, she denied the political agenda of her most political play, *A Day in Turkey; or, The Russian Slaves* (1792), in its advertisement: "Hints have been thrown out, and the idea industriously circulated, that the following comedy is tainted with POLITICS. I protest I know nothing about politics;—will Miss Wolstonecraft forgive me—whose book contains such a body of mind as I hardly ever met with—if I say that politics are *unfeminine*? I never in my life could attend to their discussion." This disingenuous claim has misled numerous critics, most recently the editor of the Garland Edition of the plays of Hannah Cowley, Frederick M. Link, who asserts that "she was no bluestocking; she knew little or no Latin, Greek, or French, and considered an interest in politics 'unfeminine'" (Link v). But an attentive reader of Cowley's plays will find a coherent and in some ways radical political agenda, one that critiques a patriarchal domestic ideology from within, and that clearly assigns to women rather than to men the primary responsibility for preserving the freedoms and welfare of the British nation. As the prologue to her *A Bold Stroke for a Husband* (1784) asserts:

> Our play holds forth the conquest of a heart,
> By one bold stroke of nature, not of art.
> A female pen calls female virtue forth,
> And fairly shews to man her sex's worth.
> Could men but see what female sense can do,
> How apt their wit, their constancy—how true;
> In vain would rakes the married state revile,
> Nor with the wanton, precious time beguile.
> Such is our aim, to rectify the age,
> By bringing rising follies on the stage;
> Be then propitious, let our fears decrease,
> While you, with plaudits, ratify the peace! (ii–iii)

The heroines of Cowley's comedies systematically foil the plots and tyrannical oppressions of older, more powerful men. In so doing, they uncover the most pervasive evil at the heart of institutionalized heterosexual marriage within a patriarchal society: the claim that elderly men have a right to the affections and the bodies of much younger women. This claim not only legitimizes what Carole Pateman has called the hidden sexual contract in liberal democratic political theory (the implicit assumption that women on the basis of their sex are not participants in Rousseau's social contract but are rather the objects of sexual exchange); but it also implicitly legitimizes a form of cultural incest. Patriarchy assumes that daughters belong to their fathers, that young females should marry father figures rather than their equals in age and power.

Many of Cowley's comedies represent the attempts of a quite elderly man, often in his sixties, to marry a girl still in her teens, often his ward. The old man is convinced not only that it is right and proper for him to marry this young girl, but that she has an *obligation,* and even the *desire,* to love him and to welcome his sexual overtures. Invariably, Cowley portrays his attempt as ludicrous, tyrannical, and self-deceived. Equally invariably, his attempt is foiled by the machinations of a resourceful, clever woman—often aided by a young man who genuinely loves and is desired by the girl, and whom she then happily marries.

In *A School for Greybeards* (1786), Seraphina—herself married to the much older Don Alexis—willingly helps the eighteen-year-old Antonia to escape marriage to the sixty-five-year-old Don Gasper so that she can marry the young, honorable Don Henry. Along the way, Seraphina, disguised as her own stepdaughter, Viola, accepts the attentions of another young man, Octavio, so that Viola can preserve herself for her true love, Sebastian. While Seraphina only pretends to elope with Octavio, her manipulations powerfully uncover the folly of the elderly men in the play: as she says, after Don Alexis has ordered her to prepare Viola to marry Signor Octavio within the week,

> poor girl! How can she receive Octavio well, with her heart devoted to Sebastian? I wonder what sort of a thing this Signor is—some wrinkled privy counsellor, like himself, I suppose. 'Tis very odd now, that those *antients* should take it into their venerable noddles, that a youthful bride is a proper appendage to their dignity; or to fancy that it requires no more talents to please a pretty wife, than to govern a stupid nation. (20–21)

Seraphina here implies that it is far easier to govern a nation than to please a woman; since women can certainly please themselves, it follows that they will have no trouble whatsoever in running the country.

Similarly, in Cowley's farce *Who's the Dupe?* (1779), Elizabeth Doiley and her cousin Charlotte easily foil Mr. Doiley's plan to marry his daughter to a learned pedant by persuading this scholar and Elizabeth's true love, the soldier Granger, to exchange roles. More difficult is Miss Archer's rescue, in *More Ways than One* (1806), of her young friend Arabella Melville from the clutches of Miss Archer's guardian, the sixty-year-old Timothy Evergreen. Having purchased the innocent young country girl Arabella from her uncle, the quack doctor Mr. Feelove, Evergreen expects to marry her at once. But with the help of Bellair, the young man whom Arabella wishes to marry, Miss Archer both saves Arabella and at the same time brings about her own marriage to her preferred lover, Mr. Carlton. Throughout this play, Miss Archer is an embodiment of the New Woman, a woman of independent spirit, intelligence, wit, and affection who produces the happy ending and thereby demonstrates the impotence of the older patriarchs.

Cowley sharply reveals the political as well as the incestuous dimensions of the patriarchal desires thwarted by Seraphina, Elizabeth and Charlotte, and Miss Archer, by cross-gendering them in *The Runaway* (1776), her first successful comedy. Here, the elderly Mr. Hargrave, rather than wishing to marry a much younger woman, tries to force his son George to marry a much older woman, the wealthy widow Lady Diana. By changing the sex of the elderly lover, Cowley allows herself to be far more explicit about the political tyranny that lies at the heart of such May-December marriages. When Lady Diana discovers that the young runaway Emily Morley—who has fled a distasteful marriage arranged by her uncle—has "stolen" George Hargrave's affections, Lady Diana immediately identifies herself with France's ancien régime, announcing "I must be rid of her, yet I know not how.—O France! for thy Bastile, for thy Lettres de Cachet!" (39). And when Mr. Hargrave's benevolent and wise brother-in-law, Mr. Drummond, takes George's side against the marriage with Lady Diana, Hargrave immediately identifies such resistance with a democratic political revolution in England: "Look'ee, Mr. Drummond, though you govern George with your whimsical notions, you sha'n't me.—I foresee how it will be as soon as I'm gone—my fences will be cut down—my meadows turned into common—my cornfields laid open—my woods at the mercy of every man who carries an axe—" (53). Mr. Justice immediately confirms that the private domestic sphere and the public sphere are the same: "This was only a political stroke, to restore the balance of power." To which Mr. Drummond responds with a defense of good sense and benevolence, the language of sympathetic feeling as opposed to that of patriarchal hubris. Echoing Mr. Hargrave, he satirically observes:

> My son shall be a great Man!—To such a vanity as this, how many have been sacrificed!—He shall be great—The happiness of love, the felicities that flow from a suitable union, his heart shall be a stranger to—but he shall convey *my name*, decked with titles, to posterity, to purchase these distinctions, he lives a wretch—This is the silent language of the heart, which we hold up to ourselves as the voice of Reason and Prudence. (54)

Since it is an elderly woman's desire that is being foiled in this play, it is a man, Mr. Drummond, who plays the role of compassion, common sense, and justice later assigned to women in Cowley's comedies. It is Mr. Drummond who generously pays the poor poacher's debts, who confirms Emily's right to choose her own husband by settling his beloved dead wife Harriet's estate upon her, and who thus makes it possible for George and Emily to marry.

If women are not exercising their wits to foil the oppressive plots of old men in Cowley's comedies, then they are using their intelligence to gain their own desires, either for freedom or for sexual gratification through marriage with a man whom they themselves have chosen. Lady Bell Bloomer, in *Which Is the Man?* (1783), a woman of "beauty, wit, and spirit; but, above all, a *mind*" (7), enjoys the pleasures of high society, yet at the same time fully acknowledges their shallowness. Pursued by several libertines, foremost among them the dissipated and vain Lord Sparkle, she cleverly evades them all. Instead, like Priscilla to John Alden, she persuades the modest, impoverished soldier Beauchamp, when he is sent by Sparkle as his emissary, to speak for himself. Telling him that if he visits her that evening, he shall see her "in the presence of the man my heart prefers," she maneuvers Beauchamp into a situation where she can openly choose him over Sparkle. As she says to Sparkle, "As caprice is absolutely necessary to the character of a fine lady, you will not be surpris'd if I give an instance of it now; and, spite of your elegance, your fashion, and your wit, present my hand to this poor soldier—who boasts only worth, spirit, honour, and love" (53).

Cowley's best-known female maneuverer, the heroine of her most often produced play, *The Belle's Stratagem* (1782), is as much a mistress of disguise and role-playing as her creator. Contracted to a marriage with Doricourt by their fathers, Letitia Hardy has not seen her intended husband since they were children. A man of fashion who has recently returned from the Grand Tour, Doricourt has learned on his travels the fascination of a French pair of eyes and an Italian grace of movement. When introduced to the beautiful, meritorious, but modest and reserved Letitia, Doricourt is profoundly bored. Observing his indifference, but at the same time realizing that she passionately desires Doricourt, Letitia decides to take matters into her own hands. She plots on the one hand to make Doricourt hate his intended bride by appearing before him as an increasingly vulgar country hoyden, gawky and rudely inarticulate. At the same time she plans to make him fall in love with a mysterious masked woman at the masquerade, a woman who exhibits before his dazzled eyes "English beauty—French vivacity—wit—elegance" (58). She then manipulates her father's own plot to rush Doricourt into the marriage—Mr. Hardy pretends to be on his deathbed, and appeals to Doricourt's sense of honor to obey the dying wish of *both* fathers. Doricourt then engages in his own masquerade, pretending to be a raving lunatic to put off this undesirable marriage. After Doricourt has been manipulated into marrying Letitia (he is told that the mysterious woman is another man's mistress), she appears before him as the masked woman of his dreams, once again arousing his passionate desire. The consummate *actress*, as she unmasks she tells the now ecstatic Doricourt, "You see I *can* be any thing; chuse then my character—your Taste shall fix it. Shall I be an *English* Wife?—or, breaking from the bonds of Nature and Education, step forth to the world in all the captivating glare of Foreign Manners?" (81). To which Doricourt then replies, "You shall be nothing but yourself—nothing can be captivating that you are not." Letitia Hardy's plotting has thus gained her exactly what she desired: a husband passionately in love with her, and complete freedom—to be "herself." By revealing to Doricourt the limits of his own perception and understanding, the "strange perversion" of his "Taste," she has assumed the mastery of their marriage: as Doricourt acknowledges, "you have now my whole soul—your person, your face, your mind, I would not exchange for those of any other Woman breathing" (81, 80). Moreover, she has amply gratified her own sexual desire. Having begun the play "enslaved" by her passionate love for Doricourt, she ends it as both his mistress and wife, the object of *his* passionate desire.

Thus I disagree with Erin Isikoff's reading of the ending of the play as a "disempowerment" of Letitia Hardy. As the male characters seize the powers of masquerade, argues Isikoff, they engage in a "strategy to repress female desire and the plot of its self-fulfillment," reducing Letitia Hardy to a "cypher" which Doricourt inscribes at his will (113–14). I would emphasize instead the degree to which Doricourt remains "charmed," even in the thrall of, his wife, who has amply gratified her own sexual desire in arousing the passion of Doricourt. I therefore also take issue with Jane Spencer, who argues that Cowley's affirmation of "a new kind of female authority in English culture" was purchased at the price of "a denial or submerging of female sexual desire and a curbing of female freedom of expression" (1995: 231). While Cowley clearly declined to follow Aphra Behn's more overtly sexual language and plots, as Spencer rightly observes, she nonetheless represented a series of heroines who both have sexual desires and also manage to fulfill them, albeit within rather than outside the institution of heterosexual marriage.

Cowley's comedies thus construct a new version of both heterosexual marriage and of the proper gender roles for the two sexes: her marriages are based on mutual respect, intense love, sexual desire, trust, and the recognition by both parties that women will have, as Jean Gagen puts it, "the deciding vote" in the selection of their husbands (115). Moreover, her female protagonists—all intelligent, well educated, resourceful, and independent—will continue to sustain these marriages, when necessary, by manipulating their husbands into more tolerant and generous behavior. In *A Bold Stroke for a Husband* (1784), the abandoned wife of Don Carlos dresses herself as a boy in order to visit her husband's mistress, successfully reclaim the fortune which her husband has given to this mistress, and in the process win his love and admiration once again.

The same female authority is represented in Cowley's two tragedies: *Albina, Countess Raimond* (1797) and *The Fate of Sparta; or, The Rival Kings* (1788). Albina, who was married at her father's desire to Count Raimond, has chastely mourned his death in battle for over a year; she is finally persuaded by her childhood lover Edward to marry him before he goes to Palestine to fight in the Crusades. Despite the machinations of Raimond's brother, Gondibert, who desires Albina and falsely accuses her of adultery with him, and of Editha, Albina's trusted friend who loves Edward and enviously promotes Gondibert's plot, Albina manages to preserve her chastity and to save Edward from destroying himself. More centrally, Chelonice, the heroine of *The Fate of Sparta*, torn between her loyalty to her father, King Leonidas of Sparta, and his former co-ruler, now sworn foe, her husband Cleombrotus, manages to negotiate a truce between these rival kings. She does so by refusing to abandon her father, and at the same time persuading her reluctant, but uxorious husband to delay his military assault. When her husband is then captured, Chelonice refuses to abandon him, even to become Queen of Sparta, insisting that she will go into exile with her husband and her son, so that her son may learn "The highest art— the art to emulate / The deeds of dignity" (83). By remaining steadfastly loyal to *both* her husband and her father, Cleonice has embodied Cowley's concept of female honor and heroism, a resourceful courage that manages to bring peace between the warring factions within both the family and the nation. The play ends with both Cleonice and her husband ascending the throne of Sparta after her father's sudden death.

Throughout her plays, Hannah Cowley promotes a coherent political ideology, one that she articulates most explicitly in that very play she claimed was not "political," *A Day in Turkey; or, The Russian Slaves* (1792). Set in a Turkish harem, where three Christian women have been trapped— the Italian coquette, Lauretta, the Russian peasant girl, Paulina, and the Russian aristocrat, Alexina, the play explores the nature of slavery and of freedom. On the one hand, Lauretta and A La Greque, the captured French valet of Alexina's husband, Orloff, proclaim the doctrine of the rights of man and of woman celebrated by the Jacobin revolutionaries in France. A La Grecque, seeing that his master Orloff has been captured, insists that they are now equals: "let us be civil to each other, as brother slaves ought to be" (4). As he later explains,

> I travell'd into Russia to polish the brutes a little, and to give them some ideas of the general equality of man; but my generosity has been lost;—they still continue to believe that a prince is more than a porter, and that a lord is a better gentleman than his slave. O, had they been with me at Versailles, when I help'd to turn those things topsey turvey there! (18)

Within the harem, the wily Lauretta engages in the same discourse of revolutionary equality. When the Turkish second-in-command, Azim, condemns the new French slave—"Frenchmen, there is no being guarded against.—They make free everywhere," Lauretta responds, "At least they have made themselves free AT HOME! and who knows, but, at last, the spirit they have raised may reach even to a Turkish harem, and the rights of woman be declared, as well as those of men" (69).

Opposed to this discourse of revolutionary natural rights is a pro-slavery discourse, articulated in the systematic oppressions of the Muslim Bassa Ibrahim and his men, Mustapha and Azim, who consider Christians as "useful cattle" and who have numerous methods for managing an "insolent female slave" (2, 8). Moreover, Azim pointedly reminds us that the institution of slavery is legal not only in Turkey but also in England. Responding to Alexina's lament that "Blest freedom here ne'er lends her ray," Azim comments: "Such a wailing about freedom and liberty! why the christians in one of the northern islands have established a slave-trade, and proved by act of parliament that freedom is no blessing at all." To which his henchman Mustapha responds: "No, no, they have only proved that it does not suit dark complexions. To such a pretty creature as this, they'd think it a blessing to *give* every freedom—and *take* every freedom" (10). Cowley's dramatic art here liberates a Bakhtinian heteroglossia, an open-ended dialogue which subtly draws connections between slavery in Turkey and the enslavement both of Africans in the West Indies and of women in England, where both black and female bodies become objects of commercial exchange.

The play focuses directly on this exchange of women. In a retelling of the traditional story of Roxanna, the Christian girl imprisoned in a Turkish harem, who wins the love—and finally the conversion to a European concept of monogamous Christian marriage—of her Turkish sultan, *A Day in Turkey* tracks the transformations within the harem achieved by three Christian women. By refusing to see Ibrahim, Alexina maintains her chastity and loyalty to her husband. At the same time Lauretta educates Ibrahim in the ways of Western love, telling him that he can never hope to "astonish" or awe Alexina into love, but must instead

> Affect humility, not greatness. You must become a suppliant, before you can hope to be a victor. . . . Yes, I know the history of the heart, and do assure you, that you must become the slave of your captive, if you ever mean to taste the sublime excesses of a mutual passion. (15)

At the same time, Lauretta coaches Paulina in the arts of the coquette—frustrating Ibrahim's sexual desire in order to be able later to gratify her own, affecting disdain and an independent indifference—so that Ibrahim will fall in love with her (thinking she is Alexina, whom he has never seen). This ruse succeeds, as another harem girl, Fatima, acknowledges: "What an odd whim it is in our master to grow fond of the *mind* of a woman! did ever any body hear of a woman's *mind* before as an object of passion?" (46).

Female Christian virtue is the power that resolves the conflicts in the play and brings all the lovers happily together. Alexina, thrown in prison by the cruel Azim, there meets Orloff and persuades him that she has been faithful to him, having sworn to kill herself rather than to "suffer the slightest violation of our sacred love" (26). At the same time, Paulina and Ibrahim declare their love for each other, and Ibrahim, in his joy, is persuaded to free both Orloff and Alexina. Ibrahim vows to marry Paulina "by sacred rites," earning Orloff's approbation: "Illustrious Turk! Love has taught thee to revere marriage, and marriage shall teach thee to honour love." When Alexina then urges Ibrahim to forgive Azim, Ibrahim comments, "Charming magnanimity! if it flows from your CHRISTIAN DOCTRINES, such doctrines must be RIGHT, and I will closely study them" (83–84).

A Day in Turkey thus negotiates its opposed discourses of freedom and slavery to a happy reconciliation, revealing Cowley's conservative feminism in its clearest form. As opposed to the Jacobin voices of unregulated freedom, whether Lauretta's or A La Grecque's or Citizen Grubb's in *The World as it Goes* (1781) who refuses to lock up his pretty young daughter—

> Liddy shan't be locked up tho'—aint I a Bill of Rights man?—aint I a London associator?—Ha'nt I joined in Petitions and Remonstrances? and shall I have Illegal Imprisonment in my own family? (*The World as it Goes, or A Party at Montpelier,* Huntington Library ms. LA 548, 17 February 1781)

—Cowley's plays consistently support the British monarchy and its political institutions. Lady Bell Bloomer consciously selects a British army officer as her husband, implicitly endorsing his uncle Fitzherbert's eulogy of Beauchamp:

> Intrepid spirit, nice honour, generosity, and understanding, all unite to form

him.—It is these which will make a British soldier once again the first character in Europe.—It is such soldiers who must make England once again invincible, and her glittering arms triumphant in every quarter of the globe. (*Which Is* 53)

Similarly, Cowley ends her comedy *The Town before You* with a rousing affirmation of the British navy. Here Asgill eagerly leaves behind even his passionately beloved Lady Horatia in order to serve his nation:

> the enthusiasm which seized me, when I trod the deck of the Victory, can never be chill'd! In the glorious tars around me, valour, intrepidity, heroism, shone forth with all their fires; they flashed through my heart! And I swear, that should my country need my assistance, I will again resume the trowsers, and sail before the mast, wherever she bids her cannon roar, or her proud pendants fly.
>   (*Advancing forward*)
> Ah! repose on *us!* and when you look on the gallant spirits, who do honour to this habit, let every fear subside; for, whilst the sea flows, and English sailors are *themselves,* ENGLAND MUST BE THE MISTRESS OF THE GLOBE! (102–103)

Within the context of this Tory British and Christian chauvinism, however, Cowley makes it clear that it is women who best understand and embody the character of true English virtue. Dedicating *The Belle's Stratagem* to the Queen, Cowley defines the purpose of her most popular comedy: "to draw a FEMALE CHARACTER, which with the most lively Sensibility, fine Understanding, and elegant Accomplishments, should unite that beautiful Reserve and Delicacy which, whilst they veil those charms, render them still more interesting." It is this very definition of female virtue which Cowley implicitly assigns to the Queen herself, thus suggesting that a "female character" is uniquely qualified to govern the nation.

Cowley further equates the skills required to govern a nation with those both of a mother and of a female artist, in her prologue to her first comedy, *The Runaway:*

> Our Poet of to-night, in faith's a—Woman,
> A woman, too, untutor'd in the School,
> Nor Aristotle knows, nor scarce a rule
> By which fine writers fabricate their plays,
> From sage Menander's, to these modern days: . . .
> Her Nursery the study, where she thought,
> Fram'd fable, incident, surprise and plot.
> From the surrounding hints she caught her plan,
> Length'ning the chain from infancy to man:
> Tom plagues poor Fan; she sobs, but loves him still;
> Kate aims her wit at both, with roguish skill:
> Our Painter mark'd those lines—which Nature drew,
> Her fancy glow'd, and colour'd them—for you;
> A Mother's pencil gave the light and shades,

A Mother's eye thro' each soft scene pervades;
Her Children rose before her flatter'd view,
Hope stretched the canvas, whilst her wishes drew.

Aligning both her own skills at fabrication and those of her heroines with
the practice of matrimony and motherhood, Cowley identifies the virtues
and freedoms of the British nation with those of the British home. As Jane
Spencer has rightly observed, Cowley's writing career attests "to the ascen-
dancy of a new kind of female authority in English culture—one that could
be both publicly visible and accorded widespread respect and attention"
(1995: 231).

Elizabeth Inchbald

In some ways the most overtly political of the major female playwrights
of the Romantic era, Elizabeth Inchbald drew subtle parallels in her plays
between the prisons of the state and the constraints of institutionalized
marriage. By revealing these connections, she hoped to reform both the
political institutions and the marital practices of her day. As she confidently
asserted in her prologue to *All on a Summer's Day,* the female playwright
may be better suited to this task than the male:

> When haughty man usurp'd fair learning's throne
> And made the Empire of the stage his own
> He rul'd a realm where Genius seldom smil'd
> And Nonsense hail'd him as her darling child. . . .
> Bard follow'd Bard, yet few coud [*sic*] justly claim
> The laurell'd trophies of a lasting name
> 'Till gentle woman seiz'd the pen and writ
> And shone not less in beauty than in wit.
> Woman! by honest emulation fir'd
> Sportive, yet elegant; tho' pointed, chaste,
> To mend our manners & refine our taste:
> Man from her learnt the fascinating art
> To please the fancy, captivate the heart
> And paint the scenes of happiness and strife
> The various scenes that chequer human life.

Inchbald's more overtly political dramas focus on the prisons of the state:
debtors' prison, the French Bastille, criminal prisons. Again and again she
shows how unjust these institutions are; how their inmates do not deserve
to be there; yet how difficult it is to free oneself from them once one is
incarcerated. In her view, it is not an appeal to the legal system or institutionalized justice but only an appeal to the quality of mercy that enables the
wrongly imprisoned to escape their chains.

In *Next Door Neighbours* (1791), the father of the beautiful, well-bred
Eleanor is in debtors' prison. Her neighbor Sir George Splendorville, catch-

ing a glimpse of her, offers her one hundred guineas to release her father—
at the price of her chastity. She is saved from rape only by the pity of Sir
George's compassionate butler, Mr. Bluntly; at the same time her father
refuses the money, preferring prison to his daughter's (even suspected) dis-
honor. When Sir George loses his estate at gambling and his fair-weather
friends desert him, his lawyer, Mr. Blackman, urges him to lie to the court,
to present falsified documents that his long-lost half-sister is dead, so that
he can collect her inheritance. Here Inchbald suggests how easily lawyers
can corrupt the judicial process. Only when the honest barrister Mr. Manly
produces evidence that Eleanor is that long-lost sister, does her father leave
prison. It is the good will of Bluntly and Manly that save Eleanor and her
father, not the workings of the law.

Similarly, in *The Wise Man of the East* (1799), adapted from Kotzebue's
The Writing Desk, the honest Mr. Metland is arrested for debt, even though
he gave a small fortune to Mr. Claransforth to invest for him; unfortu-
nately, all documentation of that transaction was in a writing desk that was
supposedly lost in a fire in the Claransforth accounting house, a fire in
which Claransforth apparently perished. For two years the Metland family
have suffered extreme poverty and misery as their well-bred daughter is
forced to work as a maid and their son to enlist in the Navy. Claransforth's
son—who knows Ellen Metland's story and has fallen in love with her—
nonetheless refuses to acknowledge his father's debt to her father; at the
same time, he tries to seduce her. Only after the mysterious dark-skinned
man from the East, Ava Thoanoa, reveals himself to be Claransforth, and
the Metland's money has been discovered in a secret compartment of a
writing desk saved from the fire, does the suffering of the Metlands end.
Again, it is not institutionalized justice that determines the ending of the
play, but the whimsical vagaries of chance and the apparent benevolence of
Ava Thoanoa, who has been "testing" his son. But that benevolence clearly
has its limits, since Claransforth was content to witness the misery and hu-
miliation of the Metlands for *two years* in order to further his self-interested
project of reforming his son.

Inchbald turns her attention to the most famous prison of the time, the
French Bastille, in *The Massacre* (1792), a play set sixty miles outside Paris.
Here the violent and unjust cruelties of the leaders of the Terror are vividly
portrayed: the well-born Eusebe's wife's family have been slaughtered in
Paris during the St. Bartholomew's Day massacre; his entire family, including his old father Tricastin, a model of charity and good sense, are arrested;
and all are condemned to death by the Montagnard Dugas and his men.
Only the last-minute intervention of the benevolent judge Glandeve saves
them from execution. Glandeve refuses to participate in a travesty of jus-

tice, and insists that "my first object is, freedom of *thought*" and "liberty joined with peace and charity" (26). While Inchbald here represents all of revolutionary France under the Terror as a prison, she also suggests that mercy and benevolence may still be able to preserve a space for freedom (although not until after Eusebe's wife and children are murdered in the streets). Whether such benevolence could be found in an *English* court of law remains an open question.

Inchbald's most extended treatment of prisons occurs in one of her finest plays, *Such Things Are* (1787), which is explicitly based on the work of John Howard, the prison reformer. By displacing the action to "India," literally Sumatra in Dutch Indonesia, Inchbald leaves open the question whether the capriciousness of the Sultan's methods of incarceration is greater or less than that of Britain's. On the one hand, the Sultan is guilty of numerous acts of arbitrary cruelty: he beheads a wife who dares to say "I won't" to him; he arrests and sells into slavery anyone who is merely suspected of disaffection from his reign, without proof; he keeps prisoners locked up without fresh air for decades at a time, never permitting others to visit them or to examine their cases. On the other hand, as the Sultan confesses to Haswell (John Howard), he is a Christian, converted by his love for the Christian Arabella who was killed (or so he thinks) by his rival (whom the Sultan then killed and is now impersonating). When Haswell gains permission to visit the Sultan's prisons, he discovers that many are there only because they lack the funds to bribe their jailers, that several have been falsely accused, and that one European woman has been kept in solitary confinement for fourteen years. Haswell persuades the Sultan to allow him to free six prisoners—among them is the European, Arabella. Devastated by the suffering he has inflicted on his own beloved, the Sultan promises to adopt every measure of prison reform that Haswell shall lay out. Moreover, he will govern his nation with the Christian benevolence, mercy, and forgiveness of the long-suffering Arabella, to whom he gives the ultimate political authority to "redress the wrongs of all my injured subjects" (71).

One might accuse Inchbald of promoting a "home-office mentality" in *Such Things Are*—the Christian Europeans, Haswell and Arabella, display a universal benevolence and willingness to turn the other cheek that is notably lacking in the Sultan and his compatriots, until they are converted by the example of the Christians. But this triumph of Christian mercy does not occur at home in England, only abroad. The implication is that Turks may make better Christians than do Europeans. In *Such Things Are,* the ferocious and vengeful Muslim prisoner Zedan steals Haswell's purse as he passes by, but after having experienced Haswell's pity, immediately returns it, feeling for the first time "something that I never felt before—it makes me like not only you, but all the world besides.—The love of my family was confined to them alone—but this sensation makes me love even my enemies" (28).

This political point is made most clearly in *The Mogul Tale* (1796), where three British balloonists—a cobbler, his wife, and a quack-doctor—inadvertently land within the Mogul's seraglio. On the one hand, Johnny the cobbler is appalled by the treatment of women in the harem; as he tells the Eunuch who tries to take his wife Fanny to the Mogul, "You are not to lay violent hands upon her, for look'ye master blacky, if you was in a certain corner of the world called Old England, you would know you dog you— that if the first Prince of the Blood was to attempt the wife of a poor Cobler, against her will and good liking—He had better take up the whole island by main force, and dash it into the sea again" (17). On the other hand, the Mogul, after having easily exposed the hubristic lies of the British visitors (who pretend to be the Pope, a nun, and a famous scientist), pronounces a judgment that establishes him as the most enlightened and merciful character in the play:

> You are not now before the tribunal of a European, a man of your own colour. I am an Indian, a Mahometan, my laws are cruel, and my nature savage—You have imposed upon me, and attempted to defraud me, but know that I have been taught mercy and compassion for the sufferings of human nature; however differing in laws, temper and colour from myself. Yes[for Yet?] from you Christians whose laws teach charity to all the world, have I learned these virtues? For your countrymen's cruelty to the poor Gentoos has shewn me tyranny in so foul a light, that I was determined henceforth to be only mild, just and merciful.—You have done wrong, but you are strangers, you are destitute—You are too much in my power to treat you with severity—all three may freely depart. (19–20)

Here, truly generous, benevolent, and enlightened rulership is embodied only in a racial other, a Turkish Muslim mogul.

Set back in England, Inchbald's domestic comedies focus on domestic tyranny, specifically the plight of the *married* woman—the consequence, perhaps, of Inchbald's own seven-year marriage to the womanizing, gambling, and much older actor Joseph Inchbald (see Boaden I: 32–59). In *Wives as They Were, and Maids as They Are* (1797), Inchbald portrays marriage as an oppressive feudal institution in which wives are prisoners. Lord Priory exacts absolute obedience from his wife. He proudly claims the title of an "unkind husband," insisting that he has always treated his wife "according to the antient mode of treating wives. . . . The antients seldom gave them the liberty to do wrong; but modern wives do as they like," and boasting of his violent temper, which is "rather of advantage to me as a husband—it causes me to be obeyed without hesitation—no liberty for contention, tears, or repining. I insure conjugal sunshine, by now and then introducing a storm" (5–6). Moreover, he keeps his wife at home under lock and key, never permitting her to attend operas, balls, or appear in public places, preventing her from having company at home or spending the night at another's house, and making sure she is in bed by 10 o'clock every night. When he breaks his rule and brings his wife to Lord Norberry's home for one evening while his furniture is moved into his London apartment, Lady Priory is exposed both to the attractions of high society, as embodied in the attractive young "heedless woman of fashion," Miss Dorrillon, and to the libertine attentions of the fop Mr. Bronzeley, who tries to seduce her. But Lady Priory foils Bronzeley's plans, first by obtaining her husband's "permission" to meet Mr. Bronzeley alone and then by steadfastly resisting his sexual advances even after he has tricked her into an "elopement." Lady Priory returns in triumph to her husband, her chastity intact, but a far wiser woman. As she observes: "I should have continued those [primitive] manners, had I known none but primitive men. But to preserve antient austerity, while, by my husband's consent, I am assailed by modern gallantry, would be the task of a Stoic, and not of his female slave" (93).

At the same time Lady Priory resubmits to this feudal marriage: "Not all the rigour of its laws has ever induced me to wish them abolished" (78). Even though several of the older men are uneasy with Lord Priory's patriarchal tyranny, the play offers no escape from this patriarchal construction of marriage. Mr. Bronzeley turns to Lady Mary Raffle, asking "if, in consequence of former overtures, I should establish a legal authority over you, and become your chief magistrate—would you submit to the same control to which Lady Priory submits?" To which the hitherto spirited, independent Lady Raffle responds, "Any control, rather than have no magistrate at all." And Miss Dorrillon ends the play by responding to *her* lover's query as to what she thinks of this, "Simply one sentence—A maid of the present day, shall become a wife like those of former times" (78).

Did Elizabeth Inchbald herself endorse this affirmation of feudal marriage? Throughout *Wives as They Were, Maids as They Are,* the female characters have been treated brutally by those very patriarchs who claim to cherish and protect them. Lady Priory has been irresponsibly exposed to the predations of a libertine rapist. Even worse, Miss Dorrillon has been arrested and taken to jail at her disguised father's behest, in order to "teach her a lesson" about the dangers of indebtedness. Only her innate generosity and filial devotion (she tells Mr. Mandred—her disguised father—to send the thousand pounds he has brought to pay her debts instead to her supposedly impoverished, dying father in India) pierces through her father's hardened heart. Many members of the audience, both male and female, may have seriously asked themselves if the domestic tyrannies practiced in this play were indeed morally defensible.

Inchbald portrays the extreme suffering that a devoted wife can endure from a vindictive husband in one of her finest plays, *A Case of Conscience* (written in 1800, first published posthumously, in 1833). Set in Spain, the play depicts the cruel treatment meted out by the Marquis of Romono to his loyal wife, Adriana. Before their marriage twenty years earlier, Adriana had been engaged to Cordunna; the rejected and vengeful Cordunna, disguised as a friar and hermit, has recently insinuated himself into the Marquis's confidence and persuaded him that Adriana was not a virgin when they married and their son Orviedo is not his but Cordunna's. This is a lie, but Adriana—never knowing why—is forced to endure daily insults from her proud, cold, embittered husband, who either refuses to speak to her at all or taunts her with accounts of her soldier son's daily dangers in battle. And when their son returns a gallant hero, the Marquis denies him his intended bride and banishes him. Not until after Cordunna has been seized by the Inquisition does the truth emerge through the agency of Father Manuel, who pronounces the play's final moral: "Wrongs before marriage cannot equal those that may follow after" (352). Although Father Manuel's words are intended to absolve Adriana from any guilt she may feel for having rejected Cordunna—"it was Virtue, not Vice, to break every promise extorted by your parents, before your judgment and experience were matured, so as to comprehend the nature of the vow you gave" (352)—they resonate at the end of this play as an indictment of the wrongs that *follow after* marriage, specifically the torments visited by the Marquis on his loving and chaste wife.

I am suggesting that Elizabeth Inchbald's portraits of marital reconciliation and enduring domestic affection—painted as they are against the backdrop of tyrannical or philandering husbands, or rigorous and unrelenting fathers[1]—may be profoundly ironic. Her plays open up a space of Bakhtinian dialogue, an arena where a liberated female desire briefly expresses itself, only to be oppressively confined by the reinstitution of patriarchal marriage at the plays' endings. This dynamic is perhaps most clearly revealed in *All on a Summer's Day* (1787), in which the exuberant young Lady Carrol, a former ward of her "now tender husband" who feels no erotic desire or deep affection for him, amuses herself by fantasizing the ideal husband, a "delightful Creature" who "in Shape, features, air, & temper" is the very "reverse" of her own husband. She is a figure of unlicensed female imagination and sexual desire, as her shocked sister-in-law Mrs. Goodley observes: "Lady Carrol, you give such scope to your imagination, & take such License in revealing it, as if you were ashamed of virtues you naturally possess, & proud to disclose every folly & indiscretion, which incessantly assail your fertile fancy" (2–3). Lady Carrol thinks her fantasy has come true when Wildlove comes to visit, but he resists her overtures out of loyalty both to her husband and to his lost first love, Louisa. At the same time Lady Carrol is carrying out a secret correspondence with another lover, the engaged son of Sir Ralph Mooneye. Her doting but unhappy husband makes explicit the parallel between the personal—Lady Carrol's liberated desires—and the political. Responding to Governor Moreton's question whether he doesn't find it more difficult to command his fine lady than a whole regiment in India, Sir William Carrol responds:

> *Sir Wm:* Oh, no—I command her with a great deal of ease.
> *Gov:* But does she obey?
> *Sir Wm:* As for that Governor—we are not in India now you know—we are in a Land of Liberty, and I will say, our Wives Liberties are as extensive as the Liberties of any set of subjects his Majesty governs. (19)

This fiction of "extensive" female liberty is brutally denied by the ending of the play. Lady Carrol's licentious desire for Wildlove is blocked by his renewed engagement to Louisa Moreton; her secret fantasizing correspondence (in which she claims to be Sir William's daughter) is uncovered by Ralph Mooneye; and her imaginative flights are once again grounded within her marriage to a man old enough to be her father. As Lord Henry sums up this still-to-be-endured marriage, "having been a witness of your conduct as man & wife, for one day only; I have seen so many sorrows and tormenting passions of every kind, incumbent on the State of Matrimony, that I here abjure the thought of Wedlock" (52). Nor does the concluding marriage between the libertinous Wildlove and the skeptical, virtuous Louisa seem to contain the recipe for marital bliss, as the ambiguous closing moral spoken by the clergyman Chrysostom underlines:

> Virtue itself turns vice being mi[s]applied.
> And Vice sometimes by action's dignified. (53)

In the world of Inchbald's domestic comedies, there is no escape from the prison of an unhappy marriage. Divorce, as Inchbald's play *I'll Tell You What* (1785) suggests, only plunges one into a second marriage more painful than the first. Unmarried women are repeatedly portrayed as unhappy with their status in life. Either they are embittered old maids desperate to marry[2] or discontented widows. In *Every One Has His Fault,* for instance, Miss Spinster eagerly accepts the reluctant proposal of Mr. Solus, even though he is "a man, of all others on earth, I dislike" while he thinks her "peevish, fretful, and tiresome" (11). Even very wealthy widows are represented as secretly unhappy. In *The Widow's Vow* (1786), the widowed Countess, despite her arranged marriage to a "bad husband" whom she hated, and despite the vow of celibacy which she has since taken, is easily fooled into meeting and then marrying her neighbor, the Marquis, who appears before her implausibly disguised as a girl. In these domestic comedies, Inchbald's only solution to the agonies of marital incompatibility, mutual distrust, betrayal, and patriarchal tyranny is an ineffective placebo: a call for tolerance and forgiveness within marriage which only her female characters seem able to answer.

Implicit in Inchbald's plays is the argument that Britain is not the land of liberty it claims to be, that its wives are prisoners, its subjects the victims of an oppressive class system that sends many honest workers to debtors' prison, and its ruling classes the slaves of dissipation and folly. Only through the agency of benevolent sensibility can social improvement come, but in Inchbald's plays the most empowered of these humanitarians tend to live elsewhere—in the East, in France, or "next door." Thus it is left to her, a female dramatist, to rouse the conscience of the British nation. "'Tis hers, the tale of sorrow to impart / And melt to sympathy the feeling heart" (prologue to *All on a Summer's Day*). As J. Taylor's prologue to *To Marry, or Not to Marry* proclaims,

> In all, her anxious hope was still to find,
> Some useful moral for the feeling mind; . . .
> An humble shrub it may, indeed, be found,
> But not a baleful weed from foreign ground.
> No!—'tis her pride, at least, if vain her toil,
> The muse has rais'd it on the British soil.

Throughout these plays by Joanna Baillie, Hannah More, Hannah Cowley, and Elizabeth Inchbald, the voices and bodies of women dominate the stage. Whether we are observing Baillie's female exemplars of rational self-control and wise advice, or More's embodiments of Christian virtue, useful learning, and compassion, or Cowley's shrewd manipulators who cleverly effect peaceful resolutions to domestic conflicts, or Inchbald's ironic vision of a more enlightened, benevolent, and just government beyond the domestic and state tyrannies of the England of her day—we see women putting forth a claim to ultimate moral, cultural, and political authority. Even when the settings of these plays are domestic, the very act of transferring to the public sphere of the legitimate stage the tyrannies and freedoms of the private sphere works to *publicize* women's capacities for rational control and virtuous behavior. Finally, these powerful female dramatists and their characters assertively occupy the discursive public sphere in order to stage intellectually and emotionally persuasive versions of a New Woman, a rational, just, yet compassionate, benevolent, and peace-loving woman, the person best suited to govern the new British nation.

3

Women's Political Poetry

Most of the recent criticism of poetry written by women in England during the Romantic period has tended to represent that poetry as the production of what critics have concurred in calling "the poetess." I am thinking especially of the analyses of the poetry of Felicia Hemans and Letitia Landon provided by Isobel Armstrong in her chapter on "Precursors" in *Victorian Poetry* (1993), by Angela Leighton in her chapters on Hemans and L. E. L. in *Victorian Women Poets* (1992), by Cheryl Walker in her chapter on "The Poetess at Large" in *The Nightingale's Burden* (1982), by Glennis Stephenson in her study of the career of Letitia Landon, *Letitia Landon: The Woman behind L. E. L.* (1995), as well as of my own attempt to locate the poetry of Hemans and Landon within the Burkean category of the "beautiful" in my *Romanticism and Gender* (1993; chap. 6). Rightly recognizing that the Victorian literary establishment defined Hemans, Landon, and their female peers as "poetesses," distinctly different from the *male* "poet," these critics have explored and defined the specific literary conventions which governed the productions of these poetesses and helped to construct a feminine "music of their own." These conventions encompassed, as Armstrong and others have shown, the adoption of the mask of the improvisatrice, the insistence on the primacy of love and the domestic affections to a woman's happiness, the rejection or condemnation of poetic fame, the embracing of Edmund Burke's aesthetic of "the beautiful" as the goal of female literary desire, and the acceptance of the doctrine of the separate spheres. At the same time, these poetesses engaged in extremely subtle rhetorical subversions of and resistances to the representation of feminine subjectivity as entirely private and domestic. They did so by identifying with such female personae as Philomela's nightingale, the Greek Pythia, or the inspired Sappho, figures which empowered their criticisms both of masculinity and of the havoc wrought by men within the public realm.

The category of the "poetess" may persuasively encompass the poetry of women like Hemans and Landon who self-consciously embraced an aesthetic of the beautiful, who celebrated, in Lydia Sigourney's description of Felicia Hemans, "The whole sweet circle of the domestic affections—the hallowed ministries of woman, at the cradle, the hearthstone, and the death-bed" (qtd. by Walker, 6) and who saw themselves as writing a specifically "feminine" poetry, however much they subverted these categories from within. I would like to suggest, however, that to consign all women's poetry published in England between 1780 and 1830 to this tradition of the poetess seriously misrepresents a great deal of it. Here I would like to focus on a female-authored poetry which does not conform to this poetic practice, a poetry which self-consciously and insistently occupies the public sphere, as Habermas defined it, a poetry which—for want of a better term—I will call the tradition of the female poet.

The Origins of the Tradition of the Female Poet

The literary tradition of the female poet is explicitly political. It originates in the writings of the female preachers or prophets who embraced seventeenth-century Quaker theology and a belief in a divine inner light that authorized them to speak in public at Quaker meetings. In *Writing Women's Literary History*, Margaret Ezell has drawn attention to the numerous seventeenth-century Quaker women who preached in public and who published over one hundred religious tracts and epistles containing accounts of their conversions, persecutions, and transcendent visions, as well as sacred verse, written in a style that was both plain and supple (Ezell, chap. 5). Christine Krueger has further documented in her study of women preachers, women writers, and nineteenth-century social discourse, *The Reader's Repentance* (1992), that by the end of the eighteenth century women preachers had learned to invoke scriptural authority for the right of women to speak in public, citing the prophet Joel who had described a time of special blessing as one in which "the sons and daughters shall prophesy"

(Krueger, part I). They further reminded their listeners that even St. Paul, in his letter to the Galatians, had acknowledged that in Christ "there is neither Jew nor Greek, there is neither bond nor free, there is neither male nor female" (Gal. 3:28).

Identifying themselves as the voice of Christian virtue, answerable to no merely mortal male, such female evangelical preachers as Mary Bosanquet Fletcher, Sarah Crosby, Susanna Wesley, Sarah Cox, Francis Pawson, Hester Ann Rogers, Mary Tooth, and scores of others, many of whom published autobiographies, memoirs, and polemical tracts, had by 1780 established both a social practice and a literary precedent for a woman to speak publicly on both religious and political issues. They had claimed and achieved the right to comment on the rectitude or unrighteousness of the government, the military, the professions of law and medicine, and especially of commerce, and to condemn in the name of the highest authority—God or Scripture—the sins of the males who surrounded them. Encouraged by John Wesley, the Methodists, and the Dissenting Academies, women preachers grew in number and influence throughout the early nineteenth century.

These female preachers taught that a careful reading of the Bible provided telling precedents for female judges (Deborah), for female rulers (Queen Esther), for female military leaders and saviors of their people (Judith). The Bible also provided authority for women to resist those fathers, brothers, and husbands who might lead them astray, for women to leave the family home in order to pursue a life of greater sanctity, for women to gather in communities that were independent of male control, even for women to laugh at God (as did Sarah).

Just as the canonical male Romantic poets claimed divine authority or "poetic genius" as the inspiration and origin of their writing, so this tradition of the female poet claimed divine authority, grounded in a revisionist reading of Holy Scripture, for their prophetic verse. They frequently defined themselves as the mouthpieces or vessels of the "Divine Word." In addition to citing the Bible, they invoked examples from written and oral history (such as Queen Elinor, Gertrude von der Wart, and the female Christian martyrs) to document an argument that, *as women*, they had demonstrated a fidelity (to Christ, to a child, or a husband) superior to that of men. Moreover, they pointed out, Christian women had traditionally been assigned the responsibility for the inculcation of virtue within the domestic sphere and for the moral and religious instruction of young children. Citing this practice, they laid claim to a more refined virtue than the average man could attain, a capacity for "right feeling" that combined a highly developed sensibility with practical morality. Again and again, the female poet insisted that she spoke on behalf of Virtue, a virtue that she consistently gendered as female, a virtue that in a Christian nation must govern both the private and the public sphere, thus taking precedence over all merely expedient considerations of government policy or commercial advancement.

Since female preachers typically spoke to the uneducated, to children, to the working classes, they consciously used a vernacular or vulgar language. Against the claims of James Harris's grammatical treatise *Hermes* (1751), Dr. Johnson's *Dictionary* (1755), and Bishop Lowth's first comprehensive grammar of English (1762), all of which attempted to regulate "proper" or "polite" speech on the basis of rules derived from Latin that only classically educated men could comprehend, they insisted on the capacity of virtue to speak in plain, everyday language, in words that even a child could hear and understand. Implicitly they engaged in the class politics which Olivia Smith has described in *The Politics of Language* (1984), in a democratizing movement which undermined the religious and social authority of learned men over the unlettered working classes or less well educated women.

Before turning to specific examples from the tradition of the female poet, I want to acknowledge the ideological limitations inherent in a literary tradition that derives its authority from the practice of the evangelical or dissenting female preacher. Because she spoke on behalf of *Christian* virtue, because she invoked the Bible as her final textual authority, the words of the female dissenting or evangelical preacher could easily be heard as an affirmation of patriarchal Christianity; indeed, much of the energy of this dissenting tradition was by 1840 absorbed within a specifically Anglican Evangelicalism that operated comfortably within the established church. Secondly, the writings of the Christian female poet could be—and often were—co-opted in the name of a British imperial expansion that also defined itself as "Christian." The female poet's jeremiads were frequently used to justify a missionary movement that imposed on other nations and cultures, whether African, American, or Asian, the assumptions of what Winthrop Jordan has called "Anglo-Africanism"—the assumptions that "to be Christian was to be civilized rather than barbarous, English rather than African, white rather than black" (94).

Nonetheless, the female poet could and did claim a moral and literary authority equal to—or even greater than—that of those male poets who worked within a neoclassical literary tradition that looked to the battlefields of the *Iliad* or the *Aeneid* for inspiration, that produced an ideology that was inherently competitive and self-aggrandizing, and that frequently sacrificed Christian virtue to national conquest or personal glory. By equating virtue with moral rectitude, a refusal to compromise, the willingness to suffer for one's beliefs, personal self-sacrifice, and compassion for others, above all with spiritual liberty and peaceful co-existence, the female poet aligned herself with Christ and his martyrs, with those who had an obligation to speak out for the greater good, even the salvation, of the nation.

However relentlessly didactic much of this tradition of female poetry seems to us today, we must remember that it inaugurated a tradition of explicitly *feminist* poetry, a poetry that insisted on the equality of women with men and the right of women to speak publicly on subjects to which they could contribute a uniquely valid perspective and which had an impact on their daily lives: specifically, the nature of good government and how best to educate children to achieve a moral society.

Defining the Tradition of the Female Poet

The female poet writes a poetry that is both political and didactic. Broadly speaking, her poetry either (1) responds to specific political events; or (2) argues more broadly for wide-ranging social and political reform; or (3) attempts to initiate a social revolution, what Mary Wollstonecraft in her *A Vindication of the Rights of Woman* called "a REVOLUTION in female manners" (192), a redefinition of gender that will ensure equal rights for women. In all these cases, the female poet grounds her social analysis on a specific political or religious ideology, one which entitles her to take up the stance of moral judge of the events transpiring around her.

Several poems written between 1780 and 1830 specifically addressed the two most influential political events of this historical period, the French Revolution and the attempts to abolish the slave trade. Let me take just two poems as representative of this type: Charlotte Smith's "The Emigrants" of 1793 and Hannah More's "Slavery" of 1788.

In "The Emigrants," Smith focuses her attention—not on the originating ideology of the French Revolution, on its battle cry for "liberty, equality, fraternity" which inspired Blake, Wordsworth, and Coleridge—but rather on the plight of the French clergymen and aristocrats who had been suddenly and violently deprived of their homes, livings, and family members by the executions of the Revolutionary Tribunal during the Terror and who had sought refuge in England. She insists that there is little difference between the oppressions of the ancien régime (mere "pampered parasites," book I, line 330), of the new French Republic (which she defines as "lawless Anarchy," I, 100), or of the British monarchy, under whose reign "equal Law is mockery" (I, 37). In her view, all the prevailing governments of western Europe are patriarchal and unjust systems constructed by "Man, misguided Man" (I, 34).

In their place, she argues, we must put a new England, one that she defines as obedient to compassion, that exercises a genuine liberty which she equates with a tolerance for diversity. In her introductory dedication to William Cowper, she argues that true "liberality" is the "annihilation of prejudices" (p. 133); she therefore urges her countrymen and women to extend their sympathy even to those French Catholic priests who do not share their religious views. Attacking both the devastations of war and the conventions of the epic genre which glorify such wars, she forswears the epic for the blank-verse Georgic pastoral, situating her poem within the English countryside near the downs of Sussex. But where Wordsworth and Coleridge found consolation in nature for the ravages of the French Terror, Charlotte Smith finds no "Content" in "rural life" (II, 176–85). When she looks into the cottages of the local shepherds and agrarian workers, she sees only "poverty," "Disease," and a myriad of insults and oppressions wrought upon the "poor but peaceful hind" by his tyrannical "rich master" (II, 63–65). Since even Mother Nature's bounty has been "stained with blood" (II, 70–71), she sees no hope for freedom in the England she knows, introducing in the second book of her poem a personal, nostalgic note, as she yearns for a forever lost childhood innocence and bliss. Although she sees no hope for a reign of "reason," "justice," or "equality" in England (II, 429, 432), she ends her poem with a reaffirmation of the moral ideology which has inspired her condemnation. Rewriting the battle cry of the French Jacobins ("liberty, equality, fraternity") in a female register—"The reign of Reason, Liberty and Peace" (all gendered female in this poem, II, 444)—she holds out the hope that the havoc wrought in France may yet, as nature's storms "drive noxious vapours from the blighted earth" (II, 442), result in a new, more compassionate and egalitarian society. As everywhere in this poem, she insists that she has spoken *on behalf of others,* that she endorses an ethic of care or "public virtue" enforced by "stern but equal Justice" (II, 432), and that Nature, if properly respected, remains a storehouse of potential bounty and happiness. It is only the "woes that Man / For Man creates" (II, 412), she concludes in a final condemnation of patriarchal militarism, that prevents both the English and the French nations from achieving that liberty and peace their citizens deserve.

In "Slavery," first published in 1788 and then expanded and retitled "The Slave Trade" in later editions, Hannah More explicitly invokes the divine authority of "Heaven" and its "bright intellectual sun," liberty, to mount her attack on the evils of the slave trade. Gendering liberty as female, she implicitly identifies her own poetic voice with that of this "sober Goddess" (line 19), and further claims as her muse Truth itself: "Fair Truth, a hallow'd guide! inspires my song" (50). Her attack on the slave trade was widely circulated; I take it here as representative of many similar poetic condemnations of both slavery and the slave trade by Ann Yearsley, Helen

Maria Williams, Anna Barbauld, and Amelia Opie. More insisted on the common humanity that Africans shared with Europeans: "Respect *His* sacred image which they bear. / . . . Let Malice strip them of each other plea, / They still are men, and men should still be free" (136, 139–40). At the same time she denounced the "WHITE SAVAGE" who, ruled by "lust of gold / Or lust of conquest" (211–12), forfeited any legitimate claim Europe might make to being either civilized or Christian.

Gender played a significant role in the poetic arguments for the abolition of slavery (see Mellor 1996). The most prominent male abolitionist poets, such as Thomas Day and William Cowper, tended to attack slavery as a violation of "natural law," the argument that all men are born equal and have certain inalienable "rights." As a man, the black African belongs to the same species as the white European, and is entitled to the same "liberty, equality and fraternity." Female poets, on the other hand, tended to condemn slavery because it violated the domestic affections. Both the slave trade and the institution of slavery in the West Indies separated mothers from their children, husbands from their wives, and subjected black women to sexual abuse from their white masters. In Hannah More's words,

> Whene'er to Afric's shores I turn my eyes,
> Horrors of deepest, deadliest guilt arise;
> I see, by more than Fancy's mirror shown,
> The burning village, and the blazing town:
> See the dire victim torn from social life,
> The shrieking babe, the agonizing wife!
> She, wretch forlorn! is dragg'd by hostile hands,
> To distant tyrants sold, in distant lands!
> Transmitted miseries, and successive chains,
> The sole sad heritage her child obtains!
> E'en this last wretched boon their foes deny,
> To weep together, or together die. (95–106)

Insisting that the "affections" are the basis of a universal morality, "in every nature, every clime the same" (117–18), More assumes the voice of righteous indignation, the voice of that "outraged goddess" Reason (145), to attack those English traders and rulers governed by a "sordid lust of gold" (127) who make "MAN the traffic, SOULS the merchandise" (146). More's target here is not only the slave trade, though that may be the most egregious example of white savagery; she extends her critique to all of what we would now call England's imperial project, the effort to conquer by trade or force the native populations of other lands; for as she insists, "conquest is pillage with a nobler name" (126).

More grounds her attack on the slave trade on Scripture and on reason, but also on sensibility, on the ability to feel what others feel, on that "nerve" which, "howe'er untutored, can sustain / A sharp, unutterable sense of pain" (159–60). By invoking sensibility as the source of morality, More lays claim to a virtue that had historically been identified with the female gender. She further identifies that same sensibility with a specifically female poetry, with what she calls the "feeling line": "Rhetoric or verse may point the feeling line, / They do not whet sensation, but define" (165–66). The responsibility of the female poet, then, is to "define" the pains, the evils, that savage white men cause, and by raising their consciousness of their wrongdoings, inspire her countrymen to repent their sins and end their crimes.

I cannot leave More's poem, and other abolitionist poems written during this period by women, without heeding Moira Ferguson's trenchant reminder that many of them embraced the discourse of Anglo-Africanism, as More's address to British slave traders reveals: "Barbarians, hold! th'opprobrious commerce spare, / Respect *His* sacred image which they bear. / *Though dark and savage, ignorant and blind,* / They claim the common privilege of kind; / Let Malice strip them of each other plea, / They still are men, and men should still be free" (135–40; my italics). As Barbara Bush and Deirdre Coleman have recently reminded us, British female abolitionist poets often shared an assumption of cultural and religious *superiority to* the black slave (Ann Yearsley's "A Poem on the Inhumanity of the Slave-Trade," 1788, is a notable exception). More conveys this in a particularly patronizing moment in the revised version of her poem, retitled "The Slave Trade" (1790), in which she summons the enslaved African to a conversion to Christianity, "Thy mental night thy Savior will not blame, / He died for those who never heard his name" (*Works* V: 350). More everywhere assumes that the Christian female poet possesses the "light" of mercy and reason that can liberate Africans from their "intellectual night" (V: 352), as she concludes her revised poem in an outburst of evangelical fervor and cultural chauvinism: "Let there be light! / Bring each benighted soul, great God, to Thee, / And with thy wide salvation make them free!" (V: 353).

For more broad-ranging political condemnations of the colonial imperialism and bourgeois capitalism hinted at in More's poem I turn first to Helen Maria Williams's *Peru*. In this, Williams's first long poem, published in 1784, she fiercely attacks the devastations wrought by Pizarro's invading troops upon the fertile lands and contented people of Peru. She opens her poem with an extended description of Peru before the Spanish conquest as a garden of Eden in which nature's abundant bounty and "love" has produced a society founded on "virtues . . . unsullied and sublime" (canto I, line 42), a "cultur'd scene" of "Joy serene" in which charity and simplicity reign. Governed by the benevolent Ataliba, in whose "pure and gen'rous heart / The virtues bloom'd without the aid of art" (I, 63–64), the Peruvians know the bliss of heaven on earth. But this Eden is destroyed by the "curse" of Europe, "the tempting bane" of gold. Williams here moves beyond the self-deceiving "anti-conquest" narratives described by Mary Louise Pratt in her *Imperial Eyes* to a full-fledged attack on European exploration, colonization, and conquest. In Williams's view, nothing can justify the treachery and brutality of Pizarro's calculated betrayal, capture, imprisonment, and finally murder of the trusting leader of the Inca, Ataliba. Pizarro's campaign of death and desolation, all inspired by a greed for gold, is hypocritically masked as a "Christian" mission by the "fanatic fury" of the Spanish Catholic priest Valverda, who eagerly puts to the sword all "heathen" shrines and their gentle worshippers.

Williams's heroic couplets celebrate, not the ideology of capitalist expansion and military glory embodied by Pizarro, but rather an ethic of love, compassion, peace, and liberty. This ethic is embodied not only by the gentle Peruvians—of whose domestic affections and fidelity even onto death she provides numerous examples—but also by the "good" priest Las Casas, who actively saves several Peruvians from the executions or enforced marriages demanded by Pizarro and his general Alphonso. His death, in canto VI, is presided over by Sensibility, who summons her followers to mourn the kind Las Casas:

> Ye to whose yielding hearts my power endears
> The transports blended with delicious tears,
> The bliss that swells to agony the breast,
> The sympathy that robs the soul of rest;
> Hither with fond devotion pensive come,
> Kiss the pale shrine, and murmur o'er the tomb; . . . (lines 247–52)

In Williams's ideology, sensibility must combine with a respect for the liberty of all peoples to produce a truly Christian world, one in which war— even battles fought for the freedom of an unjustly oppressed people, such as that waged successfully by Tupac Amaru in the closing lines of the poem —must give way to a negotiated peace. Here that peace is brought by Gasca, the benevolent Spanish Christian who comes as "the guardian minister" to end oppressions and bind up the wounds of battle.

By celebrating the Spanish Christians Las Casas and General Gasca as "messengers of peace" at the end of her poem,[1] Williams makes explicit her Eurocentric assumption that Christianity is finally superior to the religious rites of even the mild, gentle Peruvian priests whose sufferings she has so compassionately delineated. As Alan Richardson has noted in a remarkably perceptive reading of *Peru*, Williams's equation of pre-Conquest Peru with

an Edenic innocence and the "primitive" virtues of simplicity, purity, innocence, and artlessness function to suggest that Peru must, like Europe, develop through "higher" stages of religious and cultural civilization before it
can attain the ultimate "Freedom" she hails at the close of the poem (Richardson 1996). At the same time, Williams's insistent displacement of the
epic by the romance suggests that roads other than that of colonial conquest must be taken to reach the progressive goal of a social harmony me-
diated by the merciful Christianity she envisions. In her view, the "primitive" Peruvian virtues are already closer than those of an imperialist and
vindictive patriarchal culture to the domestic or relational values she hails
throughout the poem as the path to personal and national salvation—the
virtues of charity, parental nurturing, "Melting" love, and self-sacrifice for
the good of others.

The most powerful condemnation of the misguided political and commercial policies of early-nineteenth-century England by a woman occurs in
Anna Letitia Barbauld's Juvenalian satire in heroic couplets, "Eighteen
Hundred and Eleven." Written during the height of the Napoleonic campaigns and published in 1812 to broad public criticism (criticism which
did not, contrary to current scholarly belief, end her writing career),[2] Barbauld's poem dares to question Britain's commitment to war with France.
Taking up the stance of the female preacher, Barbauld defines that war as
nothing more than Famine, Disease, and Rapine which "Man" (here specifically equated with male codes of chauvinist heroism and the brutality
they produce) alone invokes, even as woman "withers." Woman is here
identified both with that "Glad Nature" who "with frantic man at strife"
pours out the bounteous "joys of life" only to have them wasted by "the
tramp of marching hosts," and also with the "fruitful" matron whose cherished "youths" are now but "fallen blossoms" on "a foreign strand" (lines
11–26).

Barbauld's jeremiad is not only a call for pacifism in the face of an increasing national militarism inspired by the successes of Nelson at sea and
Wellington on land. It is more sweepingly an apocalyptic prophecy, one
that foretells the doom of the entire nation. Inspired by Volney's *The Ruins; or Meditations on the Revolutions of Empires* (1791), Barbauld foretells
the end of the British empire: "thy Midas dream is o'er; / The golden tide
of commerce leaves thy shore" (61–62). Despite Britain's contributions
both to the sciences and the arts (Barbauld explicitly celebrates Locke,
Paley, Milton, Thomson, Baillie, and Shakespeare as Britain's greatest philosophical and poetic leaders), despite the fact that the English language has
achieved dominance "O'er half the western world," Britain's triumphant
reign is coming to an end. Barbauld envisions a time, not too distant (in-

deed, one could argue that it has now, by the beginning of the twenty-first century, arrived), when England will no longer rule the waves or control an empire, when her cities and countryside will be the haunt primarily of tourists, come from Canada and America, and "England, the seat of arts, be only known / By the gray ruin and the mouldering stone" (123–24).

In Barbauld's view, the cause of England's decline and fall is clear: her failure to preserve the very "Liberty" she so early nurtured. Wherever the "Spirit" of liberty walks, "the human brute awakes . . . thinks . . . reasons . . . feels finer wants" and cultivates with Nature's blessings "the flowers of Genius and of Art" (215–36). But when freedom is sacrificed to the demands of war or commerce, then the "Genius" of liberty "forsakes the favoured shore," "empires fall to dust . . . and wasted realms enfeebled despots sway" (241, 243–44). What Barbauld means by liberty is clarified in her earlier political tract of 1790, *An Address to the Opposers of the Repeal of the Corporation and Test Acts*. In that forcefully argued demand for the civil rights of Dissenters, she equates true liberty with the unfettered "spirit of Enquiry" and portrays the historical advance of this "genius of Philosophy" in exactly the terms she later invoked in "Eighteen Hundred and Eleven":

> The genius of Philosophy is walking abroad, and with the touch of Ithuriel's spear is trying the establishments of the earth. The various forms of Prejudice, Superstition and Servility start up in their true shapes, which had long imposed upon the world under the revered semblances of Honour, Faith, and Loyalty. Whatever is loose must be shaken, whatever is corrupted must be lopt away; whatever is not built on the broad base of public utility must be thrown to the ground. Obscure murmurs gather, and swell into a tempest; the spirit of Enquiry, like a severe and searching wind, penetrates every part of the great body politic; and whatever is unsound, whatever is infirm, shrinks at the visitation. Liberty, here with the lifted crosier in her hand, and the crucifix conspicuous on her breast; there led by philosophy, and crowned with the civic wreath, animates men to affect their long forgotten rights. With a policy, far more liberal and comprehensive than the boasted establishments of Greece and Rome, she diffuses her blessings to every class of men; and even extends a smile of hope and promise to the poor African, the victim of hard, impenetrable avarice. Man, *as* man, becomes an object of respect. (32–33)

But whereas in 1790 Barbauld could envision a triumph of liberty in England, twenty years later she had lost hope. In "Eighteen Hundred and Eleven," her feminist rewriting of a neoclassical progress poem, Barbauld represents the progress of Liberty as an inevitable geographical movement from East to West, beginning in East Asia and northern Africa and advancing to Greece, then Italy, then northern Europe, then England. But where earlier Whig progress poems ended in England, Barbauld stages the relentless movement of Liberty beyond Britain, to the Americas, and specifically to South America where Venezuela had declared its independence in 1811. For as Barbauld concludes,

> The worm is in thy core, thy glories pass away;
> Arts, arms and wealth destroy the fruits they bring;
> Commerce, like beauty, knows no second spring.
> Crime walks thy streets, Fraud earns her unblest bread,
> O'er want and woe thy gorgeous robe is spread. (314–18)

Assuming the mantle of an Old Testament prophet, Barbauld here utters one of the female poet's most devastating condemnations of nascent British imperialism as a systemic denial of individual freedom in the name of "commerce" and "progress." Unlike her male poetic predecessors (Johnson, Lyttleton, Thomson, Coleridge), Barbauld offers no salvation or escape, no turn to a "country-party" georgic idyll of enlightened leisure or a romantic concept of regeneration through Nature. Instead, like Cassandra before her, she relentlessly foretells the doom of her country, here defined as the end of that liberal public culture to which English women as well as men have contributed, that public culture which now, she implies, only female writers like herself and Joanna Baillie understand well enough to value and preserve.

For a female-authored poem which more than any other mounted a demand for a social revolution, for the initiation of a women's movement which would overthrow the existing construction of gender and ensure the equality, perhaps even the social and political superiority, of the female, I turn to Lucy Aikin's four-book *Epistles on Women* published in 1810. In this 1,200-line poem, written in heroic couplets, Lucy Aikin rewrites the history of humanity from the Garden of Eden to 1750, attributing all the major advances in "civilisation" to "Maternal Love" and the social practices of women. Deliberately responding to Pope's claim, in his epistle "To a Lady," that "Most Women have no Characters at all," and confidently taking on the challenge of the *Aeneid*, to sing "the Fate of Woman," of Milton's *Paradise Lost*, to "justify the ways of God to" women, and of Pope's *Essay on Man*, to show that whatever is, is not yet right for women, Aikin offers an alternative account of the character or nature of the female sex.

She begins, in her introduction, with a brilliant display of feminist irony: she adamantly dismisses "the absurd idea that the two sexes ever can be, or ever ought to be, placed in all respects on a footing of equality" (1810: 5), only to imply that the female may in some respects be superior to the male. After asserting that there is "no talent, no virtue . . . not an endowment, or propensity, or mental quality of any kind" (6) that the female cannot possess, she acknowledges that men have a superior physical strength that enables them to perform certain tasks (warfare, physical labor) that women cannot do. But she immediately calls the value of this physical superiority into question by suggesting that, historically, men have used their physical strength only to degrade women. "The chief 'moral of my song,'" she announces, is to show "that it is impossible for man to degrade his companion without degrading himself" (8).

After denouncing Pope's and her society's construction of women as nothing more than "a plaything and a slave," Aikin in her first epistle summons the "Historic Muse" (epistle I, line 71) in order to rewrite the story of the Creation and Fall from a radical feminist perspective. Having flatly stated in her argument to epistle I the "primary equality" of Eve with Adam, Aikin then suggests that Eve is morally superior to Adam because she, unlike Adam, has a mother, and because she will become a mother. Strategically omitting the Genesis account of Eve's creation from Adam's rib,[3] Aikin presents the origin of Eve as an overflow of Mother Nature's bounty—"When slumbering Adam pressed the lonely earth, . . . / Unconscious parent of a wondrous birth, . . . As forth to light the infant-woman sprung" (I, 75–77). Aikin's strategically placed ellipses allow us to read "unconscious parent" as referring both to Adam (asleep and therefore unconscious) and to "lonely earth," also lacking consciousness. We might thus see Adam as impregnating Earth (in a wet dream?), who then gives "birth" to a "wondrous" child, wondrous both because she is an "infant-woman" and because she is the result of man's sexual union with nature.

Since Eve has imbibed sympathy directly from her "step-dame" Nature, she is capable of nurturing and thus of *civilizing* Adam. Notably, Eve learns language, not from Adam, but rather from her mother, mimicking in "untried sounds" the sounds of "the sweet gale" and "glowing landscape" around her (I, 100). Adam, "the world's new master," on the other hand, is speechless. He roams along,

> Vainly intelligent and idly strong;
> Mark his listless step and torpid air,
> His brow of densest gloom and fixt infantile stare!
> Those sullen lips no mother's lips have prest,
> Nor drawn, sweet labour! at her kindly breast;
> No mother's voice has touched that slumbering ear,
> Nor glistening eye beguiled him of a tear;
> Love nursed not him with sweet endearing smiles. (I, 117–24)

Encountering Adam, Eve's concern and sympathy for this "moping idiot" awakens Adam's soul and *teaches* him language: "the youth, as love and nature teach, / Breathes his full bosom, and breaks forth in *speech*" (I, 150–51). The Fall, in Aikin's rewriting of the biblical and Miltonic myths, is caused not by a serpent who tempts Eve but rather by *men*. Eve succumbs, not to the serpent's words that "replete with guile / Into her heart too easie entrance won" (*Paradise Lost* IX: 733–34), but rather to Adam's words, words of love that "pierce! how swift! to Eve's unguarded heart" (I, 153). The consequence of Eve's succumbing to Adam's love of course is the engendering of children, of Abel and Cain. And, in Aikin's view, it is the "savage blood" spilt by Cain in his rivalry with Abel and Adam's "pride of power," the male capacity and desire to oppress weaker women and children, "to bruise, to slay, to ravage, to devour" (I, 87–88), that finally bring about the loss of paradise.

Demonstrating her claim to learning and intellectual authority through copious footnotes and a wide range of references to history, geography, anthropology, and the Latin and Greek classics, Aikin's second epistle tracks the consequences of masculine physical superiority for women throughout the known world, in both "primitive" and so-called "civilized" societies. Everywhere, the primary equality of women has been denied and women reduced to "female servitude" and "*homely* misery" (II, 235, 236), a slavery so severe that "the maddening mother" prefers to kill her infant daughter rather than subject her to a life of such unrelieved suffering (II, 73–74). Parodying Rousseau's celebration of the noble savage, she portrays untaught Savage Man as "half-humanized," a "monster-man" who drags "the bleeding victim bride away" (II, 42, 46).

Only motherhood and the maternal love it inspires have saved human beings from being totally annihilated by man's lawless brutality. As Aikin hails this love:

> Thrice holy Power, whose fostering, bland embrace
> Shields the frail scions of each transient race,
> To whom fair Nature trusts the teeming birth
> That fills the air, that crowds the peopled earth,
> Maternal Love! thy watchful glances roll
> From zone to zone, from pole to distant pole;
> Cheer the long patience of the brooding hen,
> Soothe the she-fox that trembles in her den, . . .
> At thy command, what zeal, what ardour, fires
> The softer sex! A mightier soul inspires . . . (II, 119–30)

Aikin here adopts an essentialist position, resting her claim for the superiority of the female on a maternal instinct found in both the animal and the human species. Note that the male of the species, in Aikin's account, is as likely to destroy as to protect his offspring:

> Ah! fond in vain, see fired by furious heat
> The jealous stag invade her soft retreat,
> Wanton in rage her pleading anguish scorn,
> And gore his offspring with relentless horn. (II, 147–50)

Aikin here implies that the survival of the species depends primarily on the female, on the maternal instinct; were it not for a mother's fond care, the male of the species would annihilate his children (whether in rage, jealousy, pride, or warfare).

Aikin's third epistle records the history of a Western culture grounded on masculine rather than feminine values. From antiquity through the Middle Ages, from the times of classical warfare to the Ottoman Empire, men have equated the advance of civilization with conquest and enslavement. Only at certain moments have women been able to assert an alternative political ideology, one focused on the preservation of peace—Aikin singles out the Sabine women, Andromache, Cornelia, and Portia as truly heroic women who opposed the continuation of war, as women who combined reason with virtue. Throughout the epistles, Aikin genders both Reason and Virtue as female, implying a special connection between women and those capacities; at the same time, she elevates female Virtue over a male God, to the "loftiest throne" of all (III, 243). She interprets classical Rome as a progressive stage in the civilizing of mankind, because it at least offered such women as Cornelia and Portia an opportunity to speak in the public realm and to articulate their alternative ethic of care and compassion; even though male lust and greed caused Rome's final decline and fall.

Her final epistle turns to modern Europe, invoking the Celtic ideal of sexual equality against those contemporary cultures which have effectively cloistered women, whether in Turkish harems, Indian suttee, or French salons. Only by modeling the public sphere on the values of the private sphere, only by inculcating the domestic virtues of compassion, love, and toleration into government policy, can the progress of civilization be forwarded. Throughout, Aikin argues that women have contributed more than men to what Norbert Elias would call the civil (as opposed to the political) society or the "civilizing process"; the only mistake that some women leaders have made is to emulate their male peers too closely. She therefore begins her history of modern women with Queens Bondica, Ethelfleda, and Elizabeth I, all of whose legendary achievements are rendered problematic for Aikin by their participation in bloody battles and acts of revenge. The execution of Mary, Queen of Scots, for instance, bares "the meanness" of "the dread Eliza"'s "selfish heart" (IV, 385).

In contrast, Aikin praises those women who carried the values of maternal love into the public realm: Jane Grey, whose acquiescence in her own execution paved the way for peace in England; Lucy Hutchinson, "high historian of the dead" (IV, 409), who corrected the public misreading of her husband's domestic virtues; Lady William Russell, whose devotion to her husband and self-control set a new standard for public morality; and finally, Margaret Roper, whose passionate display of filial devotion at the moment of her father's death called into question the authority of the king himself. In each case, Aikin contrasts the violent and deadly nature of a public sphere ruled by men with the public loyalty, love, and self-sacrifice of women.

Aikin, a highly regarded Whig historian, here equates progress with the increasing feminization of the public sphere. In her view a Golden Age of sexual equality has never existed in the past. She therefore ends her *Epistles* with a "call-to-arms" both to women and to men to reject the militaristic and competitive values of the past, to affirm the domestic affections as the noblest model for all public and private social relationships, and to educate women, who will take up the lamp of learning in order to empower mothering both as a political and a private practice.

One further point. Aikin recognizes that her revolutionary political program demands a new poetics. She includes in her last epistle a passage that might be read as her own "defense of poesy," a passage that significantly redefines the nature and function of female-authored poetry for her time. She rejects as arrogant any poetics based on originary genius, on that "godlike power" celebrated by the male Romantic poets. At the same time she forswears a concept of female art as passive imitation and "fond fancy," based on the precedent of the Corinthian maid who outlined her lover's shadow on the wall and then painted it during his absence with "cheated sight" (IV, 19–31). Instead, Aikin suggests, the best poetry is "thoughtful, cold"—rational and realistic, yet still "fostered" or sympathetically nurtured, fostered explicitly by "Friendship" (IV, 35–40). In place of a Wordsworthian overflow of powerful feeling in a solitary mind, Aikin substitutes a concept of poetry as *conversation* or linguistic mothering, as the creation and nurturing of social intercourse or public opinion, that very public opinion which Habermas defined as the foundation of political discourse in this period. Aikin therefore dedicates this poem, her defense both of the female sex and of the female poet, to a female muse, to her sister-in-law and friend, Anna Wakefield Aikin, the daughter of Gilbert Wakefield and arguably the best educated woman of her day. Anna Aikin is also that ideal female reader who will work beside her sister to bring about a "Revolution in female manners."

There are numerous other examples of political poetry by female poets—one thinks of poems by Mary Robinson, Ann Yearsley, Ann Bannerman, Mary Scott, Phillis Wheatley, Anne Grant, Joanna Baillie, Sydney Owenson, Felicia Hemans, Amelia Opie, and Letitia Landon, among many others—in addition to further pieces by the poets discussed above. Setting this large body of political poetry, intended to sway public opinion, against the more introspective and personal meditations of the tradition of the Romantic poetess enables us to better understand the myriad ways in which the women writers of the Romantic era spoke to and for the nation.

4

Literary Criticism, Cultural Authority, and the Rise of the Novel

When Anna Letitia Barbauld told Coleridge that his *Rime of the Ancient Mariner* "was improbable and had no moral," she not only articulated her shrewd critical insight into the poem's unresolved juxtaposition of a chaotic amoral universe with a Christian theology,[1] she also laid claim to a literary aesthetic that stood in sharp contrast to the concepts usually identified as "Romantic literary criticism." In this chapter I wish to suggest that the leading women literary critics of the Romantic era—Joanna Baillie, Anna Barbauld, Elizabeth Inchbald, Clara Reeve, Anna Seward, and Mary Wollstonecraft—upheld an aesthetic theory different from but as coherent as those developed by Coleridge, William Wordsworth, Hazlitt, Keats, Percy Shelley, and their male peers. At the same time, as literary critics, they asserted a claim to a powerful cultural authority: they had the intelligence and the taste to determine who writes best for the good of the nation.

I

Fifty years ago René Wellek rather simplistically categorized Romantic poetic theory as "the rise of an emotional concept of poetry, the establishment of this historical point of view, and the implied rejection of the imitation theory of the rules and genres" of a neoclassical aesthetic. Wellek further identified the Romantic aesthetic with a conception of poetry as a self-constituting system of symbols grounded on polarity, "multeity-in-unity" or the union of opposites (Wellek II: 2–3).[2] An alternative aesthetic theory developed by women writers in the Romantic era existed in the discursive public sphere, in powerful dialogue both with the competing versions of this "expressive" or organic Romantic poetics, whose constitutive trope Meyer Abrams identified as the lamp, and with the neoclassical mimetic theory it displaced—the conception of literature as holding a mirror up to nature, recording "what oft was thought but ne'er so well expressed." In place of the mirror and the lamp, we might think of Romantic-era women literary critics as sustaining the earlier Enlightenment image of literature popularized by Addison and Cowper, the trope of literature as a balance or scale that weighs equally the demands of the head and the heart, of reason and emotion. As they appropriate this aesthetic figure, however, these women literary critics redefine it in an all-important way. In their writings this balance or scale is always held—and here they rely on traditional iconic representations by Ripa and others of a female Justice/Justizia—by a woman. It is a woman, both Sybil and mother, who can most wisely judge the competing claims of thought and emotion: what she seeks, in literature as in life, is "right feeling."

Romantic-era women critics, all practicing poets, playwrights, or novelists as well as critics, thus lay claim to a cultural authority which they used to promote a specific ideology, one endorsed by the majority of the women writers of the period. In my *Romanticism and Gender* (1993) I defined this set of beliefs at length. Briefly recapitulated, the women writers of the Romantic era forswore their male peers' concern with the capacities and value of the creative imagination, with the limitations of language, with the relation of the perceiving subject to the perceived object, with the possibility of transcendence or apocalyptic vision, with the development of an autonomous self and the nature of self-consciousness, and with political (as opposed to social) revolution. Although they read the canonical male Romantic poets with interest and some approval, they often dismissed them as amoral, self-indulgent, or incomprehensible. Felicia Hemans, for instance, enjoyed Percy Shelley's "Ode to the West Wind" but thought Byron's *Don Juan* too "disgusting" to read, while Anna Seward praised Southey's *Joan of Arc* and *Madoc* effusively but found that William Wordsworth, while he had "genius," wrote a poetry that was "harsh, turgid, and obscure" (Hemans I: 243, II: 161, 147; Seward, *Letters* VI: 359–60, V: 61).

Instead, women writers of the Romantic era, whether radical or conservative, more often celebrated the workings of the rational mind, a mind relocated—in a gesture of revolutionary social implications—in the female body. Following both Mary Wollstonecraft and Hannah More, they insisted that women were as capable as men of thinking rationally and acting virtuously and should therefore be rigorously educated. They tended to endorse Wollstonecraft's argument in *A Vindication of the Rights of Woman* that the ideal marriage is one based on mutual respect, self-esteem, affection, and compatibility. Their novels, plays, and poetry repeatedly celebrate the domestic affections and marriages of equality based on such rational love.

Moreover, these women writers conceptualized a subjectivity very different from the transcendental ego standing alone, the *spectator ab extra* projected by Kant and so anxiously embodied and interrogated by William Wordsworth. They represented a subjectivity constructed in relation to other subjectivities, hence a self that is fluid, absorptive, responsive, with permeable ego boundaries, the self that Dorothy Wordsworth so memorably imaged as a floating, disappearing/reappearing island in her poem "Floating Island at Hawkeshead: An Incident in the Schemes of Nature." In their writings, this self typically locates its identity in its connections with a larger human group, whether the family or the social community.

Taking the family as the grounding figure of both social and political organization, most women writers of the Romantic era opposed violent military revolutions, especially the French Revolution, in favor of gradual or evolutionary reform under the guidance of benevolent parental instruction, a model derived from Erasmus Darwin's theory of natural evolution in *The Botanic Garden* (1789–91) and *Zoonomia, or The Laws of Organic Life* (1794). Although they endorsed Edmund Burke's image in *Reflections on the Revolution in France* (1790) of the state as "a little platoon" (Burke 41), a family, they strenuously resisted Burke's assertion that only men "of permanent property" loyal to their "canonized forefathers" (30) could lead such a platoon, and insisted that the mother played as important a role as the father in the governance of the family politic.

Here these women writers and literary critics emphatically break rank with both their male and their female eighteenth-century forebears. While they shared an Enlightenment commitment to rationality, they added to it the revolutionary claim that the female mind was not only as rational as the male but perhaps even *more* rational. This claim is based on the argument that an ethic of care, an ethic that takes as its highest value the ensuring that, in any conflict, no one should be hurt, is a more rational distribution of social goods and services than those derived from an ethic of justice, an ethic that demands that all persons, regardless of their physical and psychological needs and material assets, should be treated the same under the law.

Committed to changing the hegemonic ideology of the day, the women literary critics of the period constructed a coherent program for the production and consumption of literature, clearly defining the proper goals of literature and the correct nature of the aesthetic response. They were writing at the moment when women for the first time in Western history participated equally in the discursive public sphere. The advent of the circulating or lending library, which spread rapidly throughout England after the 1780s, ensured that books, especially novels, poems, and plays, were widely available to women readers of both the middle and the aristocratic classes. It is crucial to recognize that the bulk of the subscribers to these lending libraries were women (see Kaufman), who had by the late eighteenth century acquired the literacy, desire, and opportunity to read, and preferred to read literature, especially novels, written by women. As Edward Jacobs has documented, the circulating libraries published twice as much fiction written by women as by men. This new audience meant that women could, and perhaps for the first time did, dominate the material production of literature. Between 1780 and 1830, as cited in the introduction to the present work, more than 900 women published at least one volume of poetry; more than 500 women published at least one novel; many others published plays, essays, histories, religious, philosophical, and political tracts, travel accounts, children's books, diaries, and letters. Not only did they publish an enormous amount of writing, they also succeeded with the public. Ten of the twelve most popular novelists of the period were women. As poets, Felicia Hemans and Letitia Landon rivaled Byron and Wordsworth in popularity and sales. Joanna Baillie was everywhere hailed as the period's best playwright.[3] And the publishers of two of the most prestigious reissue series, Longman's *The British Theatre* and Rivington's *The British Novelists,* chose women as their editors (Elizabeth Inchbald and Anna Barbauld, respectively).

Since women were denied access to the higher institutions of academic learning in England and were often taught only the "accomplishments" of a well-bred young lady in their girls' schools (dancing, singing, sketching, needlework, a smattering of French and Italian, a little arithmetic and —most important—how to read and write), the women critics of the Romantic era recognized that literature—the reading of a good book—was essential to the rational education of young girls. As literary critics, they repeatedly insisted that contemporary and classical literature must assume the responsibility of educating young people, but especially young women, to be sensible, well-informed, and prudent adults. Promoting the values of the professional middle classes to which they belonged, these women critics endorsed a literature that was necessarily didactic, that demonstrated the

rewards of virtue, thrift, and self-control, while punishing the vices of will-
ful impulse, irrationality, lack of foresight, excessive sensibility, and uncontrolled sexual desire (which left girls, as opposed to boys in the days of the
sexual double standard, seduced, abandoned, pregnant, and finally condemned to the only career open to them, prostitution).

Insisting that the cultural role of literature is to instruct, these women
critics assumed the stance of the mother-teacher, selecting the appropriate
books for young people to read at different stages of their growth (Clara
Reeve concludes her *Progress of Romance* with a list of recommended novels for girls, based on their age), warning against licentious literature, and
correcting the aesthetic taste of their charges. Anna Barbauld's introduction and critical prefaces to *The British Novelists* relentlessly emphasized the
moral and pedagogical value of the novels she included. Her comments on
Frances Burney and Maria Edgeworth are typical:

> The more severe and homely virtues of prudence and economy have been en-
> forced in the writings of a Burney and an Edgeworth. . . . Where can be found
> a more striking lesson against unfeeling dissipation than the story of the *Harrels*
> [in Burney's *Cecilia*]? Where have order, neatness, industry, sobriety, been rec-
> ommended with more strength than in the agreeable tales of Miss Edgeworth?
> If a parent wishes his child to avoid caprice, irregularities of temper, procrasti-
> nation, coquetry, affectation,—all those faults and blemishes which undermine
> family happiness and destroy the every-day comforts of common life,—whence
> can he derive more impressive morality than from the same source? when works
> of fancy are thus made subservient to the improvement of the rising genera-
> tion, they certainly stand on a higher ground than mere entertainment, and we
> revere while we admire. ("Essay . . . on Novel-Writing," 50–51)

At the same time Barbauld roundly criticized those overly sentimental novels that "awaken and increase sensibilities, which it is the office of wise
restraint to calm and moderate" (52) and that give young female readers a
false notion of the importance of romantic love, which in fact "acts a very
subordinate part on the great theatre of the world" (53).

Similarly, Mary Wollstonecraft, reviewing Charlotte Smith's *Emmeline*
for the *Analytical Review* in July 1788, condemned Delamere's passion,
which "will catch the attention of many romantic girls, and carry their
imaginations still further from nature and reason." She further denounced
all novels "whose preposterous sentiments our young females imbibe with
such avidity" but that foster "vanity and affectation"; they "throw an insipid kind of uniformity over the moderate and rational prospects of life,
consequently *adventures* are sought for and created, when duties are neglected, and content despised" (*Works* VII: 24n4, 26). Throughout her reviews for the *Analytical,* Wollstonecraft insisted that novels should promote for both sexes, but especially among young women, the virtues of

moderation, reason, contentment, and the domestic affections. As Mitzi Myers has brilliantly documented, Wollstonecraft assumed a "maternal stance" in her reviews, using them as a forum from which to attack excessive feminine sensibility and to redefine the ideal woman as one who balances passion with reason, thus promoting the pedagogical and gender-role reforms she urged more directly in her *Vindication of the Rights of Woman* (Myers 1989).

The critic is a mother, educating British children; the mother thus becomes, necessarily, a literary critic. As Mary Hays urged the mothers of England, your daughters should read whatever they like so long as you

> converse with them on the merits of various authors and accustom them to critical, and literary discussions. They will soon be emulous of gaining your approbation by entering into your ideas, and will be ashamed of being pleased with what you ridicule as absurd, and out of nature, or disapprove, as having an improper and immoral tendency. You have only to persuade them that you have a confidence in their principles, and good sense, and they will be eager to justify your favourable opinion. (Hays 90)

Endorsing Samuel Johnson's view that you become what you read,[4] these female critics were anxious to instill in young people a taste for virtue and abhorrence of vice that would govern their behavior throughout their lives. Instructing the future Queen of England on what to read, Hannah More recommended Addison and Johnson, both of whom seemed to her "to have been raised by Providence for the double purpose of improving the public taste, and correcting the public morals," Cervantes for his "*right good sense,*" and Milton for his "correctness and purity" (*Works* IV: 271, 282, 291). Elizabeth Inchbald defined the goal of good comic writing thus:

> to exhibit the weak side of wisdom, the occasional foibles which impede the full exertion of good sense; the chance awkwardness of the elegant, and mistakes of the correct; to bestow wit on beauty, and to depict the passions visible in the young as well as in the aged;—these are efforts of intellect required in the production of a good comedy, and can alone confer the title of a good comic author. (*British Theatre,* preface to Richard Cumberland's *The Brothers*)

They revised the neoclassical dictum that literature must "delight and instruct" in an extremely important way. What you should read and therefore become, all these women critics agree, is a committed advocate of the domestic affections. As Anna Barbauld concluded, the best British novels endorse "our national taste and habits" which "are still turned towards domestic life and matrimonial happiness" (58). Literary instruction must therefore promote more egalitarian gender roles. Female literary critics used their writings to challenge the masculinist gender ideology promoted by Pope, Johnson, Addison, Polwhele, and a host of male writers and critics, who assumed that men were rational and should dominate the public sphere while women were emotional and should be confined to a private, domestic sphere. Instead, they developed a new image of the ideal female as one who inhabits the public sphere, most broadly defined: she is rational, morally responsible, well educated, and takes the lead in governing herself, her children, and by extension, society at large.

As a rational woman, the ideal female prudently chooses only a marriage of equality, founded on enduring compatibility or rational love, and forswears the temptations both of premarital sexuality and of adultery. As Elizabeth Inchbald repeatedly insisted in her 125 prefaces to *The British Theatre,* "conjugal love" produces the highest human happiness and "has a deeper interest in the bosom of every auditor than any other affection" (preface to Thomas Otway's *Venice Preserved*). She spelled out the way to such conjugal love in her preface to Hannah Cowley's *The Belle's Stratagem:* "The love of Sir George [Touchwood] and his wife is fervent, yet reasonable; they are fond, but not foolish; and with all their extreme delicacy of opinions, never once express their thoughts, either in ranting, affected, or insipid sentences." In contrast, the passion of Shakespeare's Romeo and Juliet is too sudden, "childish," and short lived truly to touch the heart, since to Inchbald it seemed a "matter of doubt whether they would not as quickly have fallen in love a second time, or as soon have become languid through satiety, if all obstacles to their bliss had been removed" (preface to *Romeo and Juliet*). Similarly, Inchbald found the marriage of Alphonso and Almeria in William Congreve's *The Mourning Bride* to be "merely bridal; neither cemented by long friendship, off-spring, or any of those positive ties of affection, which would infallibly win the audience to sympathize in their mutual fondness." Defying her culture's patriarchal assumption that all women must marry to be happy, Inchbald comments sardonically that "to get married, is not to obtain the summit of [the maiden auditor's] wishes, unless in wedlock she gains a friend, a companion, a counsellor, and protector" (preface to Thomas Morton's *The Way to Get Married*).

As this last comment suggests, women literary critics in this period used their writings not only to advocate new social roles and more egalitarian marriages for women but also to condemn the abuses of patriarchy and the traditional construction of masculinity. As Theresa Kelley has noted, Inchbald subtly attacked the British slave trade in her preface to Thomas Southern's *Oroonoko* (Kelley forthcoming). She recommends that the play be staged in Liverpool, where it is never performed, because the "merchants of that great city acquired their riches by the slave trade" (preface to *Oroonoko*). And she went out of her way to attack her society's tolerance for that "disease," male gambling. As Katherine Rogers points out, Inchbald was "consistently hard headed about money" and was not duped by the amorality of Edward Moore's *The Gamester,* a popular tearjerker that portrays as essentially virtuous and lovable a man who ruins his family through gambling (280). As Inchbald comments sardonically, "An audience mostly supposes, that [Beverley's wife] performs an heroic action as a wife" when she gives up her last possession, her jewels, to pay her husband's gambling debts, "but readers call to mind she is a mother; and that she breaks through the dearest tie of nature by thus yielding up the sole support of her infant child, to gratify the ideal honour of its duped and frantic father." As Inchbald concludes, in her effort to reform both genders, "a man without sense, and a woman without prudence, degrade both the masculine and the feminine character" (preface to *The Gamester*).

Anna Barbauld similarly used her prefatory remarks on the novels she included in *The British Novelists* to condemn male folly. She praised Frances Burney in particular for "her satire upon the affected apathy, studied negligence, coarse slang, avowed selfishness, or mischievous frolic by which [young men who aspire to lead the fashion] often distinguish themselves, and through which they contrive to be vulgar with the advantages of rank, mean with those of fortune, and disagreeable with those of youth" (38: viii–ix). And Mary Wollstonecraft, reviewing Thomas Holcroft's Jacobin novel *Anna St. Ives* in May 1792, took this occasion to denounce the patriarchal privileges of aristocratic rank and primogeniture, claiming that "the *moral*" of this novel "is assuredly a good one. It is calculated to strengthen despairing virtue, to give fresh energy to the cause of humanity, to repress the pride and insolence of birth, and to shew that true nobility which can alone proceed from the head and the heart, that claims genius and virtue for all its armorial bearings, and possessed of these, despises all the foppery of either ancient or modern heraldry" (*Analytical Review,* May 1792: 74).

In order to fulfill these didactic and pedagogical purposes, literature must above all be *probable,* the key term in the criticism of these women. Only a work that is realistic, that represents convincing characters in quotidian settings undergoing plausible experiences, can function effectively to educate both old and young people. Here they explicitly defend a mimetic theory of art against the inclinations of the male Romantic poets to invoke visionary experiences or supernatural events in medieval or exotic settings. Elizabeth Inchbald roundly condemns Hannah Cowley's *A Bold Stroke for a Husband* because "however fertile her imagination has been in forming a multiplicity of occurrences, and diversifying the whole exhibition by variety of character, probability is so often violated, that the effect, though powerful, is that of farce, and not a genuine comedy." The passions of the audience, whether at a comedy or a tragedy, are best moved, Inchbald insisted, by a "judicious adherence to nature and simplicity" (preface to Dryden's *All for Love*). This is an adherence that Inchbald herself did not always achieve, as Mary Wollstonecraft pointed out in her review of Inchbald's novel *Nature and Art,* which she condemned for its "improbability" (*Analytical Review,* April 1796: 511).

To be probable, literature must show how real characters change and grow *over time,* how human beings develop in relation to other people, how uncontrolled passions fester and destroy otherwise admirable people. Joanna Baillie was the first to devote her entire creative effort to representing the origin and the *growth* of the human passions. Her *Series of Plays: in which it is attempted to Delineate the Stronger Passions of the Mind, each Passion being the subject of a Tragedy and a Comedy,* begun in 1798, initiated the focus on the growth of the human mind later defined by Wordsworth, Coleridge, and their readers as the essence of Romanticism. Baillie, however, emphasized that human identity is *relational*—that subjectivity is organic, develops over time in response to external social influences, and is shaped by its connections to other selves. Focusing on the growth of the passions, she used her plays to portray both the successful control of the passions by rational thought (as I pointed out in chap. 2, in her plays such prudent self-control is located in her *female* characters) and the damage wrought when a single passion (whether hate, anger, love, jealousy, greed, etc.) takes dominance over all others. Baillie's male protagonists, like Count Basil, De Montfort, or Mr. Charleville in her comedy *The Alienated Manor,* are the ones who cannot control their emotions and wreak havoc on themselves and their families by their obsessive passions. Joanna Baillie believed that the theater could and should function as a "school" (58), to teach her audiences—by arousing their curiosity and appealing to their altruism and self-interest—that the passions must be controlled by good sense if the individual and the family are to survive and achieve happiness.

To be probable, literature must balance the mind and the heart. These women critics fully acknowledged the role played by the feelings as well as by reason in human experience. They knew that the female sex had historically been identified with passion, with "sensibility," with the emotions. They embraced the capacity of women readers to feel intensely, and argued that literature should stimulate the reader's ability to feel sympathy and disgust, pity and revulsion. They praised literary texts that used fresh plots, vivid images, scenes of pathos, all able to arouse the reader from lethargy into an alert response, to appeal to what Wollstonecraft called "the *feeling mind*" (*Analytical Review,* December 1790: 462). As Wollstonecraft explained in her essay "On Poetry and Our Relish for the Beauties of Nature," great art is produced by that "genius" (defined by her as "only another word for exquisite sensibility") which is able both to "rouse the passions" and to exercise the "understanding . . . to discriminate things" and thus to "amend the heart" (*Posthumous Works* IV: 169, 171). Wollstonecraft particularly praised Helen Maria Williams's *Letters from France,* for instance, because they so vividly displayed "the misery of [France's] prison-houses, and the tyrannic power exercised by parents . . . in a pathetic tale that did not require the aid of fiction to heighten the real distress" (*Analytical Review,* December 1790: 433).

These women critics consistently argued that sensibility must be joined with correct perception, that literature must record not flights of fancy or escapist desire but empirical truth. Even as Wollstonecraft argued that the good or "natural" writer must respond to the world immediately and powerfully, speaking "the language of truth and nature with resistless energy," she warned against a sensibility that produces libertinism, by leading one "to prefer the sensual tumult of love a little refined by sentiment, to the calm pleasures of affectional friendship, in whose sober satisfactions, reason, mixing her tranquillizing convictions, whispers that content, not happiness, is the reward of virtue in this world" ("On Poetry," IV: 164, 175). Not any feeling, but the *right feeling* must be aroused by good literature.

Probability is also a matter of craft. Both Barbauld and Inchbald were keenly aware that realistic portrayals, whether in the novel or on the stage, required specific literary techniques, techniques that could be identified, analyzed, and evaluated. As Catherine E. Moore has noted, Barbauld understood clearly the various kinds of narrative and their respective limitations (386). In her preface to Samuel Richardson's *Correspondence* (1804), Barbauld defined three possible narrative strategies or points of view, at the same time recognizing the problems inherent in each: (1) the omniscient narrator—but such narration, she observed, "will not be lively, except [the author] frequently drops himself, and runs into dialogue"; (2) first-person narration, which "confines the author's stile, which should be suited, though it is not always, to the supposed talents and capacity of the imaginary narrator"; and (3) "epistolary correspondence," which "unites, in a good measure, the advantages of the other two" but "is incompatible with a rapidstile" and "highly fictitious: it is the most natural and the least probable way of telling a story" (Barbauld, *Correspondence of Samuel Richardson* I: xxiii–xxviii). Such well-informed discussions of narrative techniques, as Catherine Moore has observed, were rare in the Romantic period; Anna Barbauld here initiates the study of what we now call narratology.

Inchbald, as a successful dramatist, was keenly aware of what worked on the stage and what succeeded only on the printed page. She recognized the role of good acting, acknowledging that a superb actor like Sarah Siddons or Mr. Lewis could rescue an inferior play, such as Thomas Morton's *A Cure for the Heart Ache.* As Katherine Rogers has noted (279), Inchbald understood the necessity of a clear exposition of the plot, as well as the need to sustain dramatic probability even when the plot becomes unbelievable by "the happy art of alluring the attention of the audience, from the observation of every defect, and of fixing it solely upon every beauty which the drama displays," as when Hannah Cowley introduces a masquerade to distract the audience from condemning her hero for falling in love with her heroine after only a few minutes of conversation (preface to *The Belle's Stratagem*). And she condemned Joanna Baillie's *De Montfort* for failing to represent the causes of De Montfort's obsessive hatred, thus rendering her protagonist unconvincing, even, in the eyes of the audience, a "lunatic." Inchbald concluded that "this drama, of original and very peculiar formation, plainly denotes that the authoress has studied theatrical productions as a reader more than as a spectator" (preface to *De Montfort*).

Anna Seward, focusing her attention as a critic exclusively on poetry, laid down what she considered the technical criteria for good poetry: "Criticism must proceed upon a large scale . . . the only requisites on which she should strongly insist are general consistence of metaphor, and happiness of allusion, appropriation as to character, vigour of idea, perspicuity of expression, accuracy and general grace of style, and picturesque power in the epithets" (*Letters* I: 244). Using these criteria, her letters abound in detailed and judicious appraisals of the superiority of Shakespeare in drama, of Milton in the epic, of Spenser in allegory, of Dryden, Pope, and Johnson in what she called the poetic sciences of "the ethic, heroic and satiric," of Thomson in the descriptive, of Prior in the narrative and epigrammatic, of Gray in the lyric and elegiac, and of Shenstone in the pastoral mode.

II

Since probability and morality were their chief literary values, these women critics of the Romantic era initiated a revolutionary reordering of the arts. In the earlier eighteenth century, the epic poem had been ranked first among the literary genres, followed by the tragic drama, the Horatian and Pindaric odes, comic dramas and satires, and the lesser poetic forms (the sonnet, the ballad). At the lowest level of the literary arts were the various forms of prose fiction: stories, legends, romances, novels. Women critics vigorously contested this hierarchy. They argued that the novel, which they traced back to the Greek romances (a claim powerfully defended by Margaret Doody in her recent study of the origin of the Western novel), was the highest literary genre because it was both the most moral and the most realistic.

In order to elevate the novel to the status they thought it deserved, without blindly endorsing Fielding's prefatory claim in *Joseph Andrews* that "a comic romance is a comic epic poem in prose," these women critics first had to deal with their culture's tendency to conflate the novel with the romance. Clara Reeve, in *The Progress of Romance* (1785), insisted both on the literary value of the romance and on the ways in which the novel had developed out of, but gone beyond, the romance. First elevating the genre of the romance, Reeve's spokeswoman Euphrasia claimed that "Epic Poetry is the parent of Romance" (Reeve I: 25). She then opposed the conventional definitions of romance as "a wild, extravagant, fabulous story" or "stories that are built upon fiction, and have no foundation in truth" (I: 6), arguing instead that the romance is "an *Heroic fable*—a fabulous Story of such actions as are commonly ascribed to heroes, or men of extraordinary courage and abilities.—Or . . . an Epic in prose" (I: 13). Surveying the history of the romance from the medieval period through the seventeenth-century French productions of Calprenède and Scudéry, Reeve emphasized their morality and civilizing influence, claiming that they all helped to inspire their readers with a love of virtue and honor, and especially that they taught young men "to look upon themselves as the champions and protectors of the weaker sex;—to treat the object of their passion with the utmost respect" (I: 68).

Yet Reeve, unlike such contemporary German proponents of the romance as A. W. Schlegel, finally condemned the romance for its failure to distinguish historical truth from fiction, and argued that the novel is a superior genre. Even though the novel originated in the plots of the romance, it has transcended this parentage by providing "a picture of real life and manners, and of the times in which it is written" (I: 111). As Reeve concluded,

> The Novel gives a familiar relation of such things, as pass every day before our eyes, such as may happen to our friend, or to ourselves; and the perfection of it, is to represent every scene, in so easy and natural a manner, and to make them appear so probable, as to deceive us into a persuasion (at least while we are reading) that all is real, until we are affected by the joys or distresses, of the persons in the story, as if they were our own. (I: 111)

Introducing the Rivington reprint series of *The British Novelists* in 1810, Anna Barbauld endorsed Reeve's claim that the novel is the highest genre of all, superior to the epic poem:

> The invention of a story, the choice of proper incidents, the ordinance of the plan, occasional beauties of description, and above all, the power exercised over the reader's heart by filling it with the successive emotions of love, pity, joy, anguish, transport, or indignation, together with the grave impressive moral resulting from the whole, imply talents of the highest order, and ought to be appreciated accordingly. A good novel is an epic in prose, with more of character and less (indeed in modern novels nothing) of the supernatural machinery. (2–3)

Like Clara Reeve, Anna Barbauld traces the origin of the novel to the romance, and argues that the cultural function of the novel is to promote the growth of morality. Both agree that the novel surpasses all other genres in its ability to describe in detail the ways that human beings interact with one another and how morally correct decisions are made and tested by experience.

Even Elizabeth Inchbald, a committed dramatist, affirmed the superiority of the genre of the novel. She first ranked drama over poetry, calling the stage "the best vehicle by which wit, poetry, and morality, could be conveyed to the good and the bad, the wise and the ignorant, of the community" (preface to John Tobin's *The Honey Moon*), whereas "Poetry, with all its charms, will not constitute a good play" (preface to George Colman, the Younger, *The Mountaineers*). Worse, whereas on stage it is very difficult to make an evil character sympathetic, "the beautiful and the base" do "combine . . . in the fiction of poetry" (preface to Nicholas Rowe's *The Fair Penitent*). Yet she went on to acknowledge the moral and psychological superiority of fiction over both poetry and the drama. In her preface to *The Iron Chest,* George Colman the Younger's dramatic adaptation of William Godwin's novel *Caleb Williams,* she commented,

> The finer details in "Caleb Williams" allow of no representation in action: the dramatist was here compelled merely to give the features of the murderer's face; while the novelist portrayed every shade of his countenance, every fibre that played in forgetful smiles, or was convulsed by the pangs of remembrance.
>
> The two arts of dramatic and of novel-writing are thus beheld at such variance, that the reader of the novel shall enter, with Falkland, into all his nice, his romantic notions of honour and posthumous fame; though the auditor, or reader, of "The Iron Chest" shall feel no concern, unless to despise it, about Sir Edward Mortimer's equal enthusiasm for the glory of reputation.
>
> The reason of this difference in consequences, from the self-same story, does not, however, betray the want of skill in the author of the play, but simply argues his want of space. Narrative, on the stage, must never be diffuse: the play must be comprised in a certain number of pages; and when the foundation of a fable is of the magnitude of murder, any abridgement of circumstances, requisite to make description both clear and probable, must be of fatal import to all the scenes so founded.

Inchbald expanded her comparison of the genre of fiction to the genre of drama in her letter to Prince Hoare's journal *The Artist* in 1807 (14: 9–19). The novel can deal directly and critically with the most pressing political issues of the day in a way the dramatist cannot, because

> The Novelist is a free agent. He lives in a land of liberty, whilst the Dramatic Writer exists but under a despotic government.—Passing over the subjection in which an author of plays is held by the Lord Chamberlain's office, and the degree of dependence which he has on his actors—he is the very slave of the audience. He must have their tastes and prejudices in view, not to correct, but to humour them. (16)

Not only was the novel capable of depicting a world that was more probable, more psychologically acute, and more politically relevant than that found in epic poetry or the earlier romances, it was also more *democratic*. The novel could be read and understood by everyone, regardless of whether one had had an education in Greek and Latin. As Anna Barbauld pointed out,

> Reading is the cheapest of pleasures: it is a domestic pleasure. Dramatic exhibitions give a more poignant delight, but they are seldom enjoyed in perfection, and never without expense and trouble. Poetry requires in the reader a certain elevation of mind and a practised ear. It is seldom relished unless a taste be formed for it pretty early. But the humble novel is always ready to enliven the gloom of solitude, to soothe the languor of debility and disease, to win the attention from pain or vexatious occurrences, to take man from himself (at many seasons the worst company he can be in) and, while the moving picture of life passes before him, to make him forget the subject of his own complaints. ("Origin and Progress of Novel-Writing" 47)

Morality, probability, right feeling—this is what the good work of literature must aim to provide its reader. Turning from the text itself to the reader, the women critics of the Romantic era developed what we would now call a "reader-response" theory. They argued that the reader approached the literary text not with Coleridge's "willing suspension of disbelief" but with something very different. Joanna Baillie provided the fullest account of an alternative concept of reader response. She argued that the "great master-propensity" of human nature is our "sympathetick curiosity," our interest in and our ability to empathize with the feelings and experiences of other human beings (Baillie 19, 4).[5] Baillie here invokes Adam Smith's concept, in his *Theory of Moral Sentiments* (1759), of sympathy as one of "the original passions of human nature" (Smith 2), the capacity that enables one person to *feel* the sufferings of another and so is inspired to acts of benevolent charity toward another. Following Smith, she further identifies "sympathy" (or what Shaftesbury called "disinterestedness") as the basis not only of all moral behavior but also of the aesthetic response, for as Smith pointed out, we experience the sufferings of others through an act of imagination; we are moved to relieve them because we imagine what it would be like to be ourselves in their situation, in exactly the same way that we identify with the heroes of tragedy and romance (Smith 2). Baillie thus anticipates both Hazlitt's concept of "gusto" and Keats's concept of "negative capability." She argues that the best art is that which most directly engages the sympathy of the audience by "faithfully delineat[ing]" human nature (24). Focusing specifically on drama, she claims that both tragedy and comedy have historically failed to represent adequately the development and the myriad effects of specific passions, passions which are felt by and exert their control over both sexes equally. Her own dramatic project, carried out in her series of *Plays on the Passions,* was to "delineate the progress of the higher passions in the human breast" in minute and subtle detail (41), since she was confident that tragedy written on this plan "is fitted to produce stronger moral effect than upon any other" (42). As the audience empathically participates in such subtle revelations of the workings of the emotions, they will be psychologically and ethically instructed, coming to recognize the ways that reason can protect one against an obsessive passion, if not entirely prevent it.

Baillie's reader-response concept of sympathetic curiosity goes beyond Smith's ethical analysis (sympathy as the foundation of benevolence or moral behavior) to anticipate what we would now call a "feminist epistemology." This epistemology assumes that every act of knowing requires an active emotional engagement of the knower with the known, that "objectivity" is a psychological and perceptual impossibility. As Mary Hawkesworth has cogently summarized this position, every act of cognition is "a human practice" that includes the full "complexity of the interaction between traditional assumptions, social norms, theoretical conceptions, disciplinary strictures, linguistic possibilities, emotional dispositions, and creative impositions" (550). One cannot perceive anything without experiencing some sort of *connection* to it, without bringing to that act of perception the full range of one's ideologically biased experiences, without locating the perceived object within a pre-existing framework of coherent meaning. Watching a play, as Joanna Baillie understood, involves an active "enlargement of our *ideas* in regard to human nature" (Baillie 37; my italics). The role of the literary critic, then, is to re-enact this sympathetic curiosity, to fuse empathic involvement with rational understanding.

Writing a criticism of their own, poised midway between a neoclassical mimetic aesthetic that was limited by its commitment to abstract universals, to the unities of time, place, and character as the definition of "realism," and to an outdated hierarchy of the arts, on one side, and on the other side, a masculine Romantic aesthetic devoted to celebrating the originality and passionate feeling of the poet, these women literary critics developed a third aesthetic. They insisted that the cultural role of literature is to educate even more than to delight, to educate by teaching readers how to take pleasure in the triumph of moral benevolence, sexual self-control, and rational intelligence. To inculcate such values and practices, literature must be both vivid and realistic, depicting events and characters rendered in sufficiently accurate and telling detail to be convincing. Generically, the novel provides the largest scope and most finely woven texture for such realistic portrayals, followed by the drama—which enables its viewers to participate sympathetically in the resolution of human conflict—and lastly by poetry that is devoted to the quotidian, that "occasional verse" which records individual responses to daily events.

Inspired by Wollstonecraft's *Vindication of the Rights of Woman* and More's *Strictures on the Modern System of Female Education,* these female literary critics assumed that the most important social revolutions occur not on the battlefield but in the home. As Elizabeth Inchbald commented,

> Whatever reason may be urged against the more elevated instruction of the sex at present, than in former days, one good consequence at least accrues from it—they are better qualified than heretofore to choose their lovers and husbands. It was in the age of female ignorance that the Lotharios, and the ye[t] viler Lovelaces, flourished. . . . Now, enlightened by a degree of masculine study, woman's taste and judgment being improved—this best consequence of all ensues—men must improve to win them. (preface to Nicholas Rowe's *The Fair Penitent*)

Their literary criticism was profoundly political, insofar as it actively encouraged women as well as men to read, to learn from their reading, and then to teach by writing, thus joining the ranks of the highest cultural authorities in the land.

We must recognize the significance of the fact that all these women critics set themselves up as *judges,* judges not just of aesthetic taste and literary excellence but also of cultural morality. As Anna Seward announced,

> Many excel me in the power of writing verse; perhaps scarcely one in the vivid and strong sensibility of its excellence, or in the ability to estimate its claims— ability arising from a fifty years sedulous and discriminating study of the best English poets, and of the best translations from the Greek, Roman, and Italian. A masculine education cannot spare from professional study, and the necessary acquisition of languages, the time and attention which I have bestowed on the compositions of my countrymen. (*Poetical Works* I: xiii)

And when George Colman the Younger attacked Elizabeth Inchbald for daring to criticize the plays of a *man* in public, and especially those of his father, who had briefly been her employer and patron (Colman compared Inchbald to a Deidama wielding "a battle-axe to slay and maim the gentlemen"), she graciously apologized. At the same time she insisted on the prerogatives of her critical craft, shrewdly observing that her very admiration for the work of both Colmans "warned me against unqualified praise, as the mere substitute for ridicule; and to beware, lest suspicions of a hired panegyrist should bring disgrace upon that production, which required no such nefarious help for its support" (preface to *The Heir at Law* and letter to George Colman the Younger). She firmly denied his charge of ingratitude, pointing out that her obligations to George Colman the Elder "amounted to no more than those usual attentions which every manager of a theater is supposed to confer, when he first selects a novice in dramatic writing, as worthy of being introduced, on his stage, to the public." Insisting on their right *as women* both to write literature and to judge it before the public eye, these women critics claimed the highest cultural authority. They claimed the right to dictate the mores and the manners of the nation, to define public opinion, to participate fully in what Habermas has called the discursive public sphere. They thus assumed full citizenship in that cultural arena or social sphere that mediates between state institutions and private domestic practices.[6] As Anna Barbauld concluded her essay on the novel, after identifying the majority of her finest contemporary writers as women:

> surely it will not be said that either taste or morals have been losers by their taking pen in hand. The names of D'Arblay, Edgeworth, Inchbald, Radcliffe, and a number more will vindicate this assertion. . . . It was said by Fletcher of Saltoun, "Let me make the ballads of a nation, and I care not who makes the laws." Might it not be said with as much propriety, Let me make the novels of a country, and let who will make the systems? ("Origin and Progess of Novel-Writing," 59–60)

Not the poet but the novelist, and a female novelist at that, here becomes the unacknowledged legislator of the world.

In raising the novel to the highest rank of the literary arts, these women critics were above all engaging in a gender politics. The novel was historically a "woman's genre"—one associated, as Terry Eagleton has shown, with "the feminization of discourse" (Eagleton 13). As the novel gained (or lost) cultural authority, so did women. Significantly, in the Victorian and modern periods, the novel increasingly pushed both poetry and the essay into the literary background, even as a Victorian backlash against female claims to literary authority tried to establish an unbridgeable divide between "highbrow" novels written by and for men and "lowbrow" (or sensationalist) novels written by and for women (see Tuchman and Fortin). This arbitrary division could not be sustained, however, and by the mid-twentieth century, female novelists finally began to achieve the same recognition and rewards as men. However marginal the positions taken by the female literary critics of the Romantic era may have seemed to René Wellek and those like him who have been invested solely in the academic canonization of male-authored literary criticism in the Romantic era, we should not forget that these women critics were highly respected by their peers, both male and female. They participated fully in the discursive public sphere in England between 1780 and 1830, in the sense theorized by Habermas. Nor should we forget that theirs were the critical positions that historically have triumphed: the novel (inextricably bound up with the formal conventions of realism) is now indisputably the dominant literary genre in Western culture, while poetry has become so marginalized that it is almost impossible for a contemporary poet to make a living solely from publishing poetry. In claiming the novel as their own, women literary critics of the Romantic era also laid claim to having carried out a revolution both in female manners and in female cultural authority.

5

The Politics of Fiction

By the end of the Romantic era, the novel had become the site of intense political debate, from the Jacobin and pro-anarchy fictions of Thomas Holcroft, Robert Bage, and William Godwin to the royalist responses of Thomas Surr and the nationalist fictions of Walter Scott and John Galt. Since by 1800 women dominated both the production and the consumption of prose fiction, it should not surprise us that they participated directly in these fictionalized political debates. I have elsewhere discussed at length the ways in which such female novelists of the Romantic era as Mary Wollstonecraft, Jane Austen, Mary Shelley, Maria Edgeworth, Ann Radcliffe, Sydney Owenson (Lady Morgan), Helen Maria Williams, and Susan Ferrier calculatedly devoted their fiction to challenging the repressive sexual politics promoted by the conduct books of the day, a politics that erected a patriarchal domestic ideology that demanded that the female be kept at home, educated only to be sexually attractive and submissive to her husband. After briefly rehearsing that argument, I wish to suggest here that the "Revolution in Female Manners" advocated by Mary Wollstonecraft was not the only political or social revolution demanded by the women novelists of the day. Several used their fiction to promote radical changes in Britain's legal system of governance, both at home and abroad.

Even perceptive feminist critics of the British novel have tended to read the female-authored fiction of the Romantic era as registering the ultimate triumph of a patriarchal domestic ideology. Basing their conclusions primarily on conduct books and religious tracts written by men and women, including Addison and Steele's *Spectator*, such critics as Mary Poovey, Nancy Armstrong, and Jane Spencer have eloquently argued that women novelists of the Romantic era were either forced to accommodate themselves to, indirectly subvert, or gain power wholly within a cultural construction of the proper lady as a modest, domesticated woman, one confined to the private sphere, one who did not speak assertively in public.

A closer look at the large number and wide range of women's fiction produced between 1790 and 1830 suggests a rather different story. Despite the powerful recent arguments by Terry Eagleton, Nancy Armstrong, Mary Poovey, and Gary Kelly to the contrary, women novelists in the Romantic era did not resign the construction of "feminine discourse" in the novel to men, obediently reproducing a hegemonic ideology of bourgeois capitalism and relocating it in an idealized middle-class patriarchal family. In this period, women novelists more frequently employed their writing as a vehicle for ideological contestation and subversion, exploiting the novel's capacity for disruptive humor and a sustained interrogation of existing social codes, for what Bakhtin called its "heteroglossia" and "dialogism." While the psychological and rhetorical accommodations noted by these critics (among many others) undoubtedly occurred in writing by women during the Romantic era, I have pointed out the existence of an equally strong female fictional practice that openly challenged and powerfully revised this domestic ideology. We can no longer assume that the doctrine of the separate spheres or the existence of a clear sexual division of labor into a public/ male versus a private/female realm was in place during the Romantic era.

The women's novel in the Romantic period played a key role in the construction of a new political ideology, one that initially grounded the salvation of the nation on the reform of the British family. This required, as I argued in *Romanticism and Gender* (1993), the construction of a new system of gender roles, one based on the fundamental equality—but not necessarily the *sameness*—of women and men. Female novelists, like the female poets, playwrights, and literary critics of the period, tended to embrace as the highest moral obligation an ethic of care, a belief that the needs of every member of the family politic must be met and that in any cultural or political crisis that demanded resolution, the fewest possible people should be hurt.

In opposition to the patriarchal domestic ideology so well described by Leonore Davidoff and Catherine Hall in *Family Fortunes: Men and Women of the English Middle Class, 1780–1850,* many women novelists of the Romantic era calculatedly used their fiction to promote a significantly different family politics. Some, as did Charlotte Smith in *The Old Manor House* (1794), rejected the masculinized political realm altogether as irredeemably brutal, corrupt, and self-destructive, and construed the ideal political state as one in which men have been entirely absorbed into a feminized domesticity. Orlando, the hero of *The Old Manor House,* is both the vulnerable dependent of a wealthy and powerful aristocratic woman and an eloquent critic of primogeniture, imperialist warfare, and the greed of modern commerce. By the end of the novel, Orlando is securely enclosed within a feminized household now run by his beloved Monimia. Amelia Opie in her novel *Adeline Mowbray* (1804) goes one step further by suggesting that benevolent love and personal self-fulfillment can flourish only within an all-female community. Opie offers as her radical political alternative, both to William Godwin's program of abstract social justice and free love and to the patriarchal domestic ideology, a compelling vision of an all-female family of choice. At the end of her novel, three unrelated and racially mixed women (the Quaker Mrs. Pemberton, the aristocratic Mrs. Mowbray, and the West Indian freed slave Savannah) take on the responsibility of rearing Editha, the dead Adeline Mowbray's daughter. Significantly, throughout this novel, it is the black woman, Savannah, who has demonstrated the greatest capacity for effective mothering, who has cherished and saved Adeline on the numerous occasions when her biological mother abandoned her. This political turn to an all-female utopia as the answer to the evils of patriarchal nineteenth-century society, a turn initiated in Sarah Scott's *Millenium Hall* (1762), occurs again at the conclusion of the last draft of Mary Wollstonecraft's *The Wrongs of Woman* (1798), where Maria—abandoned both by her husband and her lover—decides that she will "live for" her daughter, together with that daughter's "second mother," the working-class Jemima who, like Savannah, has actively preserved and cherished that daughter.

Rather than turning their backs on the public sphere to withdraw into a fictional utopia of all-female private households, many women novelists aggressively offered an alternative vision of political governance, one grounded on a radical reform of the social construction of gender. Such novelists as Mary Wollstonecraft, Ann Radcliffe, Susan Ferrier, Maria Edgeworth, Jane Austen, Mary Hays, Mary Brunton, Helen Maria Williams, and Mary Shelley, among many others, advocated the cultural production of a "new woman," one who was rationally educated, who was capable of channeling her sexual passions into a judiciously chosen egalitarian marriage, and who was equipped to carry out the responsibilities of maintaining an efficient, well-managed, and nurturing household in which the "domestic affections" guaranteed that the emotional and physical needs of every family member would be met. I further suggested that these novelists' representations of egalitarian marriages grounded on an ethic of care constituted a viable blueprint for an alternative political program, one that has much in common with a later socialist/Marxist call for the distribution of public goods and services based on needs rather than on abstract legal rights (see Mellor 1988, 1993).

The two novels I examine in this chapter entered directly into the public sphere as Habermas defined it, the arena of public opinion formed by print culture. Each offers a considered judgment on the present and future state of the British nation. I first look closely at a novel that directly engaged the burning political issue of the 1790s: the British response to the French Revolution and the preservation of constitutional liberties at home. I have chosen from among several female-authored novels dealing with this question the one that to my mind is the finest political novel published by anyone in England in the 1790s, Charlotte Smith's *Desmond* (1792). This superb and unjustifiably neglected novel has rightly been said to have marked the beginning of the historical novel in England (Doody 1975: 194). I then turn to the far better known *Persuasion* by Jane Austen, as my final example of a woman writer's observations on the political future of England following the defeat of Napoleon in 1815.

Desmond

Charlotte Smith conceived of *Desmond* as a direct response to Edmund Burke's *Reflections on the Revolution in France and on the Proceedings in Certain Societies in London Relative to that Event in a Letter Intended to Have Been Sent to a Gentleman in Paris, 1790*. Burke had presented his defense of the British constitutional monarchy as a lengthy letter written to the young scion of a family of French merchants and bankers, Charles-François Depont,[1] who in November 1789 had asked for Burke's opinion on the recent events in France (the march on Paris of 6 October 1789; the abolition of the feudal rights of the Catholic Church; and the confinement of the royal family in Paris during negotiations with the new National Federation). Burke's primary concerns, as J. G. A. Pocock has ably summarized, were with the danger that the separation of church from state might pose to the British monarchy and with the inflationary economic system introduced by the new French Republic, which was issuing a new paper currency—*assignats*—that could be fiscally sound only if it were based on the seizure of all the lands and monies previously held by the Church and the wealthier aristocrats of France. Burke's attacks on the revolutionary French government are well known. Here we need only recall that he envisioned the British monarchy as part of a sacred and natural chain of being linking man to God through the agency of the established church which had been vindicated both by history—by the demonstrable progress of English society from barbarism to the civility of the eighteenth-century gentleman—and by tradition, by the English practice of relying on precedent, custom, and common law in order to ensure that all changes to the ancient British constitution would be gradual and socially effective (Burke xlv).

Charlotte Smith signaled that she was answering *Edmund Burke's* letters to *De*pont by constructing her novel as a series of letters primarily exchanged between her hero *De*smond and his friend and mentor *Erasmus Bethel.* In adopting Burke's epistolary format (this is the only epistolary novel which Smith wrote), Smith also acknowledged the impact of Helen Maria Williams's *Letters from France* (1790–96) and the publications of the radical Corresponding Societies. By 1792, as both Mary Favret and Nicola Watson have shown, the public letter had become the major genre for political debate in England, enabling the writer to consider opposing points of view while at the same time foregrounding the role of personal experience and feeling in the determination of political ideology.

Smith answered Burke even more directly. Her protagonist Desmond explicitly condemns Burke's *Reflections on the Revolution in France* for misrepresenting the situation in France and for substituting "poetical fancy" for "matters of fact" (*Desmond* 155).[2] Desmond shrewdly observes that Burke's reliance on the Glorious Revolution of 1688 as having forever secured the liberties and rights of the British subject is arbitrary; if Burke acknowledges that one political revolution was necessary, then the constitution was not established by God from all eternity, nor is there any guarantee that future revolutions will not be equally required to protect these rights and freedoms.

Charlotte Smith here directly engages in the most powerful political debate in British history concerning the divine right of kings. Desmond first condemns Robert Filmer's arguments on behalf of unlimited governmental power in his *Patriarcha. The Naturall Power of Kings Defended against the Unnatural Liberty of the People* (1680). He then invokes the most influential refutation of Filmer, John Locke's argument for individual consent to political rule in his *Two Treatises of Government* (1690), book 2. Locke claimed, in a passage quoted at length by Desmond, that

> since a father hath not in himself a power over the life and liberty of his child, no act of his own can possibly forfeit it; so that the children, whatever may have

happened to the fathers, are free men; and the absolute power of the conqueror reaches no farther than the persons of the men who were subdued by him, and dies with them; and should he govern them as slaves, subjected to his absolute power, he has no such right of dominion over their children—he can have no power over them but by *their own consent;* and he has no lawful authority while force, not choice, compels them to submission. (Locke #189)

As Desmond then concludes, "If conquest does not bind posterity, so neither can compact bind it" (*Desmond* 156). Desmond rightly recognizes that Burke's entire argument is based on the eternal legitimacy of the "compact" made between the self-elected Parliament of 1688 and William and Mary of Orange. But since that "compact" was a matter of historical choice, why should not the future subjects of the British constitution have a similar choice? Especially if their kings should prove to be "more profligate than Charles the Second, without his wit; and more careless of the welfare and prosperity of his people than James the Second, without his piety" (157). Here Charlotte Smith clearly suggests that the two Hanoverian rulers of her time, the "mad" George the Third and the libertine, amoral, and fiscally irresponsible Prince of Wales, do not deserve the continued fealty of their British subjects.

Smith's political arguments extend well beyond this Jacobin affirmation of the natural rights of man and Rousseau's concept of the social contract against Burke's conservative defense of the constitutional monarchy. Her novel attempts to explore the relationship between the social contract, the foundation of a liberal democratic polity, and the sexual contract. As Carole Pateman has brilliantly shown in her analyses of Filmer and Locke in *The Sexual Contract,* the grounding of individual autonomy and liberty on the concept that "Every man has property in his own person," to use Locke's famous formulation, *excludes women*—whose "person" or bodies were legally constructed as under the "couverture" of men, whether fathers, husbands, brothers, or sons. As Smith recognizes, Burke's defense of the monarchy is simultaneously a defense of patriarchal privilege, of the unquestioned rights of the male to the body of the female. But she also recognizes, in a truly revolutionary insight, that Desmond's defense of the natural rights of man is every bit as much a defense of patriarchal privilege, of his right to "possess" Geraldine. Thus Charlotte Smith engages in a two-pronged radical political discourse in these letters: the first located in her eponymous hero's ongoing quarrel with Edmund Burke and other British condemnations of the French Revolution, the second located in her authorial quarrel with *both* radical and conservative apologists for British male privilege and female "slavery."

Smith's defense of the French Revolution and her condemnation of the British monarchy is registered both in the plot and in the overt political debates carried out in her novel. As Desmond travels through France in 1791 and 1792, he encounters none of the rioting, savage violence, or personal vendettas attributed to the new *citoyens* of France by British armchair journalists. He insists throughout on the necessity for eyewitness testimony; only those who have been present at the events in Paris and the French countryside since the storming of the Bastille can accurately assess their impact. As he reports to Bethel from Paris on 19 July 1790,

> I can now, however, assure you—and with the most heart-felt satisfaction, that nothing is more unlike the real state of this country, than the accounts which have been given of it in England; and that the sanguinary and ferocious democracy, the scenes of anarchy and confusion, which we have had so pathetically described and lamented, have no existence but in the malignant fabrications of those who have been paid for their mis-representations. (52)

What Desmond does encounter are happy, hardworking farmers and merchants, and *ci-devant* aristocrats like his close friend Montfleuri who sympathize with the new Republic. The "liberal and enlightened" Montfleuri is Smith's example of the way in which political revolution can produce beneficial social reorganization. Montfleuri has torn down the excessive Gothic grandeur of his country chateau, remodeled it to become a "useful" middle-class home, divided the estate into productive vineyards, cornfields, and grazing meadows, improved the living conditions and terms of employment of his workers, and transformed a former monastery into a "house of industry" in which peasants unfitted by age or disability to work in the fields are taught practical crafts. As Desmond observes,

> The effect of this is, that instead of squalid figures inhabiting cabins built of mud, without windows or floors, which are seen in too many parts of France (and which must continue to be seen, till the benign influence of liberty is generally felt), the peasantry in this domain resemble both in their own appearance, and in the comfortable look of their habitations, those whose lot has fallen in those villages of England, where, the advantages of a good landlord, a favourable situation for employment, or an extensive adjoining common, enable the labourers to possess something more than the mere *necessaries* of life, and happily counteract the effects of those heavy taxes with which all those necessaries of life are loaded. (82–83)

The text endorses Desmond's perception that the peasants of France are better off than in the past, that they are "rationally happy" because they now enjoy the certainty of remaining under a "generous and considerate" master (82). But in a brilliant display of textual and political dialoguism (or what Chris Jones has called Smith's irony [Jones 162]), Charlotte Smith adds a footnote that undercuts her protagonist's blithe assumption that these peasants can be equated with equally contented English laborers. Throughout her novel, Smith's footnotes function to display her learning and to provide documentary evidence for the claims made by her fictional correspondents. But they also—and more importantly—function to mark the difference between the political views of her characters and her own. Here her footnote asserts that the British worker is now in worse condition than Montfleuri's post-revolutionary French peasants:

> The English have a custom of arrogantly boasting of the fortunate situation of the common people of England.—But let those, who, with an opportunity of observation, have ever had an enquiring eye and a feeling heart on this subject, say whether this pride is well founded. At the present prices of the requisites of mere existence, a labourer, with a wife and four or five children, who has only his labour to depend upon, can taste nothing but bread, and not always a sufficiency of that. Too certain it is, that (to say nothing of the miseries of the London poor, too evident to every one who passes through the streets) there are many, very many parts of the country, where the labourer has not a subsistence even when in constant work, and where, in cases of sickness, his condition is deplorable indeed. (82–83n)

This footnote underlines the primary political issue at stake throughout the novel: is there now greater liberty and well-being for the majority of the people in post-revolutionary France or in England? To support his argument that life has significantly improved under the new French Republic, Desmond records numerous instances of the cruel oppressions suffered by the French lower classes under the ancien régime. He recounts the deaths of numerous Parisian pedestrians under the wheels of the huge carriages raced through the streets by the nobility, to which Smith adds a confirming documentary footnote:

> a very few years since, as a young Frenchman of fashion—one of "the very first world," was driving through the streets of Paris, with an Englishman, his acquaintance, in a *cabriolet,* in the *rue St Honoré,* which is always extremely crouded, his horse threw down a poor man, and the wheels going over his neck, killed him on the spot.—The Englishman, with all the emotions of terror, natural on such an incident, cried out—Good God, you have killed the man!—The *charioteer* drove on; saying, with all possible *sang froid*—'*Eh bien, tant pis pour lui*'—Well then, so much the worse for him. (54n)

Desmond further introduces the life history of a Breton midshipman (supposedly based on a published firsthand account)[3] who survived the tortures and jail-fevers of an English jail only to be legally but unjustly deprived of his small inherited estate by his wealthy noble neighbor who chose to exercise his droit du seigneur (113–21). The most extended portrait of the evils of the ancien régime is a scene of bad estate management. In contrast to Montfleuri's well-cultivated lands, his wealthier uncle, the Comte d'Hauteville, presides over a "long line of disfigured vegetation," miserable roads, ruined cottages, a grandiose edifice of "funereal apartments," all managed by a grotesquely overdressed, supercilious servant, Le Maire. In his desperation to recover his lost aristocratic titles and privileges, the Comte d'Hauteville has hired local ruffians to rob and assault the new armies of the republic, as well as any other passersby (including Desmond's beloved Geraldine). Thus the only physical violence that Desmond encounters on his travels through France—where, as Geraldine testifies, the towns are efficiently policed by local armed citizens (308)—are on the estates of the royalists.

Throughout her novel, Smith draws constant parallels between the ancien régime in France and the current ruling classes in England—the very parallels that Burke had fearfully imaged as a spreading fire: "Whenever our neighbor's house is on fire, it cannot be amiss for the engines to play a little on our own. Better to be despised for too anxious apprehensions than ruined by too confident a security" (Burke 9). On his travels Desmond encounters as many British nobles, gentlemen, and professionals as he does French. Burke had depicted his contented countrymen as a silent majority of "thousands of great cattle, reposed beneath the British oak, chew[ing] the cud" (Burke 75). Charlotte Smith seizes on this image of cud-chewing cattle to suggest that the ruling classes of England care for nothing but filling their own stomachs.[4] On his departure from Dover, Desmond encounters a British doctor and a former tavern keeper who first condemn the entire French nation as murderers and beggars and then happily retire, ignoring the distress of a starving Frenchwoman and her children, to glut themselves on chicken-turtle shipped from Mr. Sidebottom's slave plantation in Jamaica and specially prepared by his "negro fellow" (45–46). The "cud" that such John Bulls chew, Smith here implies, is the flesh and blood of other men and women, in particular of African slaves. This point is reinforced later in the novel when Desmond invokes the "detestable Slave Trade" as his primary evidence for the necessity of instituting major reforms in the English government (328–29).

Desmond's uncle, in parallel with Montfleuri's, illustrates the moral corruption of the British ancien régime. A retired major, he now rules his county in Somerset like a petty tyrant, boasting that he has in one year committed more prisoners to the county jail than any of his judicial brethren. Indifferent to the sufferings of his nephew or any others, he cares only for the pleasures of the table. As Bethel describes Major Danby to Desmond,

> You know, that being an old bachelor, and somewhat of an epicure, he is at home, what the vulgar call a cot; and has laid down his spontoon for the tasting spoon, converted his sword into a carving knife, and his sash into a jelly bag.—
> It is not her youth or her beauty, that recommended his present favourite housekeeper; but the skill she had acquired in studying under a French cook, at the house of a great man, who acquired an immense fortune in the American war,

by obtaining the contract for potatoes and sour crout.—But even to this gentle-woman, skilled as she is in "all kinds of made dishes, pickling, potting, and preserving," and tenderly connected with her, as the prying world supposes the Major to be; he does not leave the sole direction of that important department, his kitchen; which, when he is at home, he always superintends himself. (334)

Smith here skillfully weaves together a subtle indictment of the Major. Rather than protecting the English nation, he has reaped the benefits of war profiteering (the potatoes and sour crout sent to the British troops in the War against the American Colonies were notoriously underweight and rotten). Worse, his libidinous appetites embrace not only food but women: as Diana Bowstead has noted, the cook is also his concubine (Bowstead 243).

The three egregious examples of the excesses, waste, and abuses of privilege of the ruling classes in Britain are Lord Newminster, Mr. Stamford, and Mr. Verney. Lord Newminster is one of those "mushroom nobility" who have recently bought their titles (his father was a Mr. Grantham) and who would rather that "all the old women in the country should fast for a month" than that his dog should not be fed chocolate and biscuits (33). Mr. Stamford, a lawyer, has intrigued and bribed his way into Parliament (in part by bringing successful crim. con. [or "criminal conversation"] suits against adulterers); he has along the way acquired both a title and a large estate. As an example of the ruling British nobility, Sir Robert Stamford represents that nation of civilized gentlemen so lauded by Burke. But rather than conserving his estate for future generations, Sir Robert has laid waste to his property, cutting down woods, tearing up gardens, drowning corn-fields, all in order to build fishponds teeming with carp and tench, and hothouses designed to cultivate exotic fruits and vegetables. As Bethel concludes, "Everything is sacrificed to the luxuries of the table" (168). Verney, Geraldine's husband, epitomizes the systematic violation of Burke's image of the British gentleman as one who conserves the estate for the good of future generations. His gambling debts result not only in the loss of all his personal goods and monies, but in the necessity of leasing his inherited and entailed estate in Yorkshire away from his own sons to Colonel Scarsdale during Scarsdale's lifetime, leaving his three children virtually penniless on his death.

By refusing to distinguish between the rapacity, gluttony, insensitivity, and irresponsibility of the British ruling classes and the cruelty of the French ancien régime, Smith powerfully reinforces Desmond's arguments that the time has come for radical social reform in England, a point that even the moderate Erasmus Bethel finally concedes. After acknowledging that "a revolution in the government of France was absolutely necessary," Bethel expresses his fear that "this great and noble effort for the universal rights of the human race" will fail, perhaps because of inadequate leadership from within, but most certainly because the united armies of all other European nations, *including England,* will not allow it to succeed. For as Bethel observes, "In all these states, there are great bodies of people, whose interest, which is what wholly decides their opinion, is diametrically opposite to all reform, and, of course, to the reception of those truths which may promote it" (151). Listing all those vested interests—aristocrats, their relations, dependents, and parasites; placemen and pensioners; lawyers; and everyone who has gained a comfortable lifestyle under the existing government either from family possessions or successful commerce—Bethel pessimistically concludes that "I rather fear that liberty, having been driven away to the new world, will establish there her glorious empire—and to Europe, sunk in luxury and effeminacy—enervated and degenerated Europe, will return no more" (152).

At this point, halfway through her novel, Smith effectively concludes her debate with Burke: liberty has been momentarily achieved in republican France, but it may not be able to survive there. On the other hand, liberty does not exist under the "*yet called limited monarchies*" of England (151), either, where the slave trade flourishes and the rights and freedoms of the common person have been systematically usurped to sustain the vested interests of the aristocratic, professional, commercial, and West Indian planter classes. By having Bethel then recommend to Desmond the "sound sense . . . however bluntly delivered" (167) of Thomas Paine's *The Rights of Man* (1791), Smith firmly allies herself with Paine's republican condemnation of English despotism.

But Smith's political purposes are finally feminist more than Jacobin. Smith devotes the rest of her novel to an exploration of the gender politics that sustain both conservative and republican political ideologies. In order to uncover the most extensive and most profound oppression experienced by British subjects, namely, by women, she must turn away from abstract political theory and debate to a fictionalized account of the probable experiences of particular women. Several critics have commented on Smith's reliance on the conventions of romance and the plots of sensibility and Gothic terror in this novel (see Conway, Wikborg, Chris Jones). But they have not sufficiently appreciated the reasons for this absorption of the genre of romance into the genre of political debate.

By focusing on the devoted love of Desmond for the unhappily married Geraldine and her young children and on the miseries suffered by Geraldine at the hands of her abusive, uncaring, and spendthrift husband, Charlotte Smith does a great deal more than merely engage the reader's sympathies in the plight of a virtuous damsel in distress. She implicitly documents a powerful political argument with which we are now well acquainted: the personal *is* political, the day-to-day experiences of individuals record the subtle and myriad ways in which power is exercised by one person over another, especially in the most private and unregulated spaces of the family and the home.

Further, Charlotte Smith understands—as Mary Wollstonecraft recognized in her extremely perceptive review of *Desmond* for the *Analytical Review* in August 1792—that her various correspondents represent, in Wollstonecraft's phrase, "imbodied arguments" (*Works* 7: 451). By identifying a specific political argument with a specific character or body, Smith implicitly articulated an early version of what we would now call standpoint theory. Derived from Marxist theory, standpoint theory holds that no single "objective" understanding of social or political institutions is possible because the position that any one observer inhabits in relation to those institutions always already determines one's (necessarily limited) cognition of them. In *Money, Sex, and Power* (1983), Nancy Hartsock provided an early and still useful articulation of this epistemological argument:

> The reader will remember that the concept of a standpoint carries several specific contentions. Most important, it posits a series of levels of reality in which the deeper level both includes and explains the surface or appearance. Related to the positing of levels are several claims:
>
> 1. Material life (class position in Marxist theory) not only structures but sets limits on the understanding of social relations.
>
> 2. If material life is structured in fundamentally opposing ways for two different groups, one can expect that the vision of each will present an inversion of the other, and in systems of domination the vision available to the rulers will be both partial and perverse.
>
> 3. The vision of the ruling class (or gender) structures the material relations in which all parties are forced to participate and therefore cannot be dismissed as simply false.
>
> 4. In consequence, the vision available to the oppressed group must be struggled for and represents an achievement that requires both science to see beneath the surface of the social relations in which all are forced to participate and the education that can only grow from struggle to change those relations.
>
> 5. As an engaged vision, the understanding of the oppressed, the adoption of a standpoint exposes the real relations among human beings as inhuman, points beyond the present, and carries a historically liberatory role. (231–32)

To this argument Sandra Harding has persuasively added the caveat that the marginalized or oppressed class or gender or person has the most inclusive standpoint (or claim to strong as opposed to weak objectivity) since she is simultaneously compelled to share the ruling classes' assumptions about the nature of the social universe and yet to experience that universe in a way categorically denied to those rulers.

By assigning letters both to women and to men in her novel, Charlotte Smith "imbodies" the political arguments of *Desmond* in categorically different experiences or standpoints. Her female characters powerfully illustrate the fact that women have no power under either the ancien régime or the new French Republic. Her major female protagonist, Geraldine Verney, represents the British ideal of female sensibility, delicacy, propriety, and virtue. She has been married at her mother's demand and for "mercenary" reasons to a wealthy young libertine, Verney, who in only six years has squandered his fortune in gambling, an ostentatious lifestyle, womanizing, and alcoholism. Early in the novel, the bailiffs are in his London townhouse, threatening to evict him, his wife, and his two young children. Even though Desmond secretly pays these debts to save Geraldine's peace of mind, Verney continues his drunken excesses and gambling. To pay off his newly accrued debts, he proposes to "sell" his beautiful wife to his creditor Colonel Scarsdale. The virtuous Geraldine narrowly escapes when Verney is forced to leave the country, fleeing his other creditors. Penniless, she is supported in a modest rented cottage in a Welsh village by Bethel's benevolent generosity, while Desmond hovers nearby to ensure her safety.

Geraldine is then summoned by Verney to Paris at the height of the revolutionary events, on the Nuit de Varennes, 21 June 1791; when she explains that she has just delivered her third child, a sickly babe, and is too ill to travel, Verney sends the *ci-devant* French aristocrat, the libertine Duc de Romagnecourt to whom he has again tried to "sell" her in payment of debts, to seize her. Geraldine escapes being seized and raped by de Romagnecourt only because Desmond finances her secret journey to her mother. But her mother insists that she behave as a dutiful wife and join her husband in Paris, and Geraldine—with no money or home of her own—complies. When she arrives in Paris, Verney has once again fled with his royalist companions, and she is able to settle with her family in a small cottage at Meudon. Although she notes the improved conditions of the peasants around Meudon, she lives in constant terror of Verney's or de Romagnecourt's reappearance. At last she receives a summons to join the dying Verney at Avignon, and dutifully travels alone to his deathbed to comfort his final hours, paying her way with those very *assignats* (French Republican paper currency) which Burke had so violently denounced (Burke 171–72) but which here prove sound. En route she is captured, robbed, and almost raped by ruffians left by the Comte d'Hauteville to guard his chateau.

Geraldine's helplessness in the face of patriarchal privilege (her husband's rights to her body) and masculine brute force is first registered in the novel by Desmond's anticipatory Gothic nightmare in which Geraldine is abandoned by Verney in the midst of a storm and then dies:

> she was left exposed to the fury of contending elements, which seemed to terrify her less on her own account, than on that of three children, whom she clasped to her bosom, in all the agonies of maternal apprehension. . . . I saw her extended, pale, and apparently dying on the bed . . . with the least of the children, a very young infant dead in her arms. (99–100)

This dream locates the true source of the terror of the sublime described in Burke's *Essay on the Origin of Our Ideas of the Sublime and the Beautiful* (1757), at least insofar as women are concerned, in the brutal neglect of men who callously expose them to the cruelty of the elements or the greater cruelties of domestic violence and rape within their own homes. This dream paves the way to Smith's rejoinder to Burke's Gothic fantasy of the attack on Marie Antoinette on 6 October 1789:

> From this sleep the queen was first startled by the sentinel at her door, who cried out to save herself by flight—that this was the last proof of fidelity he could give—and they were upon him, and he was dead. Instantly he was cut down. A band of cruel ruffians and assassins, reeking with his blood rushed into the chamber of the queen and pierced with a hundred strokes of bayonets and poniards the bed, from whence this persecuted woman had but just time to fly almost naked, and, through ways unknown to the murderers, had escaped to seek refuge at the feet of a king and husband not secure of his own life for a moment. (Burke 62)

But whereas Marie Antoinette has for the moment successfully eluded her persecutors, the English Marie Antoinette, Smith's Geraldine, remains in the clutches of hers. In a scene of Gothic horror calculated to rival Burke's, Geraldine is held prisoner in the home of assassins:

> My ears were then invaded by dreadful groans, as of a person killed; groans so loud, that they were distinguishable amidst the clamour of several harsh voices, which was now increased by the hallooing of the men, and the shrieks of two of the women who had gone out from the hovel; where I sat in a state I have not language to describe; the beldam alone remaining with me, who fixed her terrible eyes upon me, and approached me in an attitude as she were about to strike me, with a long knife, which she had been using over the fire. (379)

The body of Geraldine has now become meat, about to be carved up with the kitchen knife. In the iconography of food which Charlotte Smith has developed throughout the novel, the woman becomes that which is consumed rather than that which consumes.

Despite her upper-class status, as a *femme couverte*, as a married woman, Geraldine is without money, protection, or free will. Charlotte Smith makes clear that Geraldine experiences her own self as one without identity or agency. As she explains to her sister, Fanny Waverly, she felt she had no choice but to risk her life to join her dying husband:

> Had I loved Mr. Verney, as the possessor of my first affections—as the father of my children—in short, as almost any other man might have been beloved, I should not, perhaps, have felt so very strongly the impulse of duty *only*, and should not have been urged, by its rigid laws, to incur dangers, against which, the service of pure affection, though the strongest of motives, could hardly fortify the heart.
>
> Being now, however, but too sensible, that whatever share of tenderness my young heart once gave him, he had long since thrown it away; and that duty alone bound me to him, I determined to fulfil what seemed to be my destiny—to be a complete martyr to that duty, and to follow whithersoever it led.
>
> A wretch, who is compelled to tremble on the brink of a precipice, has often been known to throw himself headlong from it, and rush to death rather than endure the dread of it.—This sort of sensation was, I think, what I felt; and as to my powers of endurance, I was like a victim, whose limbs being broken on the wheel, is, awhile, released from it, that he may acquire strength to bear accumulated tortures. (375)

Geraldine here speaks from the standpoint of one completely without power, without choice, one whose mind and body are at the service of others, of men. Under the patriarchal regimes of both republican France and monarchical England, a wife necessarily loses her psychic self, her very soul. She becomes, both legally and subjectively, a non-person. As such, she is chattel, no different from the African slaves bought and sold and tortured by their white male masters.[5]

That Geraldine's condition is universal, not particular, is suggested by the parallel story in the novel of her French counterpart, Josephine de Boisbelle, Montfleuri's sister. Josephine has also been married against her will to a man who abuses and deserts her, although she lives under the protection of her brother (as opposed to Geraldine's especially feckless, irresponsible brother, Waverly, who disdains all her pleas for help). Josephine too is attracted to Desmond, and nurses him back to health after he is wounded in a duel to protect Waverly. But Josephine enacts what the "proper lady" Geraldine is forbidden to acknowledge, female sexual desire. While nursing Desmond, she actively arouses and reciprocates his erotic passion; she bears his child, a girl, in secret in Wales; and then hands over that daughter to be raised by Geraldine. Her future is uncertain: if her husband survives, she must remain under his control; if he has been killed in the same futile royalist battle against the republican national guards in which Verney was fatally wounded, then she may be able to marry her childhood sweetheart, de Rivemont, a naval officer now in the East Indies.

Significantly, in this epistolary novel, Josephine never authors a letter (although she once writes to Geraldine a letter dictated in English by Desmond); she never speaks directly in her own voice. Whatever her destiny may be, she is left at the end of the novel *without her daughter*. Female sexual desire is here not only silenced, as Alison Conway has argued (Conway 403–404), but actively punished; under both a royalist and a republican system of patriarchal privilege, women cannot be permitted to engage openly in freely chosen sexual liaisons lest they pervert the "natural" bloodline which enables fathers to identify their children. Even the republican Desmond assumes without question that Josephine's illegitimate child belongs to him.

The most outspoken woman in the novel is Fanny Waverly. She consistently articulates her dislike for Verney, her opposition to her mother's insistence on the hollow forms of female propriety, and her horror at the cruelty and suffering that Geraldine suffers at the hands both of her husband and of her own family. She actively tries to support Geraldine, both economically and psychologically. And she aggressively seeks out the help of Bethel on Geraldine's behalf. Insofar as there is a feminist voice in the novel, it occurs in the letters that Fanny writes to her sister and Bethel. Fanny's fate is therefore particularly significant. When Desmond's friend Montfleuri meets her in Bath, he immediately falls in love, for the first time in his womanizing history. He immediately receives her mother's consent to their union and they are married posthaste. He tells Desmond that Fanny has agreed to this union and that they are both in love. But from the moment of their first meeting, we never hear directly from Fanny again: she never authors her own consent, her own desire, her own happiness. Her future is entirely constructed by others, by her mother, and by two men, Montfleuri and Desmond.

On the surface, the novel would seem to end happily, with Fanny and Montfleuri living in England next door to Desmond and Geraldine, who not only will marry in a year but will together raise her three children and Desmond's natural daughter. From the standpoint of Desmond and Montfleuri, the solution to the political debates raging between England and France, between a conservative monarchism and a radical republicanism, would seem to be a happy marriage or compromise between the two. One can preserve the constitutionally guaranteed liberties of British subjects under a limited monarchy by incorporating into the British family politic a French concern for "natural" rights, including the rights of African slaves, just as Desmond and Geraldine incorporate his "natural" daughter into their idyllic British family. Such a reading of the final politics of the novel would be consistent with Charlotte Smith's ongoing insistence, in her later

novels and in her poem *Beachy Head* (1801), on England's historical indebtedness to France since the Norman Conquest and her opposition to
the chauvinist myths of Anglo-Saxon liberties promoted by her Franco-
phobic peers (see Bray).

But Smith undercuts such a positive reading of the end of the novel by
reminding us that it represents the political standpoint only of males—of
Desmond, Bethel, and Montfleuri. Having become accustomed to reading
the letters of Geraldine and Fanny, the reader must be acutely aware of the
absence of their voices at the closing of the novel. Instead of hearing their
political endorsement of this English pastoral idyll of Anglo-French harmony, we hear instead Desmond's exultant appropriation of the mind and
body of Geraldine: "Heavens! dare I trust myself with the rapturous hope,
that on the return of this month, in the next year, Geraldine will bear *my*
name—will be the directress of *my* family—will be my friend—my mistress—my wife!" (408). As Smith's italicized pronouns alert us, Desmond
can think only in terms of possession, a male possession of the female that
he blithely extends to his male friends, as this passage continues: "I imagine
these days of happiness to come—I see the beloved group assembled at
Sedgewood:—*My* Geraldine—You, my dear Bethel—*your* sweet Louisa—
my friend Montfleuri, and *his* Fanny.—I imagine the delight of living in that
tender confidence of mutual affection, which only a circle of friends can
taste" (408; my italics). Significantly, Desmond has in effect *inherited* Geraldine. On his deathbed, Verney bequeaths his wife and children to Desmond, just as he would bequeath a piece of property: "I know you to be a
man of honour, and if Geraldine marries again, as there is certainly reason
to believe she will, it is to you, rather than to any other man, that I wish to
confide her and my children" (400).

Throughout the novel, Desmond has enacted the role of the knight of
medieval chivalry—reviving that very "age of chivalry" which Burke had
pronounced "gone" (Burke 66). He has repeatedly protected and rescued
Geraldine from the brutal assaults of her husband, his commissioned se-
ducers Colonel Scarsdale and Duc de Romagnecourt, and d'Hauteville's
licensed banditti. He has insisted throughout that his love is pure: while he
certainly desires Geraldine sexually, admiring both her physical beauty and
her personal graces, he has never acted toward her as anything but a devoted "brother." Charlotte Smith forces us to recognize that both the chivalric code and the new ideal of republican citizenship (or fraternity) openly
advocated by Desmond entail the same erasure of female political autonomy. As Joan Landes has persuasively argued in *Women and the Public Sphere
in the Age of the French Revolution,* the rhetoric of the leaders of the French
Revolution effectively reinscribed the new *citoyennes* of France within the

confined domestic sphere of the nursing mother, one who received neither the vote nor an equal education but who rather devoted herself to the bearing and rearing of male *citoyens* for the good of the Republic.

That Charlotte Smith herself did not endorse this political erasure of women from the public realm of governance and estate management is overtly announced in her opening preface. She not only claims to have firsthand reliable information concerning the events in England and France recorded in her novel, but she also insists on her right as a woman to engage in political debate:

> women it is said have no business with politics.—Why not?—Have they no interest in the scenes that are acting around them, in which they have fathers, brothers, husbands, sons, or friends engaged! Even in the commonest course of female education, they are expected to acquire some knowledge of history; and yet, if they are to have no opinion of what *is* passing, it avails little that they should be informed of what *has passed*, in a world where they are subject to such mental degradation. . . . (6)

Throughout her novel, her female characters—whether conservative or radical in their political opinions—repeatedly assert their right to hold such opinions. The pro-royalist Miss Fairfax aggressively condemns Desmond's support of the French National Assembly, insisting that "A title is as much a person's property as his estate" (37). The pro-revolution Geraldine writes at length about the improvements wrought in the French villages and towns by the republicans, citing the new national guards ("much better looking men, and much fitter to be entrusted with the care of their town than the miserable looking, half-starved soldiers, that I remember to have seen exercising on the walls when we were here before" [308]), and concluding that it may take more time before the full benefits of the revolution can be reaped.

Smith further claims that the genre of the novel—already dominated by female authors—is uniquely qualified to consider political questions. When Fanny is forbidden by her mother to read novels, Geraldine first mounts a lengthy defense of the novel as superior to drama:

> it has often struck me as a singular inconsistency, that, while novels have been condemned as being injurious to the interest of virtue, the play-house has been called the school of morality.—The comedies of the last century are, almost without exception, so gross, that, with all the alterations they have received, they are very unfit for that part of the audience to whom novel-reading is deemed pernicious; for, not only the rake and the coquette of the piece are generally made happy, but those duties of life, to which novel-reading is believed to be prejudicial, are almost always violated with impunity. . . . (200)

Geraldine then defends the genre of the novel as both more moral and more probable:

in every well-written novel, *vice,* and even *weaknesses,* that deserve not quite so harsh a name, are . . . exhibited, as subjecting those who are examples of them, to remorse, regret, and punishment—And since circumstances, more inimical to innocence, are every day related, without any disguise, or with very little, in the public prints; since, in reading the world, a girl must see a thousand very ugly blots, which frequently pass without any censure at all—I own, I cannot imagine, that novel reading can, as has been alleged, corrupt the imagination, or enervate the heart—at least, such a description of novels, as those which represent human life nearly as it is. . . . (198–99)

The novel, Smith further suggests in her preface, is a superior "vehicle of political discussion" because it need not sacrifice "truth" to the tenets of a single political party. Instead it can show "human life nearly as it is," it can engage in a "faithful representation of the manners of other countries" without indulging in "absurd" national prejudice (7). As Smith throws down the gauntlet against the phalanx of "constant pay" and "strict discipline" of her political opponents, her novel, while not yet capable of conquering this army of vested interests, nonetheless commits itself to "the powerful efforts of learning and genius . . . united in that cause which *must* finally triumph—the cause of truth, reason and humanity" (8). By drawing directly on her own experiences as the abandoned mother of twelve children left to shoulder the burden of her husband's debts and repeatedly duped by manipulating or incapable lawyers, Charlotte Smith grounded her political novel on her own standpoint, a marginalized standpoint which enabled her to see beyond the self-serving patriarchal interests that determined and sustained all the major political systems—ranging from conservative to republican to anarchical—of her historical moment. The complete erasure of female voices from the concluding letters of *Desmond* underscores Charlotte Smith's perception that the sexual contract remains in place, both in England and in revolutionary France; all women remain under *couverture.* Geraldine survives only as a wife and a mother; indeed she has been throughout the novel identified with her maternity, whether as the weeping Niobe of Desmond's Gothic nightmare (99) or as the woman who finds her only pleasures in attending to her children's needs. But her devoted and self-sacrificing motherhood here serves only to register the *distance* between republican motherhood—which serves only to supply the future citizens of France or America—and the triumphant "mother of the nation" envisioned by Mary Wollstonecraft and Hannah More, the new Britannia embodied forty years later in Queen Victoria.

Persuasion

For a compelling literary portrait of that new mother of the nation, we must turn to a novel written twenty-four years later, Jane Austen's *Persua-*

sion. Composed between 8 August 1815 and 6 August 1816, *Persuasion* is Austen's most profoundly political novel. It is explicitly set in 1813–14, after Nelson's defeat of the French fleet at Trafalgar in 1805 and just before Wellington's crushing defeat of Napoleon's armies at the Battle of Water-loo on 18–22 June 1815. The novel constitutes Austen's most extended meditation on the future of England in a post-war, post-Napoleonic cul-ture and economy. Writing during a period of intense British national self-examination, the historical period equated by Linda Colley with the emer-gence of British nationalism, Jane Austen offers a thoughtful analysis of the ideal British family politic, of the rulers best qualified to govern the new British nation. Told, with only a few exceptions, entirely from a single wom-an's point of view, the novel implicitly assigns to the female consciousness final moral and political authority in the discursive public sphere.

Persuasion begins with Austen's portrayal of the ancien régime, the Brit-ish aristocracy, here identified with Sir Walter Elliot of Kellynch Hall, who can trace his ancestry back to Charles II. As numerous readers have ob-served, Sir Walter is vain, excessively effeminate, one of those "equivocal beings" denounced by Wollstonecraft (*Vindication* 138; cf. Johnson 1995: 10–12)—"few women could think more of his personal appearance than he did" (*Persuasion* 3).[6] He surrounds himself with mirrors, both literal—so many, in fact, that Admiral Croft has to remove them, exclaiming "there was no getting away from oneself" (84)—and human, requiring his subor-dinates (his daughters, Mrs. Clay) to flatter him sycophantically. Worse, Sir Walter is fiscally irresponsible, deeply in debt, unable to "retrench," so much so that he is finally forced to lease out his ancestral mansion, which Anne Elliot rightly recognizes as a "degradation" (90). As Roger Sales has argued, Sir Walter is Austen's subtle portrait of the Prince Regent (Sales 172), also infamous for his vanity, excessive concern with fashion and style, and fiscal mismanagement. Sir Walter—and by implication the Prince Re-gent, the future King George IV—has given up the "duties and dignity of the resident land-holder" (91).

Sir Walter is joined by the putative "Queen" of Kellynch Hall, his daugh-ter Elizabeth, who for thirteen years has been "doing the honours, and laying down the domestic law" (5). Like her father, Elizabeth Elliot is con-cerned only with her personal appearance and her social status, demanding fawning attention from her inferiors but scraping obsequiously before those of even higher rank (her cousins Lady Dalrymple and Miss Carteret). Simi-larly, Mary Elliot Musgrove, the youngest sister, lives in perpetual dissatis-faction with the fact that the privileges of her rank are insufficiently ac-knowledged by her husband, in-laws, and friends. The Elliot family—with the exception of Anne—represent Austen's political judgment that contemporary British aristocracy is now infertile and stagnant (Elizabeth never marries, never has children, never changes), condemned to eternal repetition without growth, in ever more straitened circumstances, in a "state of half enjoyment" (167). The aristocracy and the landed gentry may not yet have lost all their economic power, but in Austen's eyes they have certainly lost their prestige and moral authority, as Claudia Johnson observes (Johnson 1988:145).

If the traditional aristocracy and monarchy are no longer morally viable or economically flourishing, then who is to govern the new British nation? *Persuasion* is Austen's answer to that question. She first explores the claims of the next generation of the aristocracy, the new "gentleman," Mr. William Walter Elliot. William Elliot has added economic power to the aristocracy by marrying vulgar money (the wealthy granddaughter of a butcher and daughter of a cattle-feeder), thus effectively selling his title for a price, albeit a price far higher than the £50 he originally threatened to take for it (in his letter to Captain Smith, 135). As a result, he has managed to become a man of "very gentleman like appearance" with an "air of elegance and fashion," at least in Sir Walter's view (93). Moreover, he possesses a "sensible, discerning mind" (94), good manners, and a civility sufficiently polished to persuade Lady Russell that, his wife having died, he would be a good husband for her beloved Anne. Even Anne herself is not impervious to William Elliot's charms and claims on her respect. Responding to Lady Russell's fantasy that she might become exactly what her mother had been, "Lady Elliot" of Kellynch Hall, Anne feels powerfully drawn to the traditions of old England, to the preservation of the ancien régime—"The idea . . . of being restored to Kellynch, calling it her home again, her home for ever, was a charm which she could not immediately resist" (106).

But William Elliot has a fatal flaw: he is "not open" (106). We must look closely at the failings which Austen's text assigns to William Elliot if we are to understand her political position in this novel. Summing up the case against Mr. Elliot, Anne observes:

> He certainly knew what was right, nor could she fix on any one article of moral duty evidently transgressed; but yet she would have been afraid to answer for his conduct. She distrusted the past, if not the present. The names which occasionally dropt of former associates, the allusions to former practices and pursuits, suggested suspicions not favourable of what he had been. She saw that there had been bad habits; that Sunday-travelling had been a common thing; that there had been a period of his life (and probably not a short one) when he had been, at least, careless of all serious matters; and, though he might now think very differently, who could answer for the true sentiments of a clever, cautious man, grown old enough to appreciate a fair character? How could it ever be ascertained that his mind was truly cleansed? (106)

William Elliot lacks moral principles. As his willingness to travel on Sundays suggests, he has failed Hannah More's central test of religious virtue, a rigorous Sabbatarianism combined with the consistent practice of benevolence. His fair character is only skin-deep; his mind and soul are polluted.

The events of the novel only confirm Anne's intuitive perceptions. We learn that William Elliot is all "selfishness" (138) and "insincerity" (142). He cruelly abused his first wife, perhaps hastening her early death; he led his best friend Captain Smith into debt, then abandoned him; and he refused to help the widowed Mrs. Smith reclaim her husband's property even though he was her husband's legal executor. He schemes throughout the novel to prevent Sir Walter giving birth to a direct heir: first he plans to marry Anne and produce his own heir; then he seduces Mrs. Clay (and thus prevents *her* marriage to Sir Walter). He is finally appropriately punished by becoming so completely entangled with the equally manipulative Mrs. Clay that he may have to marry her. As future rulers of England, Sir and Lady William Elliot are thus thoroughly discredited as duplicitous, selfish libertines, no better than the Prince Regent.

Instead, Jane Austen suggests, the new rulers of Britain should be those who *now* have possession of Kellynch Hall, the self-made "gentlemen," the members of the increasingly wealthy and socially powerful professional and commercial middle class who can afford to purchase titles (what Sir Walter disparagingly calls the "new creations"). In this novel, this professional class is explicitly identified with the British navy (the chosen profession of two of Austen's brothers—Francis Austen achieved the rank of Admiral of the Fleet, Charles became Rear Admiral and Commander-in-Chief of the East India Station). As role models for the future rulers of England, I wish to look first at Austen's hero, Frederick Wentworth. He exemplifies the new professional gentleman: he is the youngest son of landed gentry, with no money of his own. He is a strong believer in the value of individual effort as opposed to inherited wealth or position, who responds to Mary's snobbish pretensions with a "contemptuous glance" (58). As Marilyn Butler observed, he is a "modern-minded man" whose "personal philosophy approaches revolutionary optimism and individualism" (Butler 275–76). He rises entirely through his own exertions and merit, as recorded in his own "book" of achievement (rivaling Debrett's *Peerage*), the *Navy List* (43). By the time the novel opens, he has earned £20,000; by the time it closes his net worth has risen to £25,000.

Wentworth is clearly a man of moral principle and of benevolence. He is capable of great generosity and compassion: he sympathetically consoles Mrs. Musgrove for the loss of her ill-starred son; he is consistently kind and attentive to his friends the Harvilles and Captain Benwick; he sensitively relieves Anne of the burden of the toddler on her back (53), and aggressively procures transportation for her when she is too tired to walk further (61). He is worthy of Anne Elliot's enduring love.

Yet Wentworth is also flawed. He is "resolute" but he is also "headstrong" (19). He takes excessive risks. As a risk-taker, he is another of the Romantic era's Promethean figures, with revealing similarities to Byron's and Percy Shelley's defiant, fire-stealing rebels and to Mary Shelley's "modern Prometheus," Victor Frankenstein. Remember that Wentworth earns his fortune by theft: he literally steals or captures ships (either "privateers" running the British blockade against the French nation or French "frigates," 44) in acts of war—or equally accurately, in state-licensed piracy. Moreover, he is cavalier about the loss of life that such risk-taking acts of military piracy might incur. As he comments flippantly, "The admiralty . . . entertain themselves now and then, with sending a few hundred men to sea, in a ship not fit to be employed. But they have a great many to provide for; and among the thousands that may just as well go to the bottom as not, it is impossible for them to distinguish the very set who may be least missed" (43).

Wentworth is an overreacher, full of excessive self-confidence. As Maaja Stewart has emphasized (Stewart 92–93), he is a mercantile gambler who is convinced that lady luck is always on his side: "He had been lucky in his profession, but spending freely, what had come freely, had realized nothing. But, he was confident that he should soon be rich;—full of life and ardour, he knew that he should soon have a ship, and soon be on a station that would lead to everything he wanted. He had always been lucky; he knew he should be so still" (19). And up to the beginning of the novel, his luck has held. As Roger Sales explains, Wentworth was particularly lucky to capture "the very French frigate [he] wanted" (44) on his way home to Plymouth, while sailing under admiralty orders, since he was thus entitled to three-eighths of the prize money (the value of the ship as well as its cargo), without having to give the usual one-sixth cut to his admiral (Sales 183). Moreover, a frigate paid considerably more in prize money than did the average privateer or merchant ship, since its reinforced hull, rigging, stores, and armaments could all be sold; its crew were worth £5 each in "head-money," and the government usually paid up more rapidly for a ship captured in battle (and despite his irony, Wentworth's was a legitimate naval battle: "our touch with the Great Nation not having much improved" the condition of the *Asp* [44; see Hill, 190–91]).

But in his personal—as opposed to his professional—life, Wentworth has perhaps not been so lucky. His hope of domestic happiness has been thwarted by his excessive pride. As he finally acknowledges, he could have renewed his broken engagement with Anne Elliot in 1808, when he returned after two years from his first posting with a fortune of a few thousand pounds, but he was "too proud to ask again" (164). This pride has cost both him and Anne six additional years of unnecessary suffering.

Wentworth alone is therefore not a reliable ruler for the new British nation. He is too enthusiastic, too rash, too self-confident, too proud. He overvalues "resolution," "decision and firmness," for their own sakes, as his parable of the hard nut makes clear. Lecturing Louisa Musgrove, Wentworth insists on the evil of "too yielding and indecisive a character" on which "no influence can ever be depended on." Instead he affirms the ultimate value of "a beautiful glossy nut, which, blessed with original strength, has outlived all the storms of autumn. Not a puncture, not a weak spot any where. This nut . . . while so many of its brethren have fallen and been trodden underfoot, is still in possession of all the happiness that a hazel-nut can be supposed capable of. . . . My first wish for all, whom I am interested in, is that they should be firm" (59). Wentworth's affirmation of decisiveness for its own sake, beyond prudence or rational calculation, in effect offers a rationale for laissez-faire mercantile capitalism: for high-risk investments, aggressive entrepreneurship, and uninsured stock speculation.

As the daughter of a man who had risked a significant percentage of his inheritance on government lottery tickets and lost (Nokes 122–23), and as one well aware of the famous South Sea Bubble of 1720, Jane Austen could see the economic as well as the psychological dangers inherent in Wentworth's affirmation of resolute risk-taking. That Wentworth's values are not the values endorsed by the novel as a whole is evidenced by the case of Louisa Musgrove. High-spirited, full of "enthusiasm" (57), Louisa translates Wentworth's resolution into headstrong willfulness. She will *not* be persuaded, even to rest during a long walk (58), taking Wentworth's metaphor of the hard nut as a license for obstinacy: "Louisa, who was the most eager of the eager, having formed the resolution to go, and besides the pleasure of doing as she liked, being now armed with the idea of merit in maintaining her own way, bore down all the wishes of her father and mother for putting it off till summer; and to Lyme they were to go—" (63). The consequence of Louisa's firm resolution is of course her fall down the steep stone steps at Lyme, a fall both literal and metaphoric. She incurs a concussion to the brain, a sign of mental weakness, of wrong thinking—a concussion that leaves her with a lifelong case of excessive nervousness, the anxiety of one who has risked too much and lost, who can no longer trust the environment in which she lives. As Charles Musgrove observes, Louisa is "altered: there is no running or jumping about, no laughing or dancing; it is quite different. If one happens only to shut the door a little hard, she starts and wiggles like a young dab chick in the water" (145).

What qualities must England's ideal ruler possess, then, if not Wentworth's "firm resolution" and his willingness to take risks? Austen's answer:

the ability to combine risk-taking with rational caution and an enduring concern for the welfare of all involved. Austen sums up this ability in her title. As opposed to her earlier novels which centered their interest on persons (Emma), places (Northanger Abbey, Mansfield Park) or paired oppositions (sense and sensibility, pride and prejudice, love and friendship), *Persuasion* implies the necessity for mediation or communication between opposing standpoints or political positions (persuasions), between yes and no. Such mediation can occur either on an intellectual level—as the product of rational argument and rhetorical eloquence—or on an emotional level, as an act of self-sacrifice, sympathy, or disinterested good will. Jane Austen had specifically distinguished these two dimensions of persuasion a few years earlier in *Pride and Prejudice* (1813), in a telling conversation between Darcy and Elizabeth:

> "[Y]ou must remember, Miss Bennet, that the friend who is supposed to desire his return to the house, and his delay of his plan, has merely desired it, asked it without offering one argument in favour of its propriety."
>
> "To yield readily—easily—to the *persuasion* of a friend is not merit with you."
>
> "To yield without conviction is no compliment to the understanding of either."
>
> "You appear to me, Mr. Darcy, to allow nothing for the influence of friendship and affection. A regard for the requester would often make one readily yield to a request, without waiting for arguments to reason one into it." (34)

For Jane Austen, *persuasion* is the ability both to guide and to yield, to combine rational argument with emotional sympathy. As such, persuasion —the rhetorical art of persuasion and the willingness to be persuaded— is the quintessence of the democratic process, in which interested parties ideally learn to reconcile their opposing positions in order to arrive at a bipartisan course of action which serves the greater good of the polity as a whole.

The character in the novel who most fully embodies Jane Austen's ideal of democratic persuasion—of both persuasiveness and persuadability—is Anne Elliot. Austen herself acknowledged that Anne may be too good to be true. She wrote of *Persuasion* to her niece Fanny Knight on 23 March 1817: "You may *perhaps* like the Heroine, as she is almost too good for me" (*Letters* 335). Or as William Elliot puts it in the novel, Anne is the very "model of female excellence" (105). At the same time, Anne represents Everywoman, what any middle-class woman in England might be or might become—she is "*only* Anne" (5); "her word had no weight; her convenience was always to give way" (5). She has no money of her own—she should have a dowry of £10,000, but her father has so mortgaged his property that at her wedding she receives only "a small part" of it (165). Granted, she bears an aristocratic name, but it belongs to a family that consistently embarrasses her. And she is an old maid of twenty-seven who has lost her "bloom" (101), with no matrimonial prospects in sight.

As an aging spinster with no great expectations, Anne embodies the bleak fate of most unmarried middle-class Englishwomen—as Jane Austen commented sardonically to her niece Fanny Knight on 13 March 1817, "Single Women have a dreadful propensity for being poor—which is one very strong argument in favour of Matrimony" (*Letters* 332). And yet Anne's consciousness controls the narrative, uniquely in Jane Austen's oeuvre; as Wayne Booth noted, the only significant break in the novel's confinement to Anne's "angle of vision" between the second and final chapters of *Persuasion* occurs when Anne meets Wentworth for the first time in eight years and cannot know what he is feeling or thinking (on p. 41; Booth 169). Her mental processes become Austen's fictional model for both individual and national self-formation.

Before I discuss Anne's character in more detail, I want to look briefly at the female role models provided by the text for Anne's intellectual, emotional, and political development, role models that serve as Jane Austen's own version of Hannah More's *Hints on the Education of a Young Princess,* her "Book of the Governor" for the next presumed Queen of England, Princess Charlotte (who died on 6 November 1817, a year after Austen completed this novel). Anne is provided with two alternative mother figures (in place of her own dead mother) from whom she can seek and receive advice on how to act. The first, Lady Russell, is a "sensible, deserving" woman, of "steady age and character" (4) and "sound" abilities (8), who loves Anne as a daughter (and was formerly the best and most trusted friend of Anne's mother). Her name aligns her with Lady William Russell, that woman whom Lucy Aikin singled out in her *Epistles on Women* (1810; IV: 423) as one of England's finest "patriot hearts," famous for her devotion to the cause of a limited monarchy which preserved the freedoms of English subjects and for her heroic efforts to vindicate her husband after he was wrongly executed by Charles II in 1683. Austen's Lady Russell endorses the values of good breeding, of inherited wealth and aristocratic class privilege; as such, she takes up the position of Edmund Burke, who insisted on respect for British cultural traditions and tested governments. Because she is the voice of political conservatism, she overly values the aristocracy as such: she deeply desires that Anne *repeat* her mother's life, becoming once again the mistress of Kellynch Hall (106). Since Lady Russell wants to preserve the ancien régime of England, she advises against Anne's marrying the upstart, penniless Wentworth who has nothing but his good nature and ambitious courage to recommend him. Moreover, she urges Anne to marry the future Sir William Elliot, unable to see beyond his surface "gentlemanliness" to the lack of moral principle within.

It is Lady Russell who eight years before the novel opens persuaded Anne to break off her engagement with Frederick Wentworth. Was she right or wrong to do so? It was advice based on prudence, on caution, on the recognition that Wentworth's gamble on his own future might not pay off. Anne, eight years later, strongly believes that she would not now give the same advice to a young girl in her former position:

> How eloquent could Anne Elliot have been,—how eloquent, at least, were her wishes on the side of early warm attachment, and a cheerful confidence in futurity, against that over-anxious caution which seems to insult exertion and distrust Providence!—She had been forced into prudence in her youth, she learned romance as she grew older—the natural sequence of an unnatural beginning. (21)

But as Robert Hopkins has astutely shown, Jane Austen does not finally endorse the "consequentialism" or moral relativism of Anne's position here, the argument that the moral rectitude of an action can be judged solely by its results or consequences—in this case, that the continuation of her engagement to Wentworth was justified by his subsequent military successes. Anne herself subsequently qualifies her position, arguing that correct moral action depends more on principle, or conscience, than on consequences. As Anne finally affirms, she was right to be persuaded by Lady Russell:

> I must believe that I was right, much as I suffered from it, that I was perfectly right in being guided by the friend whom you will love better than you do now. Do not mistake me, however. I am not saying that she did not err in her advice. It was, perhaps, one of those cases in which advice is good or bad only as the event decides; and for myself, I certainly never should, in any circumstance of tolerable similarity, give such advice. But I mean, that I was right in submitting to her; and that if I had done otherwise, I should have suffered more in continuing the engagement that I did even in giving it up, because I should have suffered *in my conscience*. I have now, as far as such a sentiment is allowable in human nature, nothing to reproach myself with; and if I mistake not, a strong sense of duty is no bad part of a woman's portion. (164; my italics)

That the novel finally endorses conscience, or principle—"the strong sense of duty"—over consequentialism or the actual results of the action as the final arbiter of moral rectitude is further confirmed by Sophia Croft, Anne Elliot's second role model. As Sophia asserts, a long engagement or an uncertain engagement are both imprudent: "To begin without knowing that at such a time there will be the means of marrying, I hold to be very unsafe and unwise, and what, I think, all parents should prevent as far as they can" (154). Austen's novel thus endorses *being persuaded* as an act of rational prudence, moral principle, and finally, of love. Anne was persuaded both by her affection for her "mother" Lady Russell and, equally powerfully, by her love for Frederick Wentworth: "it was not a merely selfish caution, under which she acted, in putting an end to it. Had she not imagined herself consulting his good, even more than her own, she could hardly have given him up.—The belief of being prudent, and self-denying principally for *his* advantage, was her chief consolation, under the misery of a parting" (19).

That Sophia Croft endorses Lady Russell's position—and by implication, Anne's willingness to adopt it—affirms the ultimate value of persuadability in this novel. For Sophia—as her name suggests—is the voice of female wisdom. She is the New Woman of England upon whom Anne finally models herself, the woman who fulfills both Mary Wollstonecraft's and Hannah More's requirements for the ideal wife and mother of the nation. She is sensible and pragmatic, but capable of romance, of an impulsive and enduring love for the Admiral (whom she married after only a six weeks' engagement). She insists that women are "rational creatures" (47) and never doubts her own intellectual abilities: "Her manners were open, easy, and decided, like one who had no distrust of herself, and no doubts of what to do" (33). As a competent, rational woman, she expects and achieves an entirely egalitarian marriage with her husband. They are always together at Bath, walking arm-in-arm—indeed, her husband feels lopsided if he does not have her on his arm! As Anne observes, "Mrs. Croft seemed to go shares with him in everything" (111).

On sea, on her husband's ships, Mrs. Croft of course defers to her husband's greater professional expertise: she serves there as his helpmate, wife, and comforter, doing her best to administer to his practical and emotional needs, providing him with as homelike quarters as she can arrange. She preserves the values—the comforts and consolations—of domesticity even in an arena formerly regarded as an entirely male preserve, the military ship.

But on land, the Admiral defers to Sophia's greater expertise. She is the woman of business, as Mr. Shepherd, the lawyer who arranges the lease of Kellynch Hall, recognizes. She "asked more questions about the house, and terms, and taxes, than the Admiral himself, and seemed more conversant with business" (16). She is responsible for "improving" the estate of Kellynch Hall, as the Admiral emphasizes. Describing the new conveniences at Kellynch—a well-placed umbrella stand, a new laundry-door—he insists that "my wife should have the credit of them" (84). And when the Admiral becomes restless on land, she is the one who calls him "to order" (46). Perhaps most significant, when they go driving, she is the one who corrects their direction: "By coolly giving the reins a better direction herself, they happily passed the danger; and by once afterwards judiciously putting out her hand, they neither fell into a rut, nor ran foul of a dung-cart; and Anne, with some amusement at their style of driving, which she imagined no bad representation of the general guidance of their affairs, found herself safely deposited by them at the cottage" (62). On land, controlling the reins, Sophia Croft reigns.

As members of the professional classes who have both the practical wisdom and the economic means to improve the estate of Kellynch Hall and who attend to the needs of both the poor and the sick, the Crofts are the characters in the novel who deserve to govern the nation. They rightly replace the owners of Kellynch Hall, the old aristocrats, as the proper rulers of the new England, as Anne quickly realizes:

> she had in fact so high an opinion of the Crofts, and considered her father so very fortunate in his tenants, felt the parish to be so sure of a good example, and the poor of the best attention and relief, that however sorry and shamed for the necessity of the removal, she could not but in conscience feel that they were gone who deserved not to stay, and that Kellynch-hall had passed into better hands than its owners'. (82)

Combining Lady Russell's patriotic respect for the best traditions of the past with Sophia Croft's pragmatic, sensible household management, Anne Elliot comes to embody Jane Austen's concept of the new mother of the nation. Although not a mother herself, Anne exhibits all the skills of devoted mothering. She eagerly and effectively nurses little Charles Musgrove when his back and collarbone are injured in a bad fall. That Charles's biological mother, Mary Musgrove, is unable to respond usefully to this accident—"I am more unfit than any body else to be about the child. My being the mother is the very reason why my feelings should not be tried. I am not at all equal to it" (38)—suggests that for Austen—unlike Lucy Aikin—mothering is a learned rather than an instinctive capacity, one that can be socially constructed and reproduced. Having honed her mothering skills through frequent practice, Anne has become the "favorite" with all her nieces and nephews.

As a "mother," Anne has all the qualities required for Austen's "model of female excellence." She exhibits unceasing concern and sympathy for others. She regularly visits the poor and the sick in her parish, practicing the systematic philanthropy—"any visit of charity in the village" (88)—that Hannah More had defined as the "profession" of the upper- and middle-class woman. That Austen too regards philanthropy as the primary job of Christian Englishwomen is illustrated by the activities of Mrs. Smith, who even in her own crippled and impoverished condition devotes her free time to knitting goods that she can sell to benefit those less well off than she (102). Anne consistently sacrifices her own interests to the greater good of others, playing the piano so others may dance, staying at home to care for her nephew so that her sister may enjoy a social outing, even giving up her marriage engagement for Wentworth's sake. As Jane Nardin has persuasively argued, Anne Elliot is Austen's most self-consciously and profoundly religious heroine, the embodiment of Austen's own sincere faith in Christian beliefs and practices.

Anne Elliot is a woman of moral principle, of virtue, whose goal in life is to be "useful" to others. She can never be persuaded to do what she thinks is wrong: Charles Musgrove finds her "unpersuadable" when it is a question of abandoning her nephew to whom "she knew herself to be of the first utility" (39). She is always sincere, incapable of lying or duplicity, "only" and always Anne. She never complains: however dreary and painful her life, she accepts her fate with good humor, an exemplar of "patience and resignation" (68). Most important, she is capable of resolution and independence, of taking charge in a crisis. She is the one who sends for the surgeon when her nephew is injured; she is the one who directs the rescue operation for Louisa Musgrove after her fall down the stone steps at Lyme.

As such, she is the exemplar of excellent domestic management—both in public and at home. It is Anne who finally persuades her father to lease Kellynch Hall to pay his debts: "she considered it as an act of indispensable duty to clear away the claims of creditors, with all the expedition which the most comprehensive retrenchments could secure, and saw no dignity in any thing short of it" (9–10). As Edward Copeland has argued, Anne participates fully in the middle-class consumption of goods, but she is a wise consumer. She practices what Hannah More had preached, a Christian capitalism which insists on the honest exchange of goods and the prompt payment of debt as a matter of moral principle as well as of sound economic practice.

In taking a woman of flawless virtue as her heroine, Jane Austen subtly contested her society's definition of the ideal woman as one who possesses "accomplishments" and physical beauty. Instead Austen insists on Anne Elliot's lack of beauty—her "bloom" has faded, and when Wentworth sees her after an eight-year absence he claims that her looks were "so altered" that he should not have known her (41). By equating female virtue with the absence of physical beauty, Austen follows Ann Plumptre's lead in her novel *Something New* (1801) in constructing a new definition of female attractiveness, one based on moral character rather than on the body. Only as Anne's moral perfections reveal themselves in the course of the novel, as others come to value her more highly, does she become beautiful: Wentworth finally insists that "to my eye you could never alter," a compliment that Anne rightly recognizes to be "the result, not the cause of his warm attachment" (162). More important, Anne's exemplary virtue and growing self-confidence render her attractive to the eyes of strangers—Mr. Elliot immediately doffs his hat to her on the steps at Lyme and after her renewed engagement, she enters the crowd at her father's party "glowing and lovely in sensibility and happiness, and more generally admired than she thought about or cared for" (163). As Leilani Riehle has argued, Jane Austen is here replacing her society's identification of female beauty with the surface appearance of the face and body with a new definition of female beauty as what we would today call "inner beauty," a moral virtue that shines out from the soul.[7]

If Anne "is almost too good," as Jane Austen herself thought, why don't we envy and resent her? What makes this paragon of female excellence into a character who wins our allegiance, our willingness to follow her lead and entrust ourselves to her care? First, of course, is the fact that throughout the novel we are *confined* to Anne Elliot's consciousness, seeing events almost entirely from her point of view, and thus fully sharing her sufferings and her joys. In this sense, Anne Elliot embodies Jane Austen's meditation on the nature of romantic individualism, on what it means to be an autonomous self. Recall that in Locke's famous formulation the individual is one who owns "property in his own person" and is thereby the primary participant in a democratic polity, in which every individual has equal rights and liberties. If we are to see ourselves as holding political rights in our own persons, as autonomous participants in Rousseau's social contract, then what are the social and psychological consequences of a democracy founded on the assembly of separate selves?

Austen begins to answer such a question by emphasizing the loneliness of the autonomous individual—Anne is isolated at home, ignored by her family, undervalued by all but Lady Russell. As Tony Tanner has observed, Anne Elliot is not only the "loneliest of Jane Austen's heroines" but also the one most often displaced, dislocated, transplanted (208–10). Her isolation becomes so severe at moments in the text that it verges on self-fragmentation, a splitting in which Anne no longer knows exactly who she is or what she is feeling. When she sees Wentworth at Bath for the first time since Louisa's misfortune at Lyme, she feels cut in half—"She left her seat, she would go, one half of her should not always be so much wiser than the other half, or always suspecting the other of being worse than it was" (116). And after they meet, she cannot define her own feelings: "It was agitation, pain, pleasure, a something between delight and misery" (116). Here Anne experiences her self not as a coherent whole but rather as a chaotic flux, indefinable, contradictory, out of control.

Exploring the nature of this solitary, unknowable subjectivity, Austen's novel emphasizes the ways in which the isolated self learns to break down the boundaries between one individual and another. Austen turns first, as William Wordsworth did, to the role of memory—that memory which assures a self that it has endured through time. But where Wordsworth in *The*

Prelude or in "Lines written a few miles above Tintern Abbey" defined memory as the guarantor of the coherence of the self, however changed through time, and as the ground of an enduring belief system, in his case the faith that "Nature never did betray the heart that loved her," Jane Austen defines the function of memory very differently. For Anne Elliot, memory preserves a record of human relationships, of meaningful contact between one autonomous self and another, a record of relationships both lost and preserved. Repeatedly encountering Wentworth at the home of the Musgroves, Anne knows that "Whether former feelings were to be renewed, must be brought to the proof; former times must undoubtedly be brought to the recollection of each" (42). For eight long years Anne's memory has preserved both the times she spent with Wentworth and the intense love that she felt for him.

Communication between one autonomous self and another is enabled not only by the memory of past shared feelings but also by present activities. Anne carries on a regular correspondence with all the members of her family—she does all the "work" of preserving kinship ties through letter writing. She further devotes her time to visiting others, moving from one household to the next. As she does so, we see her performing what Keats would call an act of negative capability, displaying a profound capacity for empathy that enables her to enter fully into the concerns and experiences of those immediately around her, so much so that Bath replaces Uppercross replaces Kellynch Hall in her daily thoughts. Most important, Anne takes the initiative to preserve or create human relationships. She insists on keeping up her acquaintance with the unfortunate Mrs. Smith even over her father's objections. And once she perceives that Wentworth *might* still care for her, she assertively addresses him at the concert at Bath. Jane Austen is here insisting upon the necessity of breaking down the prison walls of the autonomous self, of developing an ego with permeable boundaries rather than one fixed in its hard-nut case of "firmness." The agency of such permeability is of course love or sympathy; hence Anne "learns romance" as she grows older (21).

Austen's argument for the necessity of overcoming the limits of the autonomous self is also an epistemological argument concerning the way we acquire knowledge. If we are locked into an isolated consciousness, how can we gain access to a universal or at least a shared truth? In this novel, trusting one's own feelings only leads to falsehood or self-deception, as when Captain Benwick insists that he can love but once or when Anne wrongly assumes that Mr. Elliot must have heard about her from Wentworth (when his informant had in fact been Mrs. Smith, 130). At the same time, Jane Austen rejects the scientific notion that one can observe the external world "objectively," without the interposition of feelings. In *Per-*

suasion, physical nature is always colored by the perceiver's emotions, in what Ruskin would later term the pathetic fallacy. As numerous readers have observed, the landscape of *Persuasion* is autumnal, mirroring the sense of loss and decay that defines Anne's consciousness of her own faded bloom:

> Her *pleasure* in the walk must arise from the exercise and the day, from the view of the last smiles of the year upon the tawny leaves and withered hedges, and from repeating to herself some few of the thousand poetical descriptions extant of autumn, that season of peculiar and inexhaustible influence on the mind of taste and tenderness, that season which has drawn from every poet, worthy of being read, some attempt at description, or some lines of feeling. (56)

Here autumn is as much a state of mind as a natural season.

If the isolated self can neither trust its feelings to gain truth nor prevent itself from imposing its feelings on and thus distorting the external world, how can the self gain reliable knowledge? In this novel, as had Charlotte Smith in *Desmond,* Jane Austen implicitly mounts the case for what feminist epistemologists have defined as "strong" (as opposed to scientific or "weak") objectivity. As Sandra Harding has explained, "weak" objectivity insists that the observer be emotionally detached from the object of knowledge, that the experiment be repeatable by different experimenters in different locations and at different times, and that the results be consistent from one researcher to the next. But such results or knowledge are thereby limited to those researchers asking the same questions, possessing the same research tools or laboratory equipment, and performing the same experiments in the same way. Such "truths" are by no means universal. Jane Austen makes just this point in the discussion between Captain Harville and Anne on the "fickleness" of woman's love. Harville, defending man's greater constancy in love, observes

> "all histories are against you, all stories, prose and verse. If I had such a memory as Benwick, I could bring you fifty quotations in a moment on my side the argument, and I do not think I ever opened a book in my life which had not something to say upon woman's inconstancy. Songs and proverbs, all talk of woman's fickleness. But perhaps you will say, these were all written by men."
>
> "Perhaps I shall.—Yes, yes, if you please, no reference to examples in books. Men have had every advantage of us in telling their own story. Education has been theirs in so much higher a degree; the pen has been in their hands. I will not allow books to prove anything." (156)

A stronger objectivity occurs when the experimenter or knowledge seeker also factors in his or her own standpoint (the emotions and life experiences which produce his or her own mental biases or way of constructing knowledge), and takes equal account of the different results reached by other knowledge seekers in other times and places, using different methods and asking differently posed questions. Only by incorporating the various standpoints of all those involved in the social production of knowledge (especially those outside as well as within the privileged arenas of the university or laboratory) can human beings begin to approach knowledge that might be universalizable. Austen wittily suggests that standpoints other than the dominant, in this case patriarchal, one are necessary to learn the truth about human love by having Wentworth *drop his pen* at the very moment Anne asserts that while man's feelings "may be the strongest," woman's "are the most tender" (155):

> a slight noise called their attention to Captain Wentworth's hitherto perfectly quiet division of the room. It was nothing more than that his pen had fallen down, but Anne was startled at finding him nearer than she had supposed, and half inclined to suspect that the pen had only fallen, because he had been occupied by them, striving to catch sounds, which yet she did not think he could have caught. (155–56)

In *Persuasion,* accurate knowledge is achieved only through such careful attending to all standpoints, through conversation or listening to others, through participating in that dialogue which forms so substantial a part of the novel itself and which Anne Elliot hails as the basis of society. "My idea of good company," she explains to William Elliot, "is the company of clever, well-informed people, who have a great deal of conversation; that is what I call good company" (99). But one must attend to the perceptions of those on the margins as well as those within the halls of social power. The most reliable truths are gained through what might be called women's ways of knowing, specifically though *gossip.* As Patricia Meyer Spacks has argued, gossip or tale-telling is a time-honored mode of understanding and communicating the range of human behaviors. In *Persuasion,* gossip is embodied in the figure of Nurse Rooke, the bearer of necessary but socially hidden or secret truths. As Mrs. Smith explains, Nurse Rooke

> is a shrewd, intelligent, sensible woman. Hers is a line for seeing human nature; and she has a fund of good sense and observation which, as a companion, make her infinitely superior to thousands of those who having received "the best education in the world," know nothing worth attending to. Call it gossip if you will; but when nurse Rooke has half an hour's leisure to bestow on me, she is sure to have something to relate that is entertaining and profitable, something that makes one know one's species better. (103)

One reaches the truth in this novel by listening to the figures on the margins of society. Mrs. Smith has gained a far more accurate account of the concert "through the short cut of a laundress and a waiter" (127) than by listening to Anne, whose feelings have distorted or blinded all her perceptions and have rendered her incapable of conveying empirical information.

In *Persuasion,* one gains knowledge as much by observing body language and facial expression as by listening to the spoken word, by attending to what the feminist linguist Deborah Tannen has called the "metaconversation" of speakers (Tannen 1990, 1994). Both Anne and Wentworth *blush,* and these uncontrollable bodily reactions communicate more than either can say. When Wentworth first sees Anne at Bath, "He was more obviously struck and confused by the sight of her, than she had ever observed before; he looked quite red" (116)—as we later learn, this is the point at which Wentworth has decided to pursue his courtship of Anne. And when Mrs. Smith observes Anne's physical appearance the day after the concert at which Anne has openly addressed Wentworth, she comments that "Your countenance perfectly informs me that you were in company last night with the person, whom you think the most agreeable in the world" (128). Anne's body then confirms the truth of this observation (even though Mrs. Smith has to herself incorrectly identified "the person"): "A blush overspread Anne's cheeks. She could say nothing" (128).

Because Anne has access to gossip, because she can read the language of the body, she gains knowledge unavailable to anyone else in her social circle. She learns from Mrs. Smith the truth about Mr. Elliot's sordid past and failed character, knowledge that prevents a possible future alliance that would have proved disastrous for her. And because she can read Wentworth's blush correctly, she is encouraged to address him at the concert, to insist on his attending her father's party. For Austen, then, truth is arrived at only when the isolated consciousness effects what Keats would call a "greeting of the spirit," only when it reaches out through both language and the body, through feelings and the imagination, to touch another. As Wentworth impulsively responds, taking up his dropped pen, "I can listen no longer in silence. I must speak to you by such means as are within my reach. You pierce my soul" (158). Through such reachings out, through the combined efforts of communication and of memory, one achieves not just truth but also a happiness so potent that Austen dares to identify it with the divine. As Anne and Wentworth stroll along the retired gravel walk, "the power of conversation would make the present hour a blessing, indeed; and prepare for it all the immortality which the happiest recollections of their own future lives could bestow" (160).

Persuasion thus serves as Jane Austen's response both to a Rousseauian or Jacobin republican politics and to a masculine Romantic poetics, both of which urged the isolated, risk-taking individual to create his own identity, his own destiny, entirely out of his own strong will and imagination. Such individuals are not safe rulers for the new England. They remain locked within a limited autonomy too willing to risk its all on a gamble, that finds security only in an ethic of justice that demands equal rights for all and in a social contract negotiated among a like-minded band of brothers, a contract that effectively excludes women from the public sphere. Instead Austen urges an alternative political model, the model of a family politic, a well-managed national household governed by a loving mother who is attentive to the needs of all her dependents.

Persuasion stands on the cusp of Britain's social and national transformation into a colonial empire on which the sun never set. Published in December 1817, a month after the death of Princess Charlotte, it engages the historical moment when England began to identify its new national identity with that of global commerce. As had Hannah More before her, Jane Austen affirmed that the project of managing or governing the motherland in a time of peaceful economic expansion is best carried out by women. The final sentences of *Persuasion* subtly but clearly make this point:

> Anne was tenderness itself, and she had the full worth of it in Captain Wentworth's affection. His profession was all that could ever make her friends wish that tenderness less; the dread of a future war all that could dim her sunshine. She gloried in being a sailor's wife, but she must pay the tax of quick alarm for belonging to that profession which is, if possible, more distinguished in its domestic virtues than in its national importance. (168)

Anne Elliot *is* tenderness, the very embodiment of a political ethic that insists that in any conflict, no one should be hurt. What rouses her greatest anxiety is the possibility of violence, of war; she would go to great lengths to resolve disputes without bloodshed, without unnecessary suffering. She is now a "tax-payer," a full-fledged citizen or member of the family politic. Most important, like Sophia Croft before her, she has chosen as her profession that of "sailor's wife"—note that Jane Austen deliberately uses the same word, "profession," to characterize both Wentworth's career and Anne's.

But Anne's profession is ranked above Wentworth's both in "national importance" and in "virtue." By patrolling the seas and protecting Britain's shores, Wentworth's profession enables Britain to expand and protect her imperial economy. But as Jane Austen had learned from her brothers in the Admiralty, the ranks of the British navy were susceptible to moral corruption and an overwhelming concern with personal financial gain, through the acquisition of prize money (see Hill 228). Henry Dundas, Viscount Melville, Pitt's Treasurer of the Navy from 1784 to 1800, had been notoriously impeached only a decade before, in 1806, for transferring the amazing amount of £8,000,000 from the Bank of England to his private account for the personal use of himself and his friends in the government and the navy. Austen was well aware of the navy's ethical failings and financial greed, as she indicates both in Mary Crawford's punning allusion in *Mansfield*

Park to her acquaintance with a circle of admirals—"Of *Rears* and *Vices*, I saw enough" (44)—and in Wentworth's unabashed reference to his own financial ambitions—"Ah, those were pleasant days when I had the *Laconia*! How fast I made money in her!" (45). In contrast, Anne's profession defines and sustains the very "domestic virtues" which constitute Britain's new sense of itself *as a nation*. It is the professional responsibility of the "wife" to construct this new "imagined community" of Britain as a harmonious family politic. It is the duty of the wife prudently to manage Britain's domestic economy of household investment and consumption, to carry out the "business" of civilized and Christian capitalism at home, and to protect the home front by ensuring offshore risk-taking against excessive speculation through the "tax of quick alarm." Even more important, as Anne Elliot and Sophia Croft demonstrate, it is the profession of women, of English wives, to define the very moral character or heart of the new British nation, to demonstrate tenderness toward all, to mother both the nation and her far-flung colonies, and thus to become the visible embodiment of Britannia herself.

That Jane Austen is here participating fully in a moment of cultural transformation, a moment in which British national identity is reconfigured as feminine, is illustrated perhaps most vividly by the change in British coinage in this period. The first widely distributed coin carrying the image of Britannia, the British copper penny, was minted in 1797, just after More published her *Cheap Repository Tracts,* and continued to be minted until the entire coinage system was revolutionized in 1816, the year Austen completed *Persuasion*. Britannia as a numismatic icon of Great Britain had first

4. British copper "cartwheel" penny, 1797.

5. British bronze penny, 1860.

appeared on the copper farthing in 1672, during the reign of Charles II (where the model for Britannia was the royal mistress Frances Teresa Stewart, later Duchess of Richmond and Lennox) and had been used again in 1714, on the extremely rare farthings struck in the last year of Queen Anne's reign; there Britannia is portrayed as a neoclassical deity, seated on rocklike clouds, floating in space, with Roman spear and olive branch. During the reign of George III, Britannia became the foremost numismatic symbol of Britain, displacing earlier mints in which the obverse of the coin had been given over to royal coats of arms. In 1797 Matthew Boulton and James Watt struck the first copper "cartwheel" penny on their new steam press in Birmingham. On the obverse to George III, who appears in Roman toga and laurel headdress, is Britannia, in a new design by Nathaniel Dance approved by the Coin Committee. Britannia here faces left (or west), holds out an olive branch and carries a trident, while her shield (sporting the Union Jack) rests beside her. She is seated on a rock surrounded by the sea, and flanked on both her front and rear (or western and eastern) borders by an English man-of-war (figure 4). In Dance's original drawing, the rock is engraved with the dates of three memorable naval victories: Lord Howe's Glorious First of June 1794; Hotham's capture of three French ships on 23 June 1795; and the defeat of the Spanish navy by Jervis off Cape St. Vincent on 14 February 1797 (Mackay 126–29). Britannia now clearly rules the waves, even as she is securely entrenched on her home turf.

After 1816, during the Regency and continuing through the reign of George IV, the new British coinage—the 1819 silver crown, the 1820 gold sovereign, the 1823 gold two-pound piece—all attempted to remasculinize British national identity by carrying on the obverse Pistrucci's image of St.

George on horseback, slaying the dragon—although the copper penny retained the image of Britannia. But when Victoria came to the throne, St. George disappeared from British coinage for almost half a century. The new mints under Victoria's reign carried on the obverse either an image of Una riding the British lion (as on the five-pound silver piece designed by William Wyon in 1839) or, in all other minted coinage, the image of Victoria as Britannia, as on the widely circulated silver groat (1838–87). On the new bronze penny of 1860, the traditional image of Britannia is reversed. Britannia now faces right or east, toward India and the British Empire (figure 5). She is helmeted, with shield and trident (but no olive branch), firmly fixed on her rock, and flanked by both a man-of-war and a lighthouse, symbols of Britain's combined military and technological imperial supremacy brought about by the care and discipline of the Mother of the Nation.

Postscript

The Politics of Modernity

I have been arguing throughout this book that the women writers of the Romantic era in Britain participated fully in the public sphere as Habermas defined it, substantively shaping public opinion during this period. Moreover, the public opinion they promoted engaged directly in the emancipatory project of enlightened rationality celebrated by Habermas. Women writers contributed significantly to the success of the abolitionist campaigns to end the slave trade and to emancipate the slaves in the British colonies in the West Indies. They successfully called for a "revolution in manners," both in female manners and in the mores of the nation as a whole. They helped to bring about a visible change in the social construction of gender, by producing the model of a New Woman—a rational, just, yet merciful, virtuous, benevolent, and peace-loving female—who was capable of providing intellectual and moral guidance both at home and in the public realm. And as the career of Hannah More documents, they radically changed the moral culture of the nation, helping to redefine Britain as a nation of Christian virtue as well as of liberty. Their interventions—through the agency of the discursive public sphere—thus had political and economic consequences so far-reaching that they call into question the prevailing scholarly assumptions that women did not participate in the public sphere or that a locatable dividing line between the private and the public sphere, however broadly or narrowly defined, existed in England between 1780 and 1830.

A striking visual confirmation of their success in redefining the image of the ideal British woman occurs in a design by Lord George Murray that was widely circulated in 1792 by the loyalist Association for the Preservation of Liberty and Property against Republicans and Levellers. Etched by Thomas Rowlandson, *The Contrast/1792/Which Is Best* visually represents two opposing modes of feminized national identity or governance: England's Britannia versus France's Marianne (figure 6). "French Liberty" is portrayed as an Amazonian harridan with Medusa-like, snaky hair, carrying a sword and triumphantly brandishing on her pitchfork the head of the decapitated male corpse beneath her foot. Another hanged gentleman swings from the lamppost behind her, emphasizing that her savage revolutionary fury is directed especially against males.

6. Thomas Rowlandson after a design by Lord George Murray: *The Contrast/1792/ Which Is Best*, 1792. Hand-colored etching. © The British Museum, London.

In contrast, "British Liberty," or Britannia, appears holding the scales of Justice in one hand, the Magna Carta in the other. Modestly dressed, wearing the helmet of Athena, the Union Jack engraved on the shield that forms the side of her chair, with the British lion sleeping beside her, Britannia is an icon of prosperous peace and happiness, guarded by the British man-of-war before her. Most notable, however, is the fact that Britannia holds the traditional staff and Phrygian cap of Liberty. This new Britannia, even as she forswears French license and violence and instead promotes the domestic virtues listed below her—"Religion, Morality, Loyalty, Obedience to the Laws, Independance, Personal Security, Justice, Inheritance, Protection, Property, Industry, National Prosperity, Happiness"—nonetheless embraces that "Independance" or "female revolution in manners" explicitly advocated by Mary Wollstonecraft in 1792.

Promoting the concept of women as the mothers of the newly reformed British nation had problematic historical consequences far beyond what Hannah More and other women writers of the Romantic era could predict. By the mid-nineteenth century, in a period of anti-feminist backlash, as had happened in post-revolutionary France (see Landes), the figure of the Mother of the Nation, even of Britannia or Queen Victoria herself (see Munich), was rewritten as the Angel in the House, a woman whose moral and intellectual roles were entirely confined to the private household. In this sense, one could argue that the feminist moral purity campaigns of Hannah More and other Romantic-era British women writers backfired. The very trope that authorized a claim to public influence—the trope of the virtuous Christian mother of the nation—could be and was used to enforce a newly hegemonic doctrine of rigidly divided and separate sexual spheres, a doctrine that confined the cultural influence of the virtuous Christian woman entirely within the bounds of the patriarchal private family.

The concept of the mother of the nation could also be—and subsequently was—used to justify Britain's colonial imperialism. As the British Empire attempted to incorporate peoples of varying racial, cultural, and political identities into a single commercial and political commonwealth, it troped that commonwealth as a harmonious and affectionate family, one presided over by a nurturing and peace-loving mother, Britannia. The British Empire thus attempted to incorporate racial and ethnic difference into what Mary Poovey, in her study of Florence Nightingale, has described as the disciplined domesticity of the British household, in which conquest and colonial rule were rewritten as "the government of love, . . . superintended by a motherly monarch" (196). The symbolic expansion of the Mother of the British Nation into the Mother of the British Empire coincided with the effort to assimilate cultural, ethnic, and racial difference into a unified family politic, one which promoted the ideological superiority of Euro-centric, Christian values and which anxiously tried to find sameness within what Homi Bhabha has seen as a practically infinite range of hybridities.

Nonetheless, Romantic-era women writers' early formulations of the concept of the Mother of the Nation often displayed a tolerance and even appreciation of cultural and racial differences far greater than that manifested by most of the male writers of this period. As Saree Makdisi has shown in his studies of Wordsworth, Scott, Burke, De Quincey, and James Mill, these writers promoted a concept of an autonomous self that defined itself in opposition, even in hostile antagonism, to the racial or ethnic other. By evincing a great deal more interest in and sympathy for racial and cultural difference, women's political writing of the Romantic period could be said to initiate what Makdisi has called the "culture of modernity," the global consciousness now characteristic of the twenty-first century.

For examples of such global consciousness or tolerance of ethnic and racial diversity in the writings of Romantic-era women, one might look first to Anna Barbauld's "Eighteen Hundred and Eleven," a poem which celebrates the heterogeneous population of London:

> The mighty city, which by every road,
> In floods of people poured itself abroad;
> Ungirt by walls, irregularly great,
> No jealous drawbridge, and no closing gate;
> Whose merchants (such the state which commerce brings)
> Sent forth their mandates to dependant kings;
> Streets, where the turban'd Moslem, bearded Jew,
> And wooly Afric, met the brown Hindu;
> Where through each vein spontaneous plenty flowed,
> Where wealth enjoyed, and Charity bestowed. (lines 159–68)

One might also look to Amelia Opie's novel *Adeline Mowbray* (1802), which sites the future salvation of the British body politic in a reconstituted family of choice, one composed of an upper-class British woman, a middle-class Quaker woman, and a working-class freed African slave woman. Or to Charlotte Smith's novel *The Old Manor House* (1794), in which the hero is saved only through the good will of a Native American chief. Or to Esme Erskine's epic poem *Alcon Malanzor* (1815), which represents the inter-racial, inter-faith marriage of the Muslim Moor Malanzor with the Spanish Catholic Rosalind as the only viable political solution to international warfare. These, and numerous other examples I might cite—from Joanna Baillie's *Raynor* to Elizabeth Inchbald's *The Way Things Are* to Hannah Cowley's *A Day in Turkey,* from Elizabeth Hamilton's *Translation of the Memoirs of a Hindoo Rajah* to Marianna Starke's *The Widow of Malabar* and Letitia Landon's "A Suttee"—all suggest that the women writers of the

Romantic era embraced the multi-ethnicity and racial intermixing of the growing British Empire with interested sympathy rather than with horror or dismay, thus introducing a new standpoint into the public debate on how the expanding British nation could best incorporate such hybridities.

The political debates initiated by women writers during the Romantic period are by no means resolved; they are waged as aggressively in our contemporary media as they were in the early nineteenth century. Does motherhood empower or confine women? Are family values a viable model for political governance? What is the proper relationship of an ethic of justice to an ethic of care, of a rights-based to a needs-based distribution of social goods and services? How should a nation respond to cultural and racial difference? By developing the concept of the Mother of the Nation, the women writers of the Romantic era should at the very least be credited with intelligently formulating such questions and entering them into the forum of open rational debate, into the discursive public sphere.

Notes

1. Hannah More, Revolutionary Reformer

1. Hannah More thus participated directly in the cultural and political process of "imagining the middle class" so well described by Dror Wahrman. The "middle class" within which she located the moral standard for the nation as a whole included the landed gentry down through the professionals and men of business to the shopkeeper who owned his own shop, those men who possessed ten pounds of capital and who were thereby qualified to vote under the Reform Bill of 1832. For More, this newly imagined, respectable middle class was unified by its commitments to Christian capitalism, the virtues of domesticity, and the imperial projects of the British nation.

Dror Wahrman rightly locates More's writing within the genre of "domestic literature," which increasingly equated this newly imagined middle class with domesticity (395–96). However, by confining himself to only one text by Hannah More, her *Strictures on the Modern System of Female Education,* Wahrman fails to recognize the degree to which the *middle-class* woman, whether embodied in the widow of modest means, Mrs. Jones of the *Cheap Repository Tracts,* or the gentleman's daughter, Lucilla Stanley of *Coelebs in Search of a Wife,* was for More the best source of social merit and spiritual virtue. The example of Hannah More thus calls into question Wahrman's insistence that the "middle-class idiom" was exclusively male before 1832 (380–90). In her works published between 1790 and 1830, More repeatedly identifies virtuous domesticity with the middle class (and especially the middle-class woman), while she represents the aristocratic woman of "Society" as one who too easily succumbs to the domination of fashion, a fashion that More finally equated with the female white slave trade in her trenchant essay "Hints towards forming a Bill for the Abolition of the White Female Slave Trade, in the Cities of London and Westminster," published in *The Weekly Entertainer* 45 (12 August 1805).

2. Theater as the School of Virtue

1. Paula Backscheider has drawn attention to Inchbald's fascination with "the stern, nearly tyrannical, father-figure" in both her fiction and her drama (Backscheider 1980: xxxii).

2. Inchbald's essays on British drama, discussed elsewhere in this volume, take a far more positive view of the spinster, as Anna Lott has observed (Lott 639–40).

3. Women's Political Poetry

1. Bartolomé de Las Casas was the single greatest defender of the rights of the AmerIndians during the Spanish Conquest in the sixteenth century, but he advocated importing slaves from Africa to replace the AmerIndians enslaved by the Spanish (Las Casas xix), a fact that Williams does not take into account.

2. The perception, first promulgated by Lucy Aikin, that the negative reviews of "Eighteen Hundred and Eleven" effectively brought Barbauld's writing career to an end (Wu 9; cf. Keach) is erroneous. Although "Eighteen Hundred and Eleven," a long poem of 334 lines, was her last *separately published* volume of verse, issued when she was 69 years old, Barbauld continued to publish individual poems under her own name in literary reviews and annuals for several more years. Her poem "On the Death of the Princess Charlotte," first titled "Elegy," was published in the *Annual Register . . . for the Year 1818* (1819) and signed "Mrs. B——d." "A Thought on Death" first appeared in Boston in the *Christian Disciple* (Nov.–Dec. 1821), and was then reprinted in Barbauld's corrected version in the *Monthly Repository* in November 1822, over her name. Moreover, she continued to edit the Rivington reprint series of novels, and during the final decade of her life, she collaborated with her niece Lucy Aikin in the preparation of her collected *Works,* which appeared shortly after her death in 1825.

3. It is possible that Lucy Aikin was familiar with the poet Jane Adams's similar omission of Eve's creation from Adam's rib in her poetic rewriting of Milton's *Paradise Lost* in her *Miscellany Poems* (Glasgow, 1734). In *"Adam* on the Formation [of] *Eve,"* Jane Adams eliminates Milton's description of Adam witnessing God's creation of Eve out of his rib while in an imaginative trance. Her Eve is still formed out of Adam's rib, but Adam sleeps through this creation; nor does God appear directly. In Jane Adams's words:

> Thus by my kind Creator an Arrest
> Was clapt on all the Organs of my Sense.
> His forming Hand he thought not fit to shew,
> Yet in his Work I could his Wisdom read;
> The fair unspotted Object met mine Eyes,
> When from my Slumber I at first awoke. (142–43)

On Jane Adams's feminist revisioning of *Paradise Lost,* see Leslie E. Moore, 74–83.

4. Literary Criticism, Cultural Authority, and the Rise of the Novel

1. For Anna Barbauld's comment on *The Rime of the Ancient Mariner,* see Coleridge's reminiscence, dated 31 May 1830, in *Coleridge's Table Talk* I: 27 and note 6. For an analysis of the unresolved contradictions in Coleridge's poem, see my *English Romantic Irony* 137–64.

2. Beyond a single citation of Clara Reeve, Wellek does not consider the contributions of women to literary criticism in the Romantic period.

3. On the impact of lending libraries on women as readers and writers, and on the popularity of women writers in the Romantic era, see my *Romanticism and Gender,* chap. 1 and conclusion. Byron, for instance, greatly admired Joanna Baillie, claiming that she "is our only dramatist since Otway & Southern—I don't except [John] Home" and has somehow "borrowed" the *"testicles"* required to write tragedy (*Letters and Journals* III: 109, V: 203).

4. The locus classicus of this argument is Samuel Johnson's fourth *Rambler* (31 March 1750), reprinted in *The British Essayists,* ed. Alexander Chalmers (London: J. Johnson, 1802), 19.

5. For detailed summaries of Baillie's theory of dramatic art, see Ross and Burroughs.

6. On the nature and function of the social sphere, located midway between a public and a private sphere, see Riley, chap. 3, and Hansen.

5. The Politics of Fiction

1. For an analysis of the family and career of Charles-François Depont, see Robert Forster, *Merchants, Landlords, Magistrates: The Depont Family in Eighteenth-Century France* (Baltimore: Johns Hopkins University Press, 1980).

2. All citations from Charlotte Smith's *Desmond* (London, 1792) are by page number, from the modern, superbly introduced and annotated edition, *Desmond,* by Charlotte Smith, ed. Antje Blank and Janet Todd (London: Pickering and Chatto, 1997). I am deeply indebted to both the notes and introduction of this edition.

3. Although Charlotte Smith ends Desmond's account of the Breton sailor with a footnote attesting that "the latter part of this narrative is a sort of free translation of parts of a little pamphlet, entitled, 'Histoire d'un malheureux Vassal de Bretagne, écrite par lui-même,' in which the excessive abuses to which the feudal system gave birth, are detailed," thus providing "evidence" for her account, Antje Blank and Janet Todd report that they have been unable to locate a copy of this pamphlet, and suggest that Smith may have "fabricated" both this pamphlet and the *Lettre aux Aristo-theocrate Français* to which she refers earlier (60n) in order "to lend greater documentary realism to her narrative" (413n48).

4. Diana Bowstead (241–45) has drawn attention to the ways in which food and agricultural cultivation (or the lack thereof) function as a marker of aristocratic excess and decay in *Desmond.*

5. Diana Bowstead has analyzed the nexus of symbolism in *Desmond* which links animals (horse, cattle, lizard) with the wife, white slave, and black slave in *Desmond* (257).

6. All citations from Jane Austen's *Persuasion* are by page number from the Norton Critical Edition of the novel, ed. Patricia Meyer Spacks (1995).

7. For an extended and insightful discussion of the emergence of "inner beauty" as a category of moral aesthetics in the Romantic era, see Leilani Riehle's *Inner Beauty, Taste and Cultural Hegemony in Early Nineteenth-Century Women's Fiction,* Ph.D. dissertation, UCLA, 2000. Also see Deirdre Shauna Lynch, *The Economy of Character: Novels, Market Culture, and the Business of Inner Meaning* (Chicago: University of Chicago Press, 1998).

Works Cited

Abrams, Meyer H. *The Mirror and the Lamp: Romantic Theory and the Critical Tradition*. New York: W. W. Norton, 1958.

Aikin, Lucy. *Epistles on Women, Exemplifying Their Character and Condition in Various Ages and Nations*. London, 1810. Reprinted in *British Literature, 1780–1830,* ed. Anne K. Mellor and Richard Matlak, 816–37. Fort Worth, Tex.: Harcourt Brace College, 1997.

Aldridge, Alfred Owen. "Madame de Staël and Hannah More on Society." *Romantic Review* 38 (1947): 330–39.

Altick, Richard D. *The English Common Reader: A Social History of the Mass Reading Public, 1800–1900*. Chicago: University of Chicago Press, 1957.

Andrew, Donna. *Philanthropy and Police: London Charity in the 18th Century*. Princeton, N.J.: Princeton University Press, 1989.

———, ed. *London Debating Societies, 1776–1799*. London: London Record Society, 1994.

Armstrong, Isobel. *Victorian Poetry: Poetry, Poetics and Politics*. London: Routledge, 1993.

Armstrong, Nancy. *Desire and Domestic Fiction: A Political History of the Novel*. New York: Oxford University Press, 1987.

Austen, Jane. *Jane Austen's Letters*. Edited by Dierdre Le Faye. 3rd ed. Oxford: Oxford University Press, 1995.

———. *Mansfield Park*. Edited by Claudia L. Johnson. New York: W. W. Norton, 1998.

———. *Persuasion*. Edited by Patricia Meyer Spacks. New York: W. W. Norton, 1995.

———. *Pride and Prejudice*. Edited by Donald Gray. New York: W. W. Norton, 1966.

Backscheider, Paula R. Introduction to *The Plays of Elizabeth Inchbald*. 2 vols. New York: Garland, 1980.

Backscheider, Paula R., and Timothy Dykstal, eds. *The Intersections of the Public and Private Spheres in Early Modern England*. London: Frank Cass, 1996.

Baillie, Joanna. *A Series of Plays: in which it is attempted to delineate the Stronger Passions of the Mind. Each Passion being the Subject of a Tragedy and a Comedy*. London: T. Cadell, 1798. Facsimile reprint, Oxford: Woodstock Books, 1990.

Baker, Keith Michael. "Defining the Public Sphere in Eighteenth-Century France: Variations on a Theme by Habermas." In *Habermas and the Public Sphere,* edited by Craig Calhoun, 181–211. Cambridge, Mass.: MIT Press, 1996.

Balfour, Clara Lucas. *A Sketch of Mrs. Hannah More and Her Sisters*. London: W. and F. G. Cash, 1854.

Barbauld, Anna Letitia. *An Address to the Opposers of the Repeal of the Corporation and Test Acts*. London: J. Johnson, 1790.

———. *The Correspondence of Samuel Richardson . . . [with] Observations on his Writings by Anna Letitia Barbauld*. London, 1804. Reprint (2 vols.), New York: AMS Press, 1966.

———. "On the Origin and Progress of Novel-Writing." In *The British Novelists; with An Essay, and Prefaces, Biographical and Critical.* Vol. 1. London: Rivington, 1810. 40 vols.

———. *The Poems of Anna Letitia Barbauld.* Edited by William McCarthy and Elizabeth Kraft. Athens: University of Georgia Press, 1994.

Barrell, John. "'The Dangerous Goddess': Masculinity, Prestige, and the Aesthetic in Early Eighteenth Century Britain." *Cultural Critique* 1989: 101–31.

Barry, Jonathan, and Christopher Brooks, eds. *The Middling Sort of People: Culture, Society and Politics in England, 1550–1800.* London: Macmillan, 1994.

Beetham, Margaret. *A Magazine of Her Own? Domesticity and Desire in the Woman's Magazine, 1800–1914.* London: Routledge, 1996.

Bell, R. C. *The Boardgame Book.* London: Marshall Cavendish, 1979.

Berg, Maxine. "Women's Work, Mechanisation, and the Early Phase of Industrialisation in England." In *The Historical Meanings of Work,* edited by P. Joyce, 64–98. Cambridge: Cambridge University Press, 1987.

Bermingham, Ann, and John Brewer, eds. *The Consumption of Culture, 1600–1800: Image, Object, Text.* Vol. 3 of *Consumption and Culture in the 17th and 18th Centuries.* London: Routledge, 1995.

Best, Geoffrey. "Evangelicalism and the Victorians." In *The Victorian Crisis of Faith,* edited by Anthony Symondson, 37–56. London: S. P. C. K., 1970.

Bhabha, Homi. "Signs Taken for Wonders: Questions of Ambivalence and Authority under a Tree outside Delhi, May 1817." In *Europe and Its Others,* edited by Francis Barker, 80–97. Colchester: University of Essex Press, 1984.

Birrell, Augustine. "Hannah More." In *Essays about Men, Women and Books,* 70–80. New York: Charles Scribner's Sons, 1894.

———. "Hannah More Once More." In *In the Name of the Bodleian and Other Essays,* 172–82. New York: Charles Scribner's Sons, 1905.

Boaden, James. *Memoirs of Elizabeth Inchbald.* 2 vols. London: Richard Bentley, 1833.

Bolt, Christine, and Seymour Dresher, eds. *Anti-Slavery, Religion and Reform: Essays in Honour of Roger Anstey.* Folkestone, Kent: William Dawson and Sons; Hamden, Conn.: Archon Books, 1980.

Booth, Wayne C. *The Rhetoric of Fiction.* Chicago: University of Chicago Press, 1983.

Bowstead, Diana. "Charlotte Smith's *Desmond:* The Epistolary Novel as Ideological Argument." In *Fetter'd or Free? British Women Novelists, 1670–1815,* edited by Mary Anne Schofield and Cecilia Macheski, 237–63. Athens: Ohio University Press, 1986.

Bradley, Ian. *The Call to Seriousness: The Evangelical Impact on the Victorians.* New York: Macmillan, 1976.

Bray, Matthew. "Removing the Anglo-Saxon Yoke: The Francocentric Vision of Charlotte Smith's Later Works." *The Wordsworth Circle* 24 (1993): 155–58.

Brewer, John. *Party Ideology and Popular Politics at the Accession of George III.* Cambridge: Cambridge University Press, 1976.

———. *The Pleasures of the Imagination: English Culture in the Eighteenth Century.* London: Harper Collins, 1997.

———. *The Sinews of Power: War, Money and the English State, 1688–1783.* Cambridge: Harvard University Press, 1988.

———. "This, that and the other: Public, Social and Private in the Seventeenth and Eighteenth Centuries." In *Shifting the Boundaries: Transformation of the Languages of Public and Private in the Eighteenth Century,* edited by Dario Castiglione and Lesley Sharpe. Exeter: University of Exeter Press, 1995.

Brewer, John, and Roy Porter, eds. *Consumption and the World of Goods.* Vol. 1 of *Consumption and Culture in the 17th and 18th Centuries.* London: Routledge, 1993.

Brewer, John, and Susan Staves, eds. *Early Modern Conceptions of Property.* Vol. 2 of *Consumption and Culture in the 17th and 18th Centuries.* London: Routledge, 1995.

Briggs, Asa. "Middle-Class Consciousness in English Politics, 1780–1846." *Past and Present* 9 (April 1956): 65–74.

Brown, Ford K. *Fathers of the Victorians: The Age of Wilberforce.* Cambridge: Cambridge University Press, 1961.

Burke, Edmund. *Reflections on the Revolution in France.* Edited with introduction and notes by J. G. A. Pocock. Indianapolis: Hackett, 1987.

Burroughs, Catherine B. *Closet Stages: Joanna Baillie and the Theater Theory of the British Romantic Women Writers.* Philadelphia: University of Pennsylvania Press, 1997.

Bush, Barbara. *Slave Women in Caribbean Society, 1650–1838.* Kingston: Heinemann; and Bloomington: Indiana University Press, 1990.

Butler, Marilyn. *Jane Austen and the War of Ideas.* Oxford: Clarendon Press, 1975.

Byron, Lord. *Byron's Letters and Journals.* Edited by Leslie A. Marchand. 11 vols. London: John Murray, 1973–82.

Calhoun, Craig, ed. *Habermas and the Public Sphere.* Cambridge, Mass.: MIT Press, 1992.

Campbell, Colin. *The Romantic Ethic and the Spirit of Modern Consumerism.* Oxford: Blackwell, 1987.

Castiglione, Dario, and Lesley Sharpe, eds. *Shifting the Boundaries: Transformation of the Languages of Public and Private in the Eighteenth Century.* Exeter: University of Exeter Press, 1995.

Chatterton, Georgiana, Lady. *Memorials Personal and Historical of Admiral Lord Gambier, G. C. B.* London: Hurst and Blackett, 1861.

Child, Philip. "Portrait of a Woman of Affairs—Old Style." *University of Toronto Quarterly* 3 (1933–34): 87–102.

Cole, Lucinda. "(Anti)Feminist Sympathies: The Politics of Relationship in Smith, Wollstonecraft, and More." *ELH* 58 (1991): 107–40.

Coleman, Dierdre. "Conspicuous Consumption: White Abolitionism and English Women's Protest Writing in the 1790s." *ELH* 61 (1994): 341–62.

Coleridge, Samuel Taylor. *Table Talk.* Edited by Carl Woodring. In *The Collected Works of Samuel Taylor Coleridge.* Vol. 14. Princeton, N.J.: Princeton University Press, 1990.

Colley, Linda. *Britons: Forging the Nation, 1707–1837.* New Haven, Conn.: Yale University Press, 1992.

Conway, Alison. "Nationalism, Revolution, and the Female Body: Charlotte Smith's *Desmond,*" *Women's Studies* 24 (1995): 395–409.

Copeland, Edward. "The Austens and the Elliots: A Consumer's Guide to *Persuasion.*" In *Jane Austen's Business: Her World and Her Profession,* edited by Juliet McMaster and Bruce Stovel, 136–53. Hampshire, England; and New York: Macmillan/St. Martin's Press, 1996.

Corrigan, Philip, and Derek Sayer. *The Great Arch: English State Formation as Cultural Revolution.* Oxford: Blackwell, 1985.

Corvey Library Catalogue of Fiction. Dienst, Germany: Belser Wissenschaftlicher, 1994.

Cott, Nancy F. *The Bonds of Womanhood: "Woman's Sphere" in New England, 1780–1835.* New Haven, Conn.: Yale University Press, 1977.

————. "Passionlessness: An Interpretation of Victorian Sexual Ideology, 1790–1850." *Signs* 4 (1978): 219–36.

Cowley, Hannah. *The Plays of Hannah Cowley*. Edited by Frederick M. Link. 2 vols. New York: Garland, 1979.

————. *The School of Eloquence, An Interlude*. Huntington Library ms. LA 515.

————. *The World as it Goes, or A Party at Montpelier*. Huntington Library ms. LA 548.

Cropper, Margaret. *Sparks among the Stubble*. London: Longmans, Green & Co., 1955.

Daunton, Martin. *Progress and Poverty: An Economic and Social History of Britain 1700–1850*. Oxford: Oxford University Press, 1995.

Davidoff, Leonore. *Worlds Between: Historical Perspectives on Gender and Class*. New York: Routledge, 1995.

Davidoff, Leonore, and Catherine Hall. *Family Fortunes: Men and Women of the English Middle Class, 1780–1850*. Chicago: University of Chicago Press, 1987.

Delicious Game of the Fruit-Basket: . . . to which are prefixed The Rules of the Game. London: William Darton, 1822.

Demers, Patricia. *The World of Hannah More*. Lexington: University Press of Kentucky, 1996.

Dickinson, H. T. "Popular Conservatism and Militant Loyalism, 1789–1815." In *Britain and the French Revolution, 1789–1815*, edited by H. T. Dickinson, 103–26. London: Macmillan, 1989.

————. "Popular Loyalism in Britain in the 1790s." In *The Transformation of Political Culture: England and Germany in the Late Eighteenth Century*, edited by Erkhart Hellmuth, 503–34. London: German Historical Institute/Oxford University Press, 1990.

Donald, Diana. *The Age of Caricature: Satirical Prints in the Age of George III*. New Haven, Conn.: Yale University Press, 1996.

Doody, Margaret Anne. "English Women Novelists and the French Revolution." In *La Femme en Angleterre et dans les Colonies Americaines aux XVIIe et XVIIIe Siècles*, 176–98. Lille: Presses Universitaires de Lille and de l'Université de la Sorbonne Nouvelle, 1975.

————. *The True Story of the Novel*. New Brunswick, N.J.: Rutgers University Press, 1996.

Eagleton, Terry. *The Rape of Clarissa: Writing, Sexuality, and Class Struggle in Samuel Richardson*. Oxford: Blackwell, 1982.

The Edinburgh Review, or Critical Journal XIV (April–July 1809). Edinburgh: Archibald Constable, 1809.

Eley, Geoff. "Nations, Publics, and Political Cultures: Placing Habermas in the Nineteenth Century." In *Habermas and the Public Sphere*, edited by Craig Calhoun, 289–339. Cambridge, Mass.: MIT Press, 1992.

Elias, Norbert. *The Civilizing Process* (1939). Translated by Edmund Jephcott. 2 vols: *The History of Manners* and *Power and Civility*. New York: Pantheon Books, 1982.

Elliott, Dorice. "'The Care of the Poor is Her Profession': Hannah More and Women's Philanthropic Work." *Nineteenth-Century Contexts* 19 (1995): 179–204.

Elliott, Pat. "Charlotte Smith's Feminism: A Study of *Emmeline* and *Desmond*." In *Living by the Pen: Early British Women Writers*, edited by Dale Spender, 91–112. New York: Teachers College Press, 1992.

Evans, M. J. Crossley. "The English Evangelicals and the Enlightenment: The Case of Hannah More." In *Transactions of the Eighth International Congress on the Enlightenment*, 458–62. Oxford: University of Oxford, 1992.

Ezell, Margaret J. M. *Writing Women's Literary History*. Baltimore: Johns Hopkins University Press, 1993.

Favret, Mary A. *Romantic Correspondence: Women, Politics and the Fiction of Letters*. Cambridge: Cambridge University Press, 1993.

Felski, Rita. *Beyond Feminist Aesthetics: Feminist Literature and Social Change*. Cambridge, Mass.: Harvard University Press, 1989.

Ferguson, Moira. *Subject to Others: British Women Writers and Colonial Slavery, 1670–1834*. New York: Routledge, 1992.

Foakes, R. A. "Coleridge, Napoleon and Nationalism." In *Literature and Nationalism*, edited by Vincent Newey and Ann Thompson, 140–51. Liverpool: Liverpool University Press, 1991.

Ford, Charles Howard. *Hannah More: A Critical Biography*. New York: Peter Lang, 1996.

Forster, Robert. *Merchants, Landlords, Magistrates: The Depont Family in Eighteenth-Century France*. Baltimore: Johns Hopkins University Press, 1980.

Foster, Charles I. *An Errand of Mercy: The Evangelical United Front, 1790–1837*. Chapel Hill: University of North Carolina Press, 1960.

Fraser, Nancy. "Rethinking the Public Sphere: A Contribution to the Critique of Actually Existing Democracy." Chap. 3 in her *Justice Interruptus: Critical Reflections on the "Postsocialist" Condition*. New York: Routledge, 1997.

Gagen, Jean. "The Weaker Sex: Hannah Cowley's Treatment of Men in her Comedies of Courtship and Marriage." *Studies in English* 8 (1990): 107–16.

George, M. Dorothy. *Catalogue of the Political and Personal Satires in the Department of Prints and Drawings, British Museum*. Vol. 8 (1801–1810). London: British Museum, 1954.

Gilbert, Alan D. *Religion and Society in Industrial England: Church, Chapel, and Social Change, 1740–1914*. London: Longman, 1976.

Gilbert, Sandra, and Susan Gubar. *The Madwoman in the Attic: The Woman Writer and the Nineteenth-Century Literary Imagination*. New Haven, Conn.: Yale University Press, 1979.

Gilmour, Ian. *Riots, Risings and Revolution: Governance and Violence in Eighteenth-Century England*. London: Pimlico, 1992.

Grogan, Claire. "Mary Wollstonecraft and Hannah More: Politics, Feminism and Modern Critics." *Lumen: Selected Proceedings from the Canadian Society for Eighteenth-Century Studies* XIII (1994): 99–107.

Habermas, Jürgen. *The Structural Transformation of the Public Sphere: An Inquiry into a Category of Bourgeois Society*. Translated by Thomas Burger with the assistance of Frederick Lawrence. Cambridge, Mass.: MIT Press, 1991.

Hall, Catherine. "The Early Formation of Victorian Domestic Ideology." In *Fit Work for Women*, edited by Sandra Burman. London: Croom Helm, 1979. Reprinted in Hall's *White, Male and Middle Class: Explorations in Feminism and History*, 75–93. London: Routledge, 1992.

Hall-Witt, Jennifer. "Women and Sociability at the Italian Opera in Early Victorian London." Paper delivered at the Clark Library, UCLA, Workshop on "Women in the Theatre, 1700–1850," 2 May 1998.

Hammond, John L., and Barbara Hammond. *The Town Labourer: The New Civilisation, 1760–1832*. London, 1917; rev. 1928. Reprinted with preface by Asa Briggs, Garden City, N.Y.: Archon Books, 1968.

Hansen, Karen. *A Very Social Time: Crafting Community in Antebellum New England*. Berkeley: University of California Press, 1994.

Harding, Sandra. "Rethinking Standpoint Epistemology: What is 'Strong Objectivity'?" In *Feminist Epistemologies,* edited by Linda Alcoff and Elizabeth Potter, 49–82. New York: Routledge, 1992.

Harland, Marion [pseud. Mary Virginia (Hawes) Terhune]. *Hannah More.* New York: G. P. Putnam's Sons, 1900.

Hartsock, Nancy C. M. *Money, Sex, and Power: Toward a Feminist Historical Materialism.* New York: Longman, 1983. Reprint, Boston: Northeastern University Press, 1985.

Harvey, A. D. *Britain in the Early Nineteenth Century.* London: B. T. Batsford, 1978.
———. *Sex in Georgian England: Attitudes and Prejudices from the 1720s to the 1820s.* London: Duckworth, 1994.

Haskell, Thomas. "Capitalism and the Origins of the Humanitarian Sensibility." Parts 1 and 2, in *The Antislavery Debate: Capitalism and Abolitionism as a Problem in Historical Interpretation,* edited by Thomas Bender. Berkeley: University of California Press, 1992.

Hawkesworth, Mary E. "Knowers, Knowing, Known: Feminist Theory and Claims of Truth." *Signs* 14 (1989): 533–57.

Hays, Mary. *Letters and Essays, Moral and Miscellaneous.* London, 1793.

Hemans, Felicia. *Memorials of Mrs. Hemans.* Edited by Henry F. Chorley. 2 vols. New York, 1836.

Hemingway, Andrew. *Landscape Imagery and Urban Culture in Early Nineteenth-Century Britain.* Cambridge: Cambridge University Press, 1992.

Hennell, Michael. "A Little-Known Social Revolution." *The Church Quarterly Review* 143 (1947): 189–207.

Hill, Richard. *The Prizes of War: The Naval Prize System in the Napoleonic Wars, 1793–1815.* London: Royal Naval Museum Publications/Sutton Publishing, 1998.

Hole, Robert. *Pulpits, Politics and Public Order in England, 1760–1832.* Cambridge: Cambridge University Press, 1989.

Hopkins, Robert. "Moral Luck and Judgment in Jane Austen's *Persuasion.*" *Nineteenth-Century Literature* 42 (1987): 143–58.

Inchbald, Elizabeth. *The Plays of Elizabeth Inchbald.* 2 vols. New York: Garland, 1980.
———. *Remarks for The British Theatre.* London: Longman, 1806–1809. Facsimile reprint of Inchbald's *Remarks* with an introduction by Cecilia Macheski, Delmar, N.Y.: Scholar's Facsimiles and Reprints, 1990. Since this facsimile does not provide consecutive pagination, I cite Inchbald's comments by author and play in my text.

Isikoff, Erin. "Masquerade, Modesty, and Comedy in Hannah Cowley's *The Belle's Stratagem.*" In *Look Who's Laughing: Gender and Comedy,* edited by Gail Finney, 99–117. Langhorne, Pa.: Gordon & Breach, 1995.

Jackson, J. R. de J. *Romantic Poetry by Women: A Bibliography, 1770–1835.* Oxford: Clarendon Press, 1993.

Jacobs, Edward. "'Circulating-Library Manufacture': Circulating Libraries and the Cultivation of Generic Writing by Female and Anonymous Authors." Paper delivered at Scenes of Writing Conference, Gregynog, University of Wales, 21 July 1998.

Jaeger, Muriel. *Before Victoria.* London: Chatto and Windus, 1956.

Jay, Elizabeth. *The Religion of the Heart: Anglican Evangelicalism and the Nineteenth-Century Novel.* Oxford: Clarendon Press, 1979.

Johnson, Claudia L. *Equivocal Beings: Politics, Gender, and Sentimentality in the 1790s: Wollstonecraft, Radcliffe, Burney, Austen.* Chicago: University of Chicago Press, 1995.
———. *Jane Austen: Women, Politics, and the Novel.* Chicago: University of Chicago Press, 1988.

Jones, Ann H. *Ideas and Innovations: Best Sellers of Jane Austen's Age.* New York: AMS Press, 1986.

Jones, Chris. *Radical Sensibility: Literature and Ideas in the 1790s.* London: Routledge, 1993.

Jones, M. G. *The Charity School Movement: A Study of Eighteenth Century Puritanism in Action.* Cambridge: Cambridge University Press, 1938. Reprint, London: Frank Cass, 1964.

———. *Hannah More.* Cambridge: Cambridge University Press, 1952.

Jordan, Winthrop D. *White over Black: American Attitudes Toward the Negro, 1500–1812.* Chapel Hill: University of North Carolina, 1968.

Kaufman, Paul. *Libraries and Their Users: Collected Papers in Library History.* London: The Library Association, 1969.

Keach, William. "A Regency Prophecy and the End of Anna Barbauld's Career." *Studies in Romanticism* 33 (1994): 569–77.

Kelley, Theresa M. "Women, Gender and Literary Criticism." In *New Cambridge History of Literary Criticism.* Vol. 9, *Romantic Literary Criticism,* edited by Marshall Brown. Cambridge: Cambridge University Press, forthcoming.

Kelly, Gary. *English Fiction of the Romantic Period, 1789–1830.* London: Longman, 1989.

———. "Revolution, Reaction, and the Expropriation of Popular Culture: Hannah More's *Cheap Repository.*" *Man and Nature: Proceedings of the Canadian Society for Eighteenth Century Studies* VI (1987): 147–55.

———. *Women, Writing, and Revolution, 1790–1827.* Oxford: Clarendon Press, 1993.

Kiernan, V. "Evanglicalism and the French Revolution." *Past and Present* I (1952): 44–56.

Klein, Lawrence. "Gender, Conversation and the Public Sphere in Early Eighteenth-Century England." In *Textuality and Sexuality,* edited by Judith Still and Michael Worton, 100–115. Manchester: Manchester University Press, 1993.

———. "Gender and the Public/Private Distinction in the Eighteenth Century: Some Questions about Evidence and Analytic Procedure." *Eighteenth-Century Studies* 29 (1995): 97–109.

Kowaleski-Wallace, Elizabeth. *Consuming Subjects: Women, Shopping, and Business in the Eighteenth Century.* New York: Columbia University Press, 1997.

———. *Their Fathers' Daughters: Hannah More, Maria Edgeworth and Patriarchal Complicity.* New York: Oxford University Press, 1991.

Kramnick, Isaac. *Republicanism and Bourgeois Radicalism: Political Ideology in Late Eighteenth-Century England and America.* Ithaca: Cornell University Press, 1990.

Kriz, Kay Dian. *The Idea of the English Landscape Painter: Genius as Alibi in the Early Nineteenth Century.* New Haven, Conn.: Yale University Press, 1997.

Krueger, Christine L. *The Reader's Repentance: Women Preachers, Women Writers, and Nineteenth-Century Social Discourse.* Chicago: University of Chicago Press, 1992.

Landes, Joan B. "The Public and the Private Sphere: A Feminist Reconsideration." In *Feminists Read Habermas: Gendering the Subject of Discourse,* edited by Johanna Meehan, 91–116. New York: Routledge, 1995.

———. "Representing the Body Politic: The Paradox of Gender in the Graphic Politics of the French Revolution." In *Rebel Daughters: Women and the French Revolution,* edited by Sara E. Melzer and Leslie W. Rabine, 15–37. New York: Oxford University Press, 1992.

———. *Women and the Public Sphere in the Age of the French Revolution.* Ithaca, N.Y.: Cornell University Press, 1988.

Laqueur, Thomas Walter. *Religion and Respectability: Sunday Schools and Working Class Culture, 1780–1850.* New Haven, Conn.: Yale University Press, 1976.

Las Casas, Bartolomé de. *A Short Account of the Destruction of the Indies.* Translated by Nigel Griffin, with an introduction by Anthony Pagden. London: Penguin Books, 1992.

Leighton, Angela. *Victorian Women Poets: Writing against the Heart.* London: Harvester Wheatsheaf; and Charlottesville, Va.: University Press of Virginia, 1992.

Link, Frederick M. Introduction to *The Plays of Hannah Cowley.* Edited by Frederick M. Link. 2 vols. New York: Garland, 1979.

Lott, Anna. "Sexual Politics in Elizabeth Inchbald." *Studies in English Literature, 1500–1900* 34 (1994): 635–48.

Lynch, Deirdre Shauna. *The Economy of Character: Novels, Market Culture, and the Business of Inner Meaning.* Chicago: University of Chicago Press, 1988.

MacKay, James. *A History of Modern English Coinage: Henry VII to Elizabeth II.* London and New York: Longman, 1984.

MacSarcasm, Rev. Sir Archibald [William Shaw]. *The Life of Hannah More, with a Critical Review of her Writings.* London: T. Hurst, 1802.

Makdisi, Saree. *Romantic Imperialism: Universal Empire and the Culture of Modernity.* Cambridge: Cambridge University Press, 1998.

Manvell, Roger. Introduction to *Selected Comedies by Elizabeth Inchbald.* Lanham, N.Y.: University Press of America, 1987.

Mason, Michael. *The Making of Victorian Sexual Attitudes.* Oxford: Oxford University Press, 1994.

McCarthy, Kathleen D. "Parallel Power Structures: Women and the Voluntary Sphere." In *Lady Bountiful Revisited: Women, Philanthropy and Power,* edited by Kathleen McCarthy, 1–31. New Brunswick, N.J.: Rutgers University Press, 1990.

McKendrick, Neil, John Brewer, and J. H. Plumb. *The Birth of a Consumer Society: The Commercialization of Eighteenth-Century England.* London: Europa, 1982.

Meakin, Annette M. B. *Hannah More: A Biographical Study.* London: Smith, Elder and Co., 1911.

Mellor, Anne K. "'Am I Not a Woman, and a Sister?': Slavery, Romanticism, and Gender." In *Romanticism, Race, and Imperial Culture, 1780–1834,* edited by Alan Richardson and Sonia Hofkosh, 311–29. Bloomington: Indiana University Press, 1996.

———. *English Romantic Irony.* Cambridge, MA: Harvard University Press, 1980.

———. *Mary Shelley: Her Life, Her Fiction, Her Monsters.* New York: Methuen; London: Routledge, 1988.

———. *Romanticism and Gender.* New York: Routledge, 1993.

Mendip Annals: or, A Narrative of the Charitable Labours of Hannah and Martha More in Their Neighborhood, being the Journal of Martha More. Edited by Arthur Roberts. London: James Nisbet and Co., 1859.

Midgley, Clare. "Slave Sugar Boycotts, Female Activism and the Domestic Base of British Anti-Slavery Culture." *Slavery and Abolition* 17 (1996): 137–62.

———. *Women against Slavery: The British Campaigns, 1780–1870.* London: Routledge, 1992.

Moore, Catherine E. "'Ladies . . . Taking the Pen in Hand': Mrs. Barbauld's Criticism of Eighteenth-Century Women Novelists." In *Fetter'd or Free? British Women Novelists, 1670–1815,* edited by Mary Anne Schofield and Cecilia Macheski, 383–97. Athens: Ohio University Press, 1986.

Moore, Leslie E. *Beautiful Sublime: The Making of "Paradise Lost," 1701–1734.* Stanford, Calif.: Stanford University Press, 1990.

More, Hannah. *Coelebs in Search of a Wife.* Bristol: Theommes Press, 1995.

———. *The Cottage Cook, or, Mrs. Jones' Cheap Dishes; Shewing the Way to do much good with little Money.* London: Cheap Repository Tracts, 1795.

———. *Sensibility: A Poetical Epistle to the Honourable Mrs. Boscawen.* London, 1782.

———. *Slavery.* London, 1788.

———. *The Works of Hannah More.* 6 vols. London: H. Fisher, R. Fisher, and P. Jackson, 1834.

Morris, R. J. *Class, Sect, and Party: The Making of the British Middle Class: Leeds, 1820–1850.* Manchester: Manchester University Press, 1990.

Munich, Adrienne. *Queen Victoria's Secrets.* New York: Columbia University Press, 1996.

Myers, Mitzi. "Hannah More's Tracts for the Times: Social Fiction and Female Ideology." In *Fetter'd or Free? British Women Novelists, 1670–1815,* edited by Mary Anne Schofield and Cecilia Macheski, 264–84. Athens: Ohio University Press, 1986.

———. "Reform or Ruin: 'A Revolution in Female Manners.'" In *Studies in Eighteenth-Century Culture.* Vol. 11, edited by Harry C. Payne. Madison: University of Wisconsin Press, 1982.

———. "Sensibility and the 'Walk of Reason': Mary Wollstonecraft's Literary Reviews as Cultural Critique." In *Sensibility in Transformation: Creative Resistance to Sentiment from the Augustans to the Romantics,* edited by Sydney McMillen Conger, 120–44. Rutherford, N.J.: Fairleigh Dickinson University Press, 1989.

Nardin, Jane. "Christianity and the Structure of *Persuasion.*" *Renascence* 30 (1977): 43–55.

Newman, Gerald. "Anti-French Propaganda and British Liberal Nationalism in the Early Nineteenth Century: Suggestions toward a General Interpretation." *Victorian Studies* XVIII (1975): 385–418.

———. *The Rise of English Nationalism: A Cultural History, 1740–1830.* London: Weidenfeld and Nicholson, 1987.

Nokes, David. *Jane Austen: A Life.* New York: Farrar, Strauss and Giroux, 1997.

Owen, David. *English Philanthropy, 1660–1960.* Cambridge, Mass.: Harvard University Press, 1964.

Pateman, Carole. *The Sexual Contract.* Stanford, Calif.: Stanford University Press, 1988.

Pedersen, Susan. "Hannah More Meets Simple Simon: Tracts, Chapbooks, and Popular Culture in Late Eighteenth Century England." *Journal of British Studies* 25 (1986): 84–113.

Philp, Mark. "Vulgar Conservatism, 1792–3." *English Historical Review* 110 (1995): 42–69.

Pickering, Samuel, Jr. *The Moral Tradition in English Fiction, 1785–1850.* Hanover, N.H.: University Press of New England, 1976.

Pindar, Peter [John Wilcot]. *Nil Admirari; or, A Smile at a Bishop; occasioned by An Hyperbolical Eulogy on Miss Hannah More, by Dr. Porteus, in his late charge to the Clergy.* London: West and Hughes, 1799.

Plumb, J. H. *The Commercialisation of Leisure in Eighteenth-Century England.* The Stenton Lecture: University of Reading, 1974.

Plumptre, James. *The English Drama Purified.* 3 vols. Cambridge, 1812.

Pocock, J. G. A. *Virtue, Commerce, and History: Essays on Political Thought and His-*

tory, Chiefly in the Eighteenth Century. Cambridge: Cambridge University Press, 1985.

Poovey, Mary. *The Proper Lady and the Woman Writer: Ideology as Style in the Works of Mary Wollstonecraft, Mary Shelley, and Jane Austen.* Chicago: University of Chicago Press, 1984.

————. *Uneven Developments: The Ideological Work of Gender in Mid-Victorian England.* Chicago: University of Chicago Press, 1988.

Pratt, Mary Louise. *Imperial Eyes: Travel Writing and Transculturation.* London: Routledge, 1992.

Prochaska, F. K. *Women and Philanthropy in Nineteenth-Century England.* Oxford: Clarendon Press, 1980.

Quinlan, Maurice J. *Victorian Prelude: A History of English Manners, 1700–1830.* New York: Columbia University Press, 1941.

Reeve, Clara. *The Progress of Romance and the History of Charoba, Queen of Aegypt.* London: Colchester Edition, 1785. Reprint, edited by Esther M. McGill. 2 vols. New York: Facsimile Text Society, 1930.

Richardson, Alan, "Epic Ambivalence: Imperial Politics and Romantic Deflection in Williams' *Peru* and Landor's *Gebir.*" In *Romanticism, Race, and Imperial Culture, 1780–1834,* edited by Alan Richardson and Sonia Hofkosh, 265–82. Bloomington: Indiana University Press, 1996.

————. *Literature, Education, and Romanticism: Reading as Social Practice, 1780–1832.* Cambridge: Cambridge University Press, 1994.

Richardson, William. "Sentimental Journey of Hannah More: Propagandist and Shaper of Victorian Attitudes." *Revolutionary World.* Vols. 11–13, 228–39. Amsterdam: Grumuner, 1975.

Riehle, Leilani. "Inner Beauty, Taste and Cultural Hegemony in Early Nineteenth-Century Women's Fiction." Ph.D. diss., University of California, Los Angeles, 2000.

Riley, Denise. *"Am I that Name?": Feminism and the Category of "Women" in History.* Minneapolis: University of Minnesota Press, 1988.

Robbins, Bruce, ed. *The Phantom Public Sphere.* Minneapolis: University of Minnesota Press, 1993.

Roberts, William. *Memoirs of the Life and Correspondence of Mrs. Hannah More.* 4 vols. London: Seeley and Burnside, 1834.

Rogers, Katherine M. "Britain's First Woman Drama Critic: Elizabeth Inchbald." In *Curtain Calls: British and American Women and the Theater, 1660–1820,* edited by Mary Anne Schofield and Cecilia Macheski, 277–90. Athens: Ohio University Press, 1991.

Rosman, Doreen M. "'What has Christ to do with Apollo?': Evangelicalism and the Novel, 1800–1830." In *Renaissance and Renewal in Christian History,* edited by Derek Baker, 301–11. Oxford: Blackwell, 1977.

Ross, Marlon B. *The Contours of Masculine Desire: Romanticism and the Rise of Women's Poetry.* New York: Oxford University Press, 1989.

Russell, Gillian. *The Theaters of War: Performance, Politics, and Society, 1793–1815.* Oxford: Clarendon Press, 1995.

Sales, Roger. *Jane Austen and Representations of Regency England.* London: Routledge, 1994.

Schmitt, Cannon. *Alien Nation: Nineteenth-Century Gothic Fictions and English Nationality.* Philadelphia: University of Pennsylvania Press, 1997.

Semmel, Bernard. *The Methodist Revolution.* New York: Basic Books, 1973.

Seward, Anna. *Letters of Anna Seward: Written between the Years 1784 and 1807.* 6 vols. Edinburgh: A. Constable, 1811.

———. *The Poetical Works of Anna Seward; with Extracts from her Literary Correspondence.* Edited by Walter Scott. 3 vols. Edinburgh, 1810.

Shiach, Morag. *Discourse on Popular Culture: Class, Gender and History in Cultural Analysis, 1730 to the Present.* Stanford, Calif.: Stanford University Press, 1989.

Showalter, Elaine. *A Literature of Their Own: British Women Novelists from Brontë to Lessing.* Princeton, N.J.: Princeton University Press, 1977.

Silvester, James. *Hannah More: Christian Philanthropist.* London: Thynne and Co., 1934.

Simpson, David. *Romanticism, Nationalism, and the Revolt against Theory.* Chicago: University of Chicago Press, 1993.

Smith, Adam. *The Theory of Moral Sentiments* (1759). 6th ed. Edinburgh: Constable, 1777.

Smith, Charlotte. *Desmond.* Edited with introduction and notes by Antje Blank and Janet Todd. London: Pickering and Chatto, 1997.

———. *The Poems of Charlotte Smith.* Edited by Stuart Curran. New York: Oxford University Press, 1993.

Smith, Olivia. *The Politics of Language, 1791–1819.* Oxford: Clarendon Press, 1984.

Spacks, Patricia Meyer. *Gossip.* Chicago: University of Chicago Press, 1985.

Spencer, Jane. "Adapting Aphra Behn: Hannah Cowley's *A School for Greybeards* and *The Lucky Chance.*" *Women's Writing* 2 (1995): 221–34.

———. *The Rise of the Woman Novelist: From Aphra Behn to Jane Austen.* Oxford: Blackwell, 1986.

Spinney, G. H. "Cheap Repository Tracts: Hazard and Marshall Edition." *The Library* XX (1940): 295–340.

Spring, David. "Aristocracy, Social Structure, and Religion in the Early Victorian Period." *Victorian Studies* VI (1963): 263–80.

———. "The Clapham Sect: Some Social and Political Aspects." *Victorian Studies* V (1961): 35–48.

———. "Some Reflections on Social History in the Nineteenth Century." *Victorian Studies* IV (1960): 55–64.

Stanton, Elizabeth Cady. *The Selected Papers of Elizabeth Cady Stanton and Susan B. Anthony.* Edited by Ann D. Gordon. Vol. I. New Brunswick, N.J.: Rutgers University Press, 1997.

Stephenson, Glennis. *Letitia Landon: The Woman Behind L. E. L.* Manchester: Manchester University Press, 1995.

Stevens, George Alexander. *A Lecture on Heads, with Additions by Mr. Pilon, as delivered by Charles Lee Lewes, with 47 Heads by Nesbit, from designs by Thurston.* London: 1802.

Stewart, Maaja A. *Domestic Realities and Imperial Fictions: Jane Austen's Novels in Eighteenth-Century Contexts.* Athens: University of Georgia Press, 1993.

Stratford, Joseph. *Robert Raikes and Others: The Founders of the Sunday Schools.* London: Sunday School Union, 1880.

Sussman, Charlotte. "Women and the Politics of Sugar, 1792." *Representations* 48 (1994): 48–69.

Sutherland, Kathryn. "Hannah More's Counter-Revolutionary Feminism." *Revolution in Writing: British Literary Responses to the French Revolution,* edited by Kelvin Everest, 27–64. Milton Keynes and Philadelphia: Open University Press, 1991.

Tannen, Deborah. *Gender & Discourse*. New York: Oxford University Press, 1994.

———. *You Just Don't Understand: Women and Men in Conversation*. New York: Ballantine Books, 1990.

Tanner, Tony. *Jane Austen*. Cambridge: Harvard University Press, 1986.

Taylor, Thomas. *Memoir of Mrs. Hannah More: with Notices of Her Works, and Sketches of her Contemporaries*. London: Joseph Rickerby, 1838.

Thompson, E. P. *The Making of the English Working Class*. London: Victor Gollancz, 1963. Rev. ed. Pelican Books, 1968.

Thompson, Henry. *The Life of Hannah More: with Notices of Her Sisters*. London: T. Cadell; and Edinburgh: Blackwood, 1834.

Tuchman, Gaye, with Nina Fortin. *Edging Women Out: Victorian Novelists, Publishers, and Social Change*. New Haven, Conn.: Yale University Press, 1989.

Vallone, Lynne. "'A humble Spirit under Correction': Tracts, Hymns, and the Ideology of Evangelical Fiction for Children, 1780–1820." *The Lion and the Unicorn* 15 (1991): 72–95.

Vaughn, William. "The Englishness of British Art," *The Oxford Art Journal* 13, no. 2 (1990): 11–23.

Vickery, Amanda. "Golden Age to Separate Spheres? A Review of the Categories and Chronology of English Women's History." *The Historical Journal* 36 (1993): 383–414.

———. *The Gentleman's Daughter: Women's Lives in Georgian England*. New Haven, Conn.: Yale University Press, 1998.

Wahrman, Dror. *Imagining the Middle Class: The Political Representation of Class in Britain, c. 1780–1840*. Cambridge: Cambridge University Press, 1995.

Waldron, Mary. Introduction to Hannah More's *Coelebs in Search of a Wife*. Bristol: Theommes Press, 1995.

Walker, Cheryl. *The Nightingale's Burden: Women Poets and American Culture before 1900*. Bloomington: Indiana University Press, 1982.

Walpole, Horace. "The Text of Horace Walpole's Correspondence with Hannah More." Edited by Charles H. Bennett. *The Review of English Studies*, new series 3 (1952): 341–45.

Watson, Nicola J. *Revolution and the Form of the British Novel, 1790–1825: Intercepted Letters, Interrupted Seductions*. Oxford: Clarendon Press, 1994.

Webb, R. K. *The British Working Class Reader, 1790–1848: Literacy and Social Tension*. London: Allen and Unwin, 1955. Reprint, New York: Augustus M. Kelley, 1971.

Weintraub, Jeff, and Krishan Kumar. *Public and Private in Thought and Practice: Perspectives on a Grand Dichotomy*. Chicago: University of Chicago Press, 1997.

Wellek, René. *A History of Modern Criticism: 1750–1950*. 2 vols. New Haven, Conn.: Yale University Press, 1955.

Wikborg, Eleanor. "Political Discourse versus Sentimental Romance: Ideology and Genre in Charlotte Smith's *Desmond* (1792)." *English Studies: A Journal of English Language and Literature* 78 (1997): 522–31.

Williams, Helen Maria. *Letters from France* (1790–96). 8 vols. in 2. Facsimile edition with introduction by Janet Todd. Delmar, N.Y.: Scholars' Facsimiles and Reprints, 1975.

———. *Peru, A Poem in Six Cantos*. London, 1784.

Williams, Raymond. *Keywords: A Vocabulary of Culture and Society*. London: Fontana/Croom Helm, 1976.

Wollstonecraft, Mary. "On Poetry and Our Relish for the Beauties of Nature." In *Post-

humous Works of the Author of a Vindication of the Rights of Woman, edited by William Godwin. Vol. IV, 165–74. London, 1798.

———. *A Vindication of the Rights of Woman* (1792). Edited by Carol Poston. New York: Norton, 1988/1975.

———. *The Works of Mary Wollstonecraft.* Edited by Janet Todd and Marilyn Butler. London: Pickering and Chatto; New York: New York University Press, 1989.

Wu, Duncan, ed. *Romantic Women Poets: An Anthology.* Oxford: Blackwell, 1997.

Yeazell, Ruth Bernard. *Fictions of Modesty: Women and Courtship in the English Novel.* Chicago: University of Chicago Press, 1991.

Index

Italicized page numbers refer to illustrations.

abolitionist movement, 6, 35, 75, 142
Abrams, Meyer, 86
absence: in Baillie's *Count Basil,* 43–44
Adams, Jane, 148n3.3
Addison, Joseph, 86, 90, 104
Adeline Mowbray (Opie), 105, 145
Aikin, Anna Wakefield, 84
Aikin, Lucy, 84, 131, 148n3.2–3; *Epistles on Women,* 32, 80–84, 128
All on a Summer's Day (Inchbald), 61, 66–67
Altick, Richard, 3–4
Andrew, Donna, 4
Andromache, 83
Angel of the House, 144
aristocracy, British: in Austen's *Persuasion,* 122–124; reform of in More's works, 19–21, 24–25; in Smith's *Desmond,* 108–113
Armstrong, Isobel, 69
Armstrong, Nancy, 7, 104
Ataliba, 77
Austen, Charles, 124
Austen, Francis, 124
Austen, Jane, 4, 103, 105; *Persuasion,* 121–139, 149n5.6
autonomous self: in Austen's *Persuasion,* 133–134

Backscheider, Paula, 8, 147n2.1
Bage, Thomas, 103
Baillie, Joanna, 84, 85, 95, 145, 148n4.5; popularity of, 88, 148n4.3; sympathetic curiosity, 98–99; theater as school for social reform, 40–42, 93
Baillie, Joanna, works: *Count Basil,* 42–46
Baker, Keith, 2
Bakhtin, M. M., 58, 104
Balfour, Clara, 15

Bannerman, Ann, 84
Barbauld, Anna Letitia, 75; on Coleridge, 85, 148n4.1
Barbauld, Anna Letitia, works: *British Novelists, The,* prefaces, 88, 89, 90, 92, 94, 96–97; "Eighteen Hundred and Eleven," 78–80, 145, 148n3.2; "Origins and Progress of Novel-Writing," 98, 101
Barry, Jonathan, 24
Bastille, 61
beauty, inner: in Austen's *Persuasion,* 132–133
Beetham, Margaret, 3
Behn, Aphra, 56
Belle's Stratagem, The (Cowley), 55–56, 60, 95
Bentham, Jeremy, 30, 40
Berg, Maxine, 9
Bermingham, Ann, 9
Bhabha, Homi, 145
biblical women, 10, 71, 80–82
Birrell, Augustine, 18
Blake, William, 73
Blank, Antje, 149n5.3
Blessington, Marguerite, Countess of, 4
board games, 10–11
body language: in Austen's *Persuasion,* 137
Bondica, Queen, 83
Booth, Wayne, 128
Boulton, Matthew, 140
Bowdler, Thomas, 47
Bowstead, Diana, 149n5.4, 149n5.5
Brewer, John, 7–8, 9, 11
Britannia, 139–141, 143–144
British chauvinism. *See* chauvinism, cultural
British Novelists, The (Barbauld), 88, 89, 90, 92, 94, 96–97

ANNE MELLOR is Professor of English, Above Scale, at UCLA, where she is a Faculty Affiliate at the Center for the Study of Women. She is author of *Blake's Human Form Divine* (1974), *English Romantic Irony* (1980), *Mary Shelley: Her Life, Her Fiction, Her Monsters* (1988), and *Romanticism and Gender* (1993); editor of *Romanticism and Feminism* (1988); and co-editor (with Richard Matlak) of *British Literature, 1780–1830*.